"*Swimming with the Sharks* gives a glimpse of ho[ ] division within American Christianity that is ex[ ] litical and secular influences. With insights cultivated over fifty years of pastoral ministry and a commitment to fostering unity across denominations and ideologies, Jack Haberer provides a vital resource for all believers seeking a better way forward in embodying the Good News of Jesus."

—**MARK BATTERSON**, lead pastor, National Community Church

"When Jack Haberer speaks, I listen. Whatever he writes, I read. Most denominational discourse is predictable and scripted. But Jack is unpredictable. He loves Jesus and the church—especially local congregations—more than ecclesiastical tribalism. This book is a masterpiece of bridge-building that celebrates the diversity and unity of the body of Christ. Read it and rejoice."

—**GREG ANDERSON**, graduate chaplain, Wheaton College

"The church model that Jack unveils in this very readable book helped our church to flourish in the 1980s and 90s and still works today. His publication of what he did with us and with subsequent congregations around the country is a gift for all who will read it."

—**BECKY CAVALLUCCI**, elder, Trinity Wellsprings Church

"If you're heading into shark-infested waters—and that includes everyone in ministry in this day and age—Jack Haberer's book belongs in your survival pack. His insights and breadth of pastoral experience will enrich any voyage to which you've been called."

—**GLENN MCDONALD**, author of *Morning Reflections*

"Jack Haberer acknowledges the many different ways we understand who Jesus is and what Jesus most deeply calls the church to be. He makes a strong case that to be the most faithful expression of the church, every congregation and denomination needs to allow for that wide diversity within its own beloved community. Haberer's book is a must-read for pastors and church leaders in this era of theological and political hyper-partisanship."

—**JIM KITCHENS**, co-founder, PneuMatrix

"Leadership is a challenge, especially during polarized times when institutions are often cracked, broken, and seemingly on the verge of tearing themselves apart. In such times, church leadership becomes even harder as faith communities struggle to live up to their ideals. Drawing on his personal journey across America's complicated spiritual landscape, Jack Haberer offers practical advice rooted in deep theological thinking, providing a path toward achieving St. Paul's admonition in Galatians 5:13: '*By love serve one another.*'"

—**JONATHAN ADDLETON**, rector/ president, Forman Christian College

Swimming with the Sharks

Swimming with the Sharks

Leading the Full Spectrum Church in a Red-and-Blue World

Jack Haberer

Foreword by Will Willimon

CASCADE *Books* • Eugene, Oregon

SWIMMING WITH THE SHARKS
Leading the Full Spectrum Church in a Red-and-Blue World

Cascade Books
An Imprint of Wipf and Stock Publishers
199 W. 8ᵗʰ Ave., Suite 3
Eugene, OR 97401

www.wipfandstock.com

PAPERBACK ISBN: 979-8-3852-1040-4
HARDCOVER ISBN: 979-8-3852-1041-1
EBOOK ISBN: 979-8-3852-1042-8

Cataloguing-in-Publication data:

Names: Haberer, Jack, author. | Willimon, Will, foreword.

Title: Swimming with the sharks : leading the full spectrum church in a red-and-blue world / Jack Haberer; foreword by Will Willimon.

Description: Eugene, OR: Cascade Books, 2024 | Includes bibliographical references.

Identifiers: ISBN 979-8-3852-1040-4 (paperback) | ISBN 979-8-3852-1041-1 (hardcover) | ISBN 979-8-3852-1042-8 (ebook)

Subjects: LCSH: Christianity and politics—United States. | Polarization (Social sciences)—United States. | Right and left (Political science)—United States.

Classification: BR516 H15 2024 (paperback) | BR516 (ebook)

VERSION NUMBER 06/19/24

My first three books were dedicated to the persons
who have shaped my faith, my ministry, and my life above all others:

Barbie Haberer, the love of my life for forty-eight years!
Maureen Haberer, my first teacher, role model, and coach.
Betty Moore, my mentor in all matters of church renewal.
I now add a PS: Kelly Haberer, the daughter who has taken my best
to the next generation.

This book I dedicate to two groups:

First, to the scholars who have most influenced the way
I have formulated my faith, my proclamation,
and my churchmanship:
Dr. Roger Nicole, Professor of Theology
Dr. Joseph Pirone, Professor of Psychology
Dr. Gordon Fee, Professor of New Testament
Dr. Michael Peterson, Professor of Philosophy
Dr. J. Arthur Baird, Professor of New Testament
Dr. Robert Johnson, Fellow Pastor and Theologian
Dr. Richard Lovelace, Professor of Church History
Dr. Walter Brueggemann, Professor of Old Testament
Dr. Joseph Small, Retired Director of Theology &Worship

Second, to the thousands of church members in congregations I have
served who have worked alongside me in my laboratory to test and
reformulate how best to launch them into ministry partnerships,
who have delivered proof positive that I was right to believe that God
has gifted them to do such significant service, and who have made
real the unspeakable joy of being their pastor and friend.

If you find anything of value in this book,
do know that the best ideas came
from them, with God's help.
I was just taking notes.

Contents

Foreword

"If you aspire to be a pastoral leader these days, you better learn to swim with the sharks," I declared to my Introduction to Ordained Leadership class at Duke. "Got an excessive need to float in placid waters? Then ask God to call you to be president of General Motors. But if you persist in your hunch that Christ wants you to carry his church into the future, I've got just the book to show you how."

I had spent the day before reading Jack Haberer's *Swimming with the Sharks.*

Having profited from Jack's earlier *GodViews,* in which Jack argued, in best Reformed fashion, that our notions of God make all the difference in the way we behave in, and lead forward the body of Christ, I knew what to expect of Jack: lively, well-written, beguiling, wise counsel for those of us who are called to lead churches.

Because he has given his life to leading the church in turbulent times, diving into troubled ecclesiastical waters as pastor, writer, editor, and nationally recognized church leader, Jack knows what he is talking about.

Jack the theologian tells us to use administration, management, and leadership books wisely, utilizing some, but not all of their advice. Good advice. Our theological authorization and commitments mean that we church leaders are called to lead in a way that's congruent with our vocation. The essence of what we are called to do, the content of our preaching and teaching, Jack characterizes as "the grace of our Lord Jesus Christ, the love of God and the fellowship of the Holy Spirit" (2 Cor 13:14).

He writes from the point of view of a lifetime of joyful experience in the ministry, "However, all of these joys have been accompanied by the heartbreaks caused time and again when I have found myself pressed into the place of choosing sides. Us versus Them. Right versus Wrong. Right versus Left. Red versus Blue." Therefore, one of Jack's recurring themes is that we've got to get over our binary, us-versus-them thinking. He urges us to raise our right hand and repeat after him, promising that we will never, ever again make the simplistic statement, "Well, there are always two sides to every story."

Jack says that, when wading into troubled church or community waters, leaders (negotiator, orchestrator, referee, pastor) must keep our point of view as complex and multifaceted as people really are. "Binary thinking—breaking all issues down to a two-choice debate or dichotomy—may make for fun rivalries, but it seldom leads to serious questions in order to find intelligent answers."

"When you're convinced that they are really, really bad, you can be sure that they're not as bad as you fear. And when you're convinced that you are really, really good, you can be sure that you're not as good as you claim." Ouch.

Although Jack's journey through many denominations (Catholic, Baptist, Assemblies of God, Free Methodist) and movements (which he aggregates as "fundapentacharisgelical") led ultimately to being thoroughly, irretrievably Reformed and Presbyterian, I'm telling my fellow Wesleyans, caught in our mudslinging divorce: Read *Swimming with the Sharks*. Methodists of all stripes will find that Jack gives them a way to rebuild relationships in family, church, and community that were damaged by the polarizing accusations and counter-accusations that always drive denominational divisions.

Swimming with the Sharks manages to be simultaneously realistic, honest, and hopeful. "There *are* real threats out thar in them waters," and yet we can all learn to lead in ways that give the community the optimum opportunity to move forward. Jack urges us to take Ephesians 4:15–16 as our watchword, "speaking the truth in love" via the mutual-affirmation-and-mutual-admonition available to us amid the dysfunctional community of faith as it helps us "to grow up in every way into him who is the head, into Christ, from whom the whole body, joined and knit together by every ligament with which it is equipped, as each part is working properly, promotes the body's growth in building itself up in love."

The way to free a congregation from its red-against-blue, conservative-versus-liberal binary disputes is for pastors to "urge, to facilitate, and to equip every one to discern their gifts, to find potential partners with whom to cultivate them, to scout out possible recipients and sharers of them, and to go and do accordingly. And then, the whole momentum of the congregation can rise like a phoenix." In other words, we can move forward by recovery of our originating sense of a vocation to participate in Christ's mission.

"Stop being a leader and choose instead to be a launcher," Jack tells pastors in his beguiling, positive invitation to missional engagement. "Launch all those folks into whatever direction God is sending them—even if they are going out in ways that are contrary to others on the same team. God's mission is not linear, not a straight, one-dimensional line, but one going in 360 degrees of directions all at once." Just what we ought to expect from an "omni-directional mission of God, fueled by the omnipotent Holy Spirit, motivated by the omni-benevolent God, and made possible by the omni-gracious Savior."

In the present moment, effective pastoral leaders don't need to be those who pour oil on troubled waters or who frantically search for safe harbors. Jack says we need to be good at two things: Preaching the full gospel and commissioning people to go. That means learning how to lead in the name of Christ by swimming with the sharks. I promise that you'll find encouragement and practical guidance for how to accomplish that in this wonderfully helpful, theologically based book.

Will Willimon

Professor of the Practice of Christian Ministry,
Duke Divinity School,
United Methodist Bishop, retired.
Author of *Listeners Dare: Hearing God in the Sermon.*

Acknowledgments

It takes a faith community to write an individual's personal testimony. So, too, it takes a Venn diagram of overlapping faith-friendship communities to cast a vision to write a book like this. The most obvious circle of friends is the group who read through the manuscript offering insights to improve the product. Grammar experts like my life partner Barbie Haberer and my sister Tobi Doty, writer types like magazine editor Barb Robertson, devotional writer Glenn McDonald, and pastoral theologians Robert Johnson, Sheldon Sorge, and Mark Achtemeier, and outside-the-box psychologist-activist Joe Pirone all poured many hours into helping me write this book. And there's my Cascade editor Rodney Clapp, who poured the fruits of a lifelong career in theological and devotional writing into this project. I can't thank you all enough for your contributions to the cause.

Overlapping the above, current Venn circle includes pastoral leaders and consultants with whom I have been comparing notes on how they have been promoting all-member empowerment and equipping: Presbyterian consultant and author Sue Mallory (a 1980s pioneer in equipping ministry); pastor and *discernmentarian* Jessica Moffatt (a Methodist pioneer in tandem with Sue); Mark Batterson, pastor of National Community Church and author of many books; associate pastors Mary Anne De La Torre and Charles Taylor of North Jersey Vineyard Church; Pastor Eric Barton, Bethel Bible Church, Tyler, Texas; Ramin Gibbs, Connections Minister at Oak Hills Church, San Antonio, Texas; blogger and edgy religiopolitical commentator Nathan Manderson.

At the fifty-years-ago beginning of my Venn diagram is the circle of friends who first taught me how to live in Christian community wherein everybody's gifts mattered. It started with John Bolster and Tim Pendry, best friends in the offensive backfield of the freshman football who helped me launch the Mustard Seed Coffeehouse in Ramsey, New Jersey. We weren't even old enough to drive! But the vestry of St. John's Episcopal Church trusted us to start that Saturday evening teenagers' gathering, which took off like a rocket at the outset of the Jesus movement, i.e., the eastern version of it. In that circle we were joined by my three siblings Tobi, Beth Haberer Beale, and Geoff Haberer; by Laura Templeton, Larry and Lynette Stephan, Steve Silverstein, Donna Bedlivy Cain, Carl and Skip Miller, Martha and Gina Knight, Steve Jensen; and gained adult guidance from Ken and Barb Stuhr and Bob and Betty Steele—all of us being empowered to exercise our gifts and fulfill God's callings in our lives.

Another Venn circle includes faculty members of Elim Bible Institute such as Paul Johansson, David Edwards, Stuart Dahl, and Edgar Parkyns, plus faculty at Roberts Wesleyan College: Dr. Mike Peterson, who downright taught me how to think; and Dr. Stanley Magill, who injected a love of biblical texts in the original languages. Then, another circle showcases professors at Gordon Conwell Theological Seminary, such as Drs. Gordon Fee, who exegeted all the major texts relating to the Presence and Power of the Holy Spirit; Roger Nicole, who embodied ecumenical theology—modeling how to explain others' theological convictions better than they could do so for themselves; Dan Jessen, who introduced me to the task of facilitating the ministries of all members; Richard Lovelace, who mentored me in the promotion of Unitive Evangelicalism and spiritual awakenings in mainstream denominational traditions; and others like Gordon McDonald, John Jefferson Davis, and David Scholer.

Another Venn circle adds those church members who have embodied not only the pure empowerment of the Holy Spirit but also the spiritual giftings the variety of which exceed any gift list or gifts inventory others have enumerated: Sid and Carol Ditkowski, Becky Cavallucci, Bud Earhart, Walt Weber, Renee Bryant, Linda Howard, David Schechter, Bill Burch, Doug and Ruth Paauwe, Carol and Jim Rootsey, Scott and Trisha Jordan, Kristine Roberts Jones, Edith Comer, Dot and Ken Vance, Pete and Fran Peterson, Bill and Grace Nelson.

The next Venn circle includes Barbara Carmichael, Craig and Nancy Goodwin, Connie and Larry Nyquist, Jimmy and Marilu McGregor, George and Joyce Coyer, Julie and Lynn Calhoun, Will and Allison

Groten, Jimmy and Suzette Connell, Mike and Susie Ray, Judy Franklin, Mary-Anne Collins, Barb Henkel, Byder Wilde, Laura and Lee Huebel, Lynne Kaley, Mary and Tom Basich, Sharon Jenkins, Perry and Carole Westerfield, Sarah Korkowski Duncan, Dave and Melissa Johnson, Katrina Pennington, Doug and Judy Blanchard, Paul and Mary Anne Marshall, Brady and Suzanne McCollum, Jim and Kathy Luther, Pam and Bill Merrill, Don and Patti Metzler, Leroy and Joyce Schlechte, Cliff and Nicky Cunningham, Reg Brown, Becky Baxter, Barb and Fred Robertson, Dana Park, Betty Templeton, Georga Thomas, Mac and Anne Wallace, Linda and Marty Meador, Michelle Vass, Jeanne and Terry Stone, Jim and Bonnie Keith, Mike and Holly Kincaid, Mike and Karla Lawson.

Yet another Venn circle encompasses Susie and Dick Hilton, Jim Cochran, Pete and Kathleen Dent, Deb Palmer, Bob and Elaine Martin, Gary and Joyce Stone, Dennis Dries, Mike and Gwen Loomis, Donna Barnwell, Dana Yashou, Dick and Shirley Cahn, Barbara Culp, Deb Palmer, Larry and Sherry Deal, Moufid and Afaf Khoury, Chuck and Kelly Hess, Pam and Andy Weiss, Roger and Kathy Yott, Anita Kraus Dave and Pat Hoffman, Ron DeLong, Vincent DiCicco, Alan Jennings, Abraham Pa Cawi, Ken Sabotta, Glenn and Becky Short, Mark and Erica Simmons, Bill and Jane Townsend, Helen and Charley Underwood, Bill and Mary-Ellen Valentine, John and Sue VanDenElzen, Greg and Carol Wampole, Becky and John Tacca.

Another Venn circle: John and Nancy Mallory, Judy and Warren Ferguson, Bob Schmerbeck, Sabrina Adrian, Susan Montoya, Ann Reynolds, Clarice Amann, Dayton and Sam Baublit, Sam and June Begeman, Verna Benham, Frank and Julie Dunlap, BK and Fred Gamble, Tim and Becca Huchton, Richard and Meg Scott-Johnson, Wes and Gini Norris-Lane, Alice Lerp, Carroll and Jane Pickett, Dick and Lynne Powell, Don and Jane Priour, Jane Ragsdale, Tom and Sharon Richardson, Tim and Gretchen Rye, Eldon and Barbara Sheffer, Bobby and Cheryl Sieker, Andriena Silguero-Valles, Blake and Cheryl Smith, Tim and Mary Ellen Summerlin, Tommy and Donna Tait, Mark and Shannon Tuschak, Ed and Nancy Wallace, Alicia Martin, and Mary Stone.

Yet one more Venn circle: pastoral and denominational colleagues George Callahan, John Lyles, Mike Cole, Rick Young, Bob Bonham, Tammy Mitchell, Mike Loudon, Jack Baca, John Gable, Bob Henley, Agnes Brady, Ed Hurley, Doug Hucke, Shawn Smith, Brent Eelman, Barbara Wheeler, Gary Demarest, Rich Mouw, Woody Brown, Cliff Kirkpatrick, and John Wilkinson.

Introduction

Incredulous

"Ignorance can be cured, but stupidity is forever."

—ARISTOPHANES

"ARE YOU KIDDING ME? You're making this up, right?" I was incredulous. Unhappy. Even mad. "Are you telling the truth? I moved fifteen hundred miles to serve Jesus here by the beach and nobody told me this?"

Being raised in the northeast US, I enjoyed swimming in my north Jersey town's Crystal Springs Lake, and once in awhile on the Jersey shore, on Cape Cod, and the North Shore above Boston. But I always salivated when my wealthier friends got to talking about their summer vacations down on the Florida beaches—Miami, Ft. Lauderdale, Daytona.

So when a dynamic, charismatic church, which had grown from a dozen members to over eight hundred in just five years, invited me to join the staff of the powerful preaching pastor George Callahan, in Pompano Beach, Florida, I was over-the-moon elated—not just about the church and pastor, but also the location. Paradise was calling.

Paradise, however, threw me two curves in that very first week.

On that first Monday morning, George welcomed me to my office and then said, "I'll see you at the end of day. I have to do a burial at sea first." He headed out the door.

At about 5:00 PM he returned, looking ashen.

My office mates and I had experienced a downpour outside our office suite in a local shopping center, but on board the cabin cruiser off shore, that same storm turned ferocious. The deceased church member, an elderly man who had been an avid deep-sea fisherman, had been cremated. George's assignment was to pour his ashes off the back of the boat.

The man's widow was insistent that they needed to motor out past the horizon; and like a child in the back seat of a car, he told us, he kept asking the widow, "Are we there yet?"

"Not yet, George," she would say. "I still can see buildings back on the land."

"Meanwhile," George editorialized, "every one of us onboard was tossing our cookies over the side."

Finally, they'd motored far enough, and turned off the engine. George climbed over the transom, down onto the casting platform, and read a brief prayer. After offering some words about "ashes to ashes" and "dust to dust," he poured them out over the water. At that very second, a wind gust rushed in and blew the ashes right back onto the boat, covering George and spraying over all the rest.

Which is why, upon his return, he looked ashen. Literally. Even shaken. But after hearing our giggly expressions of pseudo-sympathy, with a shrug he offered his first bit of advice to this young upstart: "Jack, first lesson for scattering ashes: check the wind direction."

With that, the patina of the Florida paradise dulled a bit. Perhaps the environment might not be quite as welcoming as I had imagined. But that wasn't what drove me to incredulity.

That reaction followed three days later. George had been given an admission ticket to fly on the famous Goodyear Blimp that was parked on a landing strip a few miles from the church offices. Chagrined by the ashes experience, his enthusiasm had faded, so he gave the ticket to Guy Shepherd, the young music director. And Guy took flight.

When Guy returned to the offices, he wasn't ashen. He was glowing with pleasure. But he also threw a curve. "We flew up and down the coast. The water was beautifully blue and clear. But, one thing caught me by surprise," he said. "As we soared a few hundred feet above the land and sea, we saw hundreds of people sunbathing on the beach, hundreds more wading and body surfing in the shallow waters, and farther offshore, surfers taking rides on the outside waves. But between the waders and the surfers there was a wide stretch of water. And it was filled with sharks. In one school of sharks alone I counted twenty-four. And no matter how far we traveled north up to Palm Beach and south past Fort Lauderdale, they were there."

He concluded, "I'm never going out in the water again."

That's when I burst into the aforesaid rant of incredulity. And I was not just incredulous, but—I daresay—unhappy. Even mad. Sharks in my dream-come-true, new home in paradise? How could this be? Is this a sign of things to come?

Little did I imagine it at the time, but indeed—it was but a tiny hint of things to come . . . both in the water and outside it.

However, it wasn't long before my family and I chose to ignore the threats in the waters. We soon were dipping toes and diving through the dangerous waves, risking the possibility of direct shark encounters. And a few we did have (we'll come to that forthwith). But that was then . . .

. . . This is now. And the sharks are out there still. In fact, there are other sharks here among us in churches and faith fellowships all across the country. I want to talk with you about those sharks. But before doing so, please allow me to extend a personal welcome to you, my reader.

From My Heart to Yours

First: if you are one of those who have read my earlier book, *GodViews: The Convictions that Drive Us and Divide Us:*[1] Thank you! Thanks for reading, viewing, or at least considering those twentieth-century thoughts. Just today I received an email from somebody who had recently heard of *GodViews*. She bought it, read it, raved about it, and thanked me for it. A newish Episcopal pastor. Yay! Perhaps other Episcopalians will read it, too. It made my day, some twenty-three years after its publication.

It also makes my day to have you, a *GodViews* veteran, be willing to risk swimming with the sharks. You swam there somewhat when *GodViews* made its debut. There, however, we weren't chancing encounters with the most ferocious fish in the sea. Oh, we did visit the edge of the sea, the coastline of the eastern end of the Mediterranean. We saw the Holy Land sites of Caesarea, the port city of inclusiveness, right on that coast, and Mt. Carmel, the citadel of truth, overlooking the same coast.

In this book we will revisit those locales briefly a few chapters into our new conversation. But this time around we will be diving into the ocean waves that frame the east, west, and south sides of the dear ol' USA. And, these waves will be highlighting a ferocity beyond the force of the moderate Mediterranean currents' typical ebb and flow. We will be getting stoked while hangin' ten, and getting caught inside the sick

---

1. Haberer, *GodViews*.

barrels of the gnarly swell breaks, getting wiped out, bombed, shredded, even rag-rolled.

Surfer lingo aside, our beach adventures will be thrilling. Dangerous. Even life-threatening. Because we won't just be surfing in powerful waves. We will be swimming . . . indeed, surfing . . . with the sharks.

In the process we will take a close look at a broader read of *GodViews*, than we did in that earlier text. You will find the best ideas there reformulated here in even more pointed, perhaps unnerving, and memorable ways. Hopefully, you will see how those basic ideas can play out in your world of church life in these far more complicated twenty-first century years.

Second: To you who are a *GodViews* rookie: Let me spell out the context of this writing. *GodViews* was birthed out of the conflicts pulsating around my own denomination, the Presbyterian Church (USA). It was published by our own denominational book company in the hope of quelling an earthquake that was threatening to drive a deep chasm between us Presbyterians.

I wish I could say it prevented the earthquake. It did not. But the resulting fallout was more a splintering than a schism. Just about 5 percent of our churches split away, many less than the prognosticators predicted. I want to think that *GodViews* helped in mitigating the damage. Some friends have reported that the *GodViews* paradigm helped them to better understand the "other side" of the pressing arguments. Some tell me that the framework outlined in *GodViews* helped them to find a respectable and mutually beneficial way to hold on to one another while still holding on to their differing convictions.

To all of you: This new retelling of *GodViews* arises out of the fierce polarization across all American Christianity that has escalated from DEFCON 3 to DEFCON 1. Whereas in the 1990s I had the luxury of focusing on one denomination's conflicts, now in the 2020s I am compelled to speak to the extreme polarizations, harsh accusations and counteraccusations, and the shrinkage besetting all branches of the Christian faith across the country, and frankly, wherever partner churches serve around the globe. This new volume tackles these challenges across all denominations and nondenominational movements. It hopes to shed light on all who range across the spectrum of faiths from passionate Pentecostals to somewhat apathetic SBNRs (spiritual but not religious).

More than that, this volume spells out what the first version left out: an approach to church ministry that I have cultivated in full-spectrum churches in such a way as to learn from my own congregation members how to be together in one family, one body, one fellowship.

In writing the 2001 book, I didn't want to set myself up as the expert on church leadership and management. I simply wanted to show how the different voices in the church are needed for any one congregational church to be a true microcosm, an embodiment of the larger, worldwide church—thereby being what Jesus dubbed (parenthetical commentaries mine): ". . . my witnesses in Jerusalem (locally), Judea (regionally), Samaria (across the tracks with *those* people) and to the end of the earth (all people-groups around the world)." *GodViews* put that all in a single denomination's context, which was a big enough apple to bite.

But this volume has been begging to be written for the larger church, aiming for all believers to be witnesses to Jesus and his good news. It requires me to reflect the frames of reference of multiple denominations, multiple movements, multiple cultures, multiple ethnicities, and multiple ideologies. For fifty years I have been discussing, visiting, researching, formulating, theologizing, testing, modifying, adapting, broadening, refocusing, retheologizing, and reformulating this model of ministry—engaging in conversation and observation of churches in many traditions, denominations, and movements. I feel a fire in my belly, an inner demand to write down and share the lessons I've learned.

Churches all around are becoming less of what they once were, largely by becoming pawns in the wars and seductions of raw secular, political power, as well as emotional exploitation. The losses are not inevitable nor unstoppable. They can be turned around. We need to address and redress that fact. We need to spell out a better way.

Across forty years of pastoral ministry, I have served bipartisan, even multipartisan congregations, and have addressed many issues within American churches that are swirling all around us in the larger culture. Yet we haven't suffered significant losses over them. Oh, those churches weren't conflict-free. But most conflicts were driven not by such political differences, but by personality clashes and/or programmatic changes, and/or dumb judgment calls, mostly by me, that have been quickly resolved by an apology and a handshake. Issues weren't raised by theological or ethical disagreements either, even though we had them, too. With relative ease we have addressed the big issues of the day, which has fostered a spirit of mutual respect and a readiness to learn from one another in ways that wouldn't have happened if we were cordoned off into partisan enclaves of agreement. All along the way, those conversations were building upon a model of ministry I formulated, mostly from intense study of the New Testament churches and reinforced by a careful reading and sifting of secular business leadership skills.

The resulting lessons beg to be put into print. Which leads to . . .

A second fire is burning white hot inside me as I read on social media and hear from fellow pastors the counsel they are reading or hearing from so-called experts on how to lead their churches through the overwhelming changes afoot in their congregations and surrounding culture. That fire burns extra hot due to the idiocy that keeps coming from many of those sources. Yes, that's the word I used: idiocy. Oh, great value can come to us who read and learn from great leaders in the world of business management. But for every great one there are others who are blowing smoke, spinning clichés that other business leaders are wise enough to ignore. But, pastors, trained in Bible colleges and/or seminaries too often take such voices' bumper-sticker slogans at face value. We even treat such consultants as having the final word on how to do what we do.

Prodded by Aristophanes' hope about curing ignorance, I am compelled to write this book. And, therefore, I thank you, the *GodViews* veteran or rookie that you are, for giving me a chance to pour out my learnings and accumulated counsels gained from better sources, beginning with the Scriptures themselves.

A Circuitous Route in a Journey of Faith

I did discover and formulate a comprehensive paradigm for local church ministry while in seminary, especially through my elective courses and independent studies in the areas of church ministry, exploring sources as far back as the ancient churches and getting reformulated through the medieval, reformation, and recent eras. This model—indeed, my whole ministerial education—was built on the messy foundation of the circuitous route that launched me into church ministry:

- a tender child's faith as one baptized and confirmed in the Roman Catholic church, shaped especially by a mom who was educated by Jesuit scholars from kindergarten through college;

- a teenage rocket ship of fanatical, enthusiastic evangelism as a born-again, charismatic Jesus Freak and coffeehouse co-founder which brought hundreds of teens to Christ over its ten years of soul-winning via Jesus music and personal testimonies;

- a passionate and devout Pentecostal Bible college student;

- a Free Methodist college's religion-and-philosophy-degreed undergraduate;

- a piano-playing leader of a praise band that had launched a nondenominational church and then, after it split; . . .

- a member of both the praise band and the leadership team (board of deacons, we called ourselves) that launched its offshoot—a second, joy-filled (but somewhat directionless) nondenominational church;

- then, a student in a large, multidenominational, evangelical seminary, whose students and faculty ranged from Anglican to Assemblies of God, and whose board chair was Billy Graham;

- a student intern and music director (organist, pianist, guitarist—the lone musician) in a tiny, federated American Baptist and Disciples of Christ church, until I finally was hired to serve . . .

- in a Presbyterian Church, whose elder board both hired me and initiated my candidacy to be ordained in this venerable denomination before I'd actually worshiped in it. They didn't even think to ask me if I wanted to do so . . . and, as a newbie fresh out of seminary, I was too intimidated to tell them I wasn't looking to become a Presbyterian;

- and a newly ordained, young pastor to a beach community near the Kennedy Space Center.

It was while riding on the rising and crashing waves of my theological and ecclesiastical tides that I searched intently to find some model of ministry that could help me avoid the shark attacks that had preceded and followed my seminary studies. Having formulated a plan for such a model, I began testing my hypotheses within months of my arrival in the Florida Space Coast community. I modeled and promoted it throughout a spirited—dare I say, "Holy Spirited?"—ten-year tenure there. And the congregation grew gradually but steadily (over 10 percent net increase per year in every form of measurement) against all odds (the local population grew less than 1 percent per year).

Then and there I refined, promoted, implemented, and further refined that model. Then, after completing that, I continued to adjust, rerefining, retheologizing, and managing the model over twelve years in a second church next to Johnson Space Center (as I often said, "It doesn't take a rocket scientist to run a church, but we have one in every pew in case the need should arise"), and thereafter in four other ministry contexts.

And, you know what? Against all odds and trends, those churches were functioning as full-spectrum churches without me even thinking to call them that. You could also call us "Big Tent churches," although that sounds to me a little bit too much like, "Don't worry, be happy." We had Republicans and Democrats serving together in all kinds of leadership roles. We had outspoken pro-lifers and pro-choicers in major leadership positions. Pro-gay and family-values voters. Military brass and enlisted and civilians. Corporate executives and union laborers. Working together. Liking each other. Loving one another.

I inherited, hired, and supervised associate pastors, Christian educators, musicians, youth directors, and other staff members whose theology, ethical convictions, and lifestyles were widely varied. And yet, almost every one flourished in their areas of giftedness and calling, and we flat-out enjoyed each other's friendships and our collective esprit de corps. Our elders, deacons, and other leaders thrived in their service and discipleship. And members throughout those congregations did so, too. The churches grew in every category of measurement.

In 2005 (four years after *GodViews'* publication), when the trustee board of the venerable *Presbyterian Outlook* (the leading independent "thought leader" magazine in Presbyterianism)—sought an editor, they approached me . . . an odd choice, given my erratic journey of faith—especially the parts that bespoke a conservatism to the right of their publication's somewhat progressive history. But they sought my help and even hired me. The board chair's rationale? "The prophetic voice we've always offered the church needs today to be one that can make the case for us staying together, and Pastor Jack Haberer is the only one we know who's doing that." I got the job by default.

In that role, I was entrusted with the task of writing weekly editorials—we actually published forty-three times per year—to thousands of church leaders, our primary audience, about how to wrestle with the church's controversies and to thrive in ministry amid such debates. In the process, I was provided a megaphone from which to try to strengthen "the tie that binds our hearts in Christian love," so that "the fellowship of kindred minds [could be] like to that above."

That was my endeavor then and there. This is my aim here and now with you.

So how will I accomplish all this in this book? I will attempt to correct some misdiagnosing of the problems ailing the churches across the country. I will invite you to break out of the binary, two-party mentality that dominates Americans' public discourse. Then I will reintroduce you to Jesus of Nazareth. That is, I will introduce you to a set of roles and functions he carried out while being raised in the north country of Palestine/Israel, and both there and in the big city of Jerusalem in his mature years that followed. In the process, we'll bring GodViews out into the open, and see how those views of God's mission match up to Jesus' personality and ministry. We'll then consider how to create a culture that not only survives but thrives, despite the differences in ministry passion that can too easily create competition and rivalries among God's family. We will unpack the craziness of the early church with its multiple models for us to emulate as we seek to partner with God's mission here and now.

Spoiler alert: this will lead us to the too-little-tried-and-tested biblical model of congregational ministry I call *the Empowerment Church Model*, one that can help you, my reader and new friend, to fulfill these hopes right where you are.

Huh? Bringing GodViews out into the open?

GodViews. It is an odd word. Really, it's two words. And, it's a title. Hence, two capital letters. But I converged the two into one word back in 2001 when my book editor, Tom Long at Geneva Press (the second Presbyterian Publishing Corporation imprint alongside Westminster John Knox), allowed me to contract the words together. For those readers of Presbyterian ecclesiastical associations, it's been circling around ever since, and it's generated a few, individual "aha" moments. It has prompted conversations. Even debates. For me it has generated hundreds of speaking engagements, bunches of questions, and lots of book sales.

But today, GodViews needs to go interdenominational. And multidenominational. And nondenominational. And pandenominational. And international.

- GodViews: A vocabulary word that I hope will circulate among the Methodists, you who are trying to recover from the largest ecclesiastical divorce since the Civil War—to offer pathways to reconcile severed family and neighborhood friendships.

- GodViews: An idea that I hope will circulate among the Southern Baptists, you whose loss of the "Cooperative Baptist Fellowship" in the early 1990s introduced a trickle of losses from America's largest and fastest growing Protestant denomination; but thereafter, the tide turned. Departures escalated to a rate of 400,000 per year in the 20-teens and 2020's. And, as we go to print, the shrinkage shows no signs of abating.

- GodViews: Perhaps this idea will ping around the Roman Catholic parishes, seminaries, and orders—not just in the USA but around the world—so that you all may find a language of conversation that can work within a church that pays a singular homage to the Bishop of Rome, but, within the US churches, has a huge number of adherents who are personally offended by the political leanings of the current pope.

- GodViews: I hope this thinking will regain use among the peacemaking Mennonites. The first *GodViews* text was embraced by a wave of your kin, especially those of you in Canada. You have dedicated yourselves to help churches of all denominations to find the missing peace. How about bringing the American Mennonites on board—and especially so, since this edition is aiming to de-escalate the hottest wars and rumors of wars you have faced in generations?

- GodViews: I pray these thoughts can take hold in all of you congregationalists and Cambellites, Lutherans and Anglicans, dispensationalists and Reformed, all of you serving in other denominations wherein church splits multiply like rabbits, but generate many more losses than gains.

- GodViews: Perhaps most of all, may the term take hold among you nondenominational, multidenominational, and interdenominational Christians in whose congregations passion for the Lord often rides high. Such passion prompts your new churches to grow like weeds, especially some of the multiple campus church plants. But, like the wheat seeds in shallow or thorny ground, those early spurts often plateau or are even singed by conflagrations that can rage unchecked by pretested fire-fighting strategies, full-force fire hydrants, or even rules of thumb with which to bring reconciliation and resolution.

Back in the year 2000, when I first proposed to the editor that a book to be called *GodViews,* he asked me to address "The Convictions that Drive Us and Divide *All of* Us," in ways that would help the whole range of American churches. But he gave me just four months to move from proposal to completed manuscript . . . and I was serving as pastor of a hyper-busy congregation at the time.

I demurred. "Tom, I once was a part of a whole bunch of those denominations and movements, and I'm indebted to them all; but for the past twenty years I've lived only among us Presbyterians. I simply don't have the time in four months to do credible enough work for the sakes of all those others." He conceded my point, and that 2001 volume focused on the "us" who are Presbyterian.

But I've circulated through and kept tabs of what's been happening all around the country in churches of all brands, drawing upon friends I'd made throughout my circuitous journey through each of them. That was helped especially when in 2006 I began a nine-year stint as editor and publisher of *The Presbyterian Outlook*, which prompted me to publish news of all kinds of churches, denominations, and movements, with any one of which you, my reader, may identify. And I did publish those news reports and commentaries not just weekly in print, but daily online on that new invention, the internet. In the meantime, more and more church-related news reports kept hitting the major secular news outlets because, well, we've generated more community organizing efforts, get-out-the-vote door-knocking, partisan polarizations, and—oh, yes—more and more scandals than ever before.

I've been doing my homework to better understand you all. And for my post-editorial service years, I've been back in congregational life, serving churches in three parts of the country—another Florida beach community, a northeast industrial city, and a rural Texas town—pouring my heart into these varied front lines of ministry.

Yes, the front lines of local congregational life have always been my central calling, and the proclaiming of the gospel of Jesus and his grace has continued to be my central message. It still wakes me up in the morning with fresh anticipation. Indeed, in many a church lobby (a.k.a. foyer, vestibule, narthex), I have heard some version of the query, "You are the most energetic and enthusiastic preacher I've ever heard; how can you at your age be the Eveready Energizer Battery Bunny Pastor that you are?" I usually just laugh, especially because they were mostly comparing me with other Presbyterian preachers, and "enthusiastic" is not our middle name; if they were Pentecostals, they would probably call me sedate. Still, I smile when I hear such comments. And, on one occasion a couple of years ago I responded spontaneously, "I still believe this stuff."

Once those words slipped out, they became my byline. I have repeated that answer often. I really do believe this stuff. And for that reason, I continue to be energetic and enthusiastic in my proclamation of the good news of Jesus and his love.

The Depth of Our Dilemma

Sad to say, "More than 4,000 churches closed in America in 2020. Over that same time, over 20,000 pastors left the ministry and 50 percent of current pastors say they would leave the ministry if they had another way of making a living."[2] Pastors have burned out, worn out, been drained out, been thrown out. Some have lost their faith, or at least their passion for the faith. Some have stayed in ministry nevertheless, if only because they had no other skill set by which to put food on the table. They continued faking it ("til they feel it") as best they could, even though they knew that they were quietly becoming SBNRs—spiritual but not religious—and looking forward to the day when Sundays would be days off from all duties, even worship itself.

But while I've faced my own conflicts along the way—with some of them deeply painful and debilitating—I have never tired of preaching and teaching the good news of Jesus, the full gospel of "the grace of our Lord Jesus Christ, the love of God and the fellowship of the Holy Spirit" (2 Cor 13:14), the essence of which I will proclaim later on in this book. And, most of the time, I've loved serving most of the people God has brought into the diverse churches I've served through five decades (the first ten years of which preceded ministerial ordination and compensation). And, it's out of that love, and the yearning to share what truly has worked to bring folks together across their disparate GodViews, that I offer the following chapters to help you thrive in ways to match or even exceed what I have experienced.

2. Brody, "New Barna Survey Finds."

And So, How Will We Get There?

I will begin by reintroducing you to the wide, wide world in which we find ourselves, highlighting the ecclesiastical islands to which many of us have fled and against which many of us have contended. The outside world is speaking of us in categories we've too easily seconded and adopted as the Right or the Left, the Conservatives or the Liberals, the Red or the Blue. We have worn those labels as four-inch-round lapel pins. And, accordingly, we've become accomplices in our own polarization. Oh, those labels aren't new, but they once were humming along as background noise. Today they shout out in fortissimo. We simply can't seem to rise above the great divide. We will look closely at what's going on here.

I will offer you the five GodViews as an alternative paradigm and construct by which to better understand ourselves and one another. I'll also reintroduce you to the ways Jesus himself comes across in the Gospels, as one we not only encounter but as one we also emulate. I'll draw help from Thomas à Kempis by turning the title of his major work into a question: "The Imitation of *Which* Christ?"

I'll also add more present specificity to the ideological passions and repulsions that you likely feel in your alliances and oppositions in your own church experience. You readers of more Catholic or Lutheran, Baptist or Moravian, Reformed or Restorationist, Methodist or Messianic, COGIC or AME, Pentecostal or Charismatic, Calvary Chapel or Willow Creek or Bethel or Purpose-Driven congregations will find your place in the narrative as it unfolds. My critique of all GodViews/Christ-Images will be more pointed than before (you'll surely enjoy my criticisms of the GodViews that aggravate you).

Then I will launch into a whole new body of work, specifically spelling out a paradigm to implement church leadership in ways whose rationale you will hopefully agree is pretty much unimpeachable and truly self-evident, but whose implementation may feel challenging and radical. It will require a lot of you who are a present, past, or future leader—not by increasing your workload, but by demanding that you upgrade your tolerance, your respect, and your empowerment of others doing their work in your church.

Beware!

Control freaks beware! Those controlling tendencies will feel threatened as I take you on a tour through several of the first-century churches to show how those new believers participated in the Holy Spirit's launch of a movement instead of building a denomination, a hierarchy, a governing body, a clerical class of leaders, a set liturgy, a publishing house, a parliamentary procedure, or any singular model for anything they did. To borrow a book title from management guru Tom Peters, whose work I will reference, they were *"Thriving on Chaos."*[3] And, sure enough, in the process, they "turned the world upside down" (yes, that's a real quote from one of their critics right in the book of Acts—17:6).

But the chaos that they experienced was a chaos of joy, a riot of spiritual passion, a cacophony of biblical study, an explosion of evangelism, a pandemonium of worship, a revolution of mercy, justice, grace, and peace—all to the glory of God.

And for you who feel threatened not only at the thought of giving up some control but also after reading the above line, "It will require a lot of you . . . ," take heart. If you join into this chaos, you will discover ways to make your life more orderly, your workload a bit lighter, your performance anxiety eased.

We will look at faithful ways to follow those ancient churches' lead in the here and now, and thereby empower the full breadth of folks Christ Jesus has brought together to be his body—i.e., the full, universal body of Christ, the congregations bounded together in nations and/or associations and/or denominations and/or particular movements, and each individual congregation, which is a microcosm of the fuller expression of his body. In the process, we also will see that such a biblical model of church movement forms the best context within which the reds and blues, plus the oranges, yellows, greens, indigos, and violets . . . er, uh, purples . . . can find full expression.

This model lived in real time will help better approximate Jesus' model of valuing every one of the one hundred sheep of his parabolic flock—willingly leaving the ninety-nine to win back the one wandering away—than many of our churches have been doing. It also will open wide the fields in which those sheep can exercise their particular gifts to fulfill their particular callings, so that the stagnant, plateaued institutional churches can again become movements, contagions of faith and faithfulness, in living

3. Peters, *Thriving on Chaos.*

forth the full gospel of "the grace of the Lord Jesus Christ, the love of God, and the communion of the Holy Spirit" (2 Cor 13:14).

I know that the above promises and predictions sound grandiose. But in an era of diminishing expectations, program cancellations, and a theology of scarcity, the time has come for the church to elevate its expectations, its vision, its hope. As Yale biblical scholar Leander E. Keck declared in the 1960s, and as recorded in *The Church Confident*, "Christianity Can Repent, but It Must Not Whimper."[4]

So, put on your seat belt. Soar with your friends, family, and me into the full-spectrum church of our full-spectrum Savior to radically transform the red-and-blue world that needs so desperately to rediscover the other colors of the spectrum and to shine that light to the uttermost parts of the earth.

---

4. Keck, *Church Confident*, subtitle.

— Part I —

Two Is the Dangerest Number

— 1 —

The Seas in Which We Swim

Close Encounter of the Fishy Kind

IT'S ONE THING TO hear secondhand the report about dangerous sharks down below a person soaring a few hundred feet above the waters. While those razor-toothed predators may look ferocious, the observer is (usually) safely far above the fray. It's a different thing when encountering the sharks, even just one shark, up close and in person. So it was for this Haberer family two years into our introduction to the Florida paradise.

The off-putting blimp report faded in memory as we dipped toes, then knees, then bellies, and then shoulders into those beautiful waters. Even our young kids found beach time to be rapturous . . . until one particular summer morning.

David was now seven years old, Kelly was five. Barbie (not the doll but their mom and my bride) took them to the beach. As they walked out into waist-to-chest waters, the waves ebbing and flowing such as they do, she stood guard nearby in toe- to ankle-deep water.

Then somebody shouted, "Shark! Shark! Shark!" A cacophony of voices joined the chorus, shouting from every direction. Barbie looked out to the waters, and sure enough, that unmistakable fin was cutting through the foot-deep waters heading straight for our babies.

Instantly, the swimmers and waders turned toward shore and raced to escape the threat. All except David and Kelly. Oh, David was trying to get out. But his little sister was intent on holding her ground. He wrapped both hands around one of her wrists, and tugged on her, trying to drag her to the shore, but was making little progress. She was pulling away from him with all her might. With an internal shot of adrenaline, Barbie gave chase to them, reached out, wrapped her arms around both, and carried them onto dry ground. Then the shark carved right through the waters they had just escaped.

"Kelly, what were you thinking?" Barbie panted, heart pounding. "Didn't you see the shark coming after you?'

Kelly shook her head sheepishly.

"Didn't you hear everybody shouting at you?"

She shrugged her shoulders sheepishly.

"Didn't you hear people shouting, 'Shark, shark'?"

"Yeah," she said, as she nodded sheepishly.

"Why didn't you come out of the water?"

She just stared at Mom nervously.

"Why didn't you come out of the water?" Barbie asked again, more sternly.

Fighting back tears, Kelly answered, "I didn't hear a shark."

"You what?"

"I didn't hear a shark."

"What do you mean, you didn't hear a shark?"

"You know . . ." and her words turned from speech to song, singing in high-pitched staccato notes an unmistakable melody: "Duh, DUH! Duh, DUH! Duh, duh, duh, duh, duh, duh . . . ," the opening notes of the theme song to the movie *Jaws*.

At that, Barbie's tone of voice quieted, her face transformed from stressed to smiling, from intense to tender, from frightened to reassuring, and her words to both kids turned from horrified to prayerful, "Thank God you're both okay."

The Problem of Diagnosis

Kelly was a very advanced child. We knew that the minute she was born. "Oh, she's so advanced," we said when she opened her eyes, when she cried, when she breathed. Yes, we were typical, proud parents. Long term, she showed great intelligence, earning two academic degrees, the first one from an Ivy League college. But on that day in the waters, she didn't show advanced judgment about the fish swimming around her. Her diagnostic skills were wanting—dangerously so.

In fact, she didn't run from danger because she didn't realize she was in danger. She thought that the shark alarm to which she must respond was a two-note theme song from a videotaped movie that some babysitter had played for her. She was oblivious to the real, critical, must-be-obeyed alarm, the screaming voices of panicked swimmers and sunbathers. (Note to the babysitter: it took forty years for Kelly to finally divulge who played that prohibited "R-rated" *Jaws* movie; but we know your name now, and we know where to find you! Hahahaha!)

We laugh about that story now, but at the time it wasn't funny. Likewise in our nation today: All around America people are shouting "Shark, shark, shark!" in fortissimo, but we are not united in our discernment. The creatures that you perceive to be life-threatening, others consider to be allies in battle. Some that others fear most are the ones you trust implicitly.

And therein lies one of our greatest problems . . . we are a divided people—divided most of all by not knowing which alarms signal peril and which alarms are no big deal.

For myself, a kid raised in a typical suburban, middle-class town, some of the warnings heard in my childhood were false, like those older boys warning me, "Stay away from girls; they have cooties," or the older girls warning my sisters, "Stay away from boys; they're stupid."

For this kid raised in the Roman Catholic Church, some of the warnings were exaggerated, like those my classmates and I heard from our sweet, kind first-grade teacher Sister Catherina, who warned us to stay away from dangerous Protestants. Of course, we believed her.

Then again, as a born-again, fundamentalist teenager, my Baptist pastor Larry Magill warned us youth members to stay away from dangerous Catholics. I kinda believed him, but blood running thicker than water, I couldn't exactly disown the folks putting a roof over my head and food in my belly.

Then after high school, I went to a Pentecostal Bible school, where I heard that the Baptists were lacking the Holy Spirit. And that the mainline Protestants and the Roman Catholics weren't born again; at best, they could be categorized merely as "nominal Christians"—i.e., Christian in name only.

Then in a Methodist college, I learned that our Wesleyan theology embraced the God-given gift of human free will, whereas the Reformed churches' theology of predestination was wrong to teach that people who had no free will when it came to matters of salvation.

In a more relatively "broad-minded" evangelical seminary I learned that many denominations and many movements were truly Christian, but only if they affirmed such fundamentals of the faith as the virgin birth of Christ, the inerrancy of Scripture, and Jesus' resurrection. At every point in time, I may not have been able to spell out exactly what I believed in all its particulars, but I knew for sure who all else were wrong, who constituted the "opposition," who represented the field of mission to whom I was being called and sent to convert to the true faith.

Oh, I was willing to live dangerously. When an evangelical pastor serving in one of those nominal mainline denominational churches asked me to join his church staff, I jumped aboard. When the regional leaders of that denomination examined me to see if I was a fitting candidate, I acknowledged that evangelicals like me are in the minority in that denomination. When asked "Why in the world should we let you lead one of our churches?," I responded that I believed that folks like me can bring greater and clearer conviction to the proclamation of the gospel as summarized in their constitution, which they too often taken for granted; and I added that I need folks like them to help people like me avoid a blindness that comes from hanging around single-minded allies clustered together in our theological echo chambers.

They let me in. And the "living dangerously" mode has continued for forty-plus years.

'Tis Been Something of a Battleground

Some fights ought not to be fought. Some alliances ought not to be forged. Sometimes negotiations ought not to be entered. Sometimes we need to stand up and fight . . . or if possible, to take flight.

As we heard in first grade, "Don't get into the cars of strangers!" No negotiation. No consideration. "Drawing a line in the sand" is just the thing to do. Then, again, lines in the sand soon get blurred, smoothed out, washed away. That's really a stupid cliché, if it's intended to mean a final conclusion, a final point of non-compromise has been reached, isn't it?

Still, in my youthful and young adult worlds, a multiplicity of warnings was expressed so repeatedly, so emphatically and with such great threat that we divided our world instinctively between friends and foes, between allies and enemies, between our kind of people and those other kinds of people. Many of those kinds of warnings, those kinds of demarcations, have stuck with us forever.

Going back to my own narrative—swimming with sharks . . . As young adult parents who didn't want to be permanently prohibited from going into the ocean, we knew we needed to do a better job of teaching our children to better listen and respond to signs of danger in the future.

Then again, as a young adult pastor of a church of Bible-believing Christians, I was pretty adept at defining our kind of people—fellow lovers of Jesus—as over against the other kind of people—those who are not lovers of Jesus, but really are wolves in sheep's clothing—fake believers, false believers.

Indeed, in the years preceding and following that close encounter with a shark, I was honing my skills in drawing the lines between true believers on the theological right and false believers on the left . . . or so I thought. Until I took my first trip, already a lifelong dream trip, to the land of Jesus' sojourn on earth: Israel, the Holy Land.

Carmel and Caesarea: Citadel of Truth . . . Port City of Inclusiveness

I expected my first trip to Israel to be an eye-opening experience, one that would illumine the ancient God-stories. I did not expect it to open my eyes to today's God-story.

Every nerve screamed with excitement on that first morning of discovery. After years of searching the depths of Scripture, the bus ride winding up Mt. Carmel proved almost more than my imagination could grasp. Here. Right here Elijah dueled with the prophets of Baal. Here the God of Abraham and Sarah, Isaac and Leah, Jacob and Rachel shut out the gods of the Canaanite pantheon. Here divinity proved itself. Here I was now encountering the very "here" of God's visitation.

Our trans-Atlantic flight had delivered us to Israel the night before. Now, just eighteen hours later, we were ascending to a place whose history had captivated me for years. A major research paper in seminary had led me through the study of the ancient Baal epic, discovered in 1928. I had parsed every Hebrew word and retranslated every phrase. I had learned that the drought brought on by Elijah's prophecy had targeted Baal for personal humiliation, since he was not only the prime minister of Canaanite mythology but also the god allegedly possessing the power over the elements of sun, lightning, and rain. I had learned that Queen Jezebel, who had imported such paganism, was driven by her ambition for unchallenged control in Israel that demanded putting Elijah's "troublemaking" out of the way forever. I had learned that Elijah's final success in calling fire down from heaven would prove the undoing of the queen's paganism and her power. Indeed, Elijah's faith was validated, God was shown to be almighty, and the prophets of Baal were brought to their fateful end. Truth had won.

Here we now were re-engaging that truth-conquest. The bus driver parked just outside the gate of the monastery atop the mountain. Walking through the gate, we entered the courtyard. To our right rose the small monastery and to our left stood a tall statue of the sword-bearing prophet slaying a defeated pagan priest (a rather violent-looking image by today's standards). We walked across the courtyard and ascended steps around the left side of the monastery. Arriving at an open terrace, a wide panorama opened before us: to the west, the blue Mediterranean Sea, to the east, the Valley of Armageddon, and to the south, a row of mountains heading toward Jerusalem.

Ronnie, our tour guide, pointed toward the southwest, along the coastline. "Look over there," he said. "Can you see those smokestacks?" We squinted to see. Readjusting our focus we blurted a chorus of, "Yes," "I see them," "There they are."

He continued, "That's Caesarea, where we were an hour ago."

My thoughts catapulted about eight hundred years from the days of Elijah to the time of Peter. I thought about the stories we had just read while in Caesarea's open theater on our first stop up the coast from our Tel Aviv hotel. My thoughts ran particularly to that one story—the conversion of Cornelius, the Roman soldier. Being a God-fearer, a Roman who followed Jewish practices, his desire for God caused him to send messengers down the coast to Joppa to urge the apostle Peter to come and tell him the news of Jesus. Just before those messengers reached Joppa, Peter was shown a vision of a sheet filled with unkosher foods descending from heaven, and was told to eat what was there. Upon protesting its unlawfulness, he heard a voice command, "What God has called clean let no one call unclean." Released from those Levitical standards, Peter traced the coast northward a day's journey to Caesarea and led Cornelius to faith. In the process, the wall of exclusion between "God's Chosen

People" and the outsiders was destroyed, and the division between Jew and gentile abolished.

Standing now upon the terrace, my thoughts suddenly caught up to the present. I found myself thinking about the church entering the twenty-first century. "Here it is," I thought. "This is where we live now," I pondered, though feeling disrupted by its potential implications. "This is where the church is . . . living in the tension between Carmel, the citadel of truth, and Caesarea, the port city of inclusiveness."

The timing could not have been more uncanny. Just a couple weeks before I had celebrated a Presbyterian triumph of truth—*at least, truth as I understood it at the time.* As moderator of the Presbyterian Coalition, I had helped encourage votes across my denomination to block ratification of Amendment A, the "fidelity-integrity" amendment, as it was known, which would have weakened the denomination's prohibition against the ordination of "avowed, unrepentant, sexually active homosexuals," as it was most often phrased. For three years I had spent an enormous amount of energy helping establish that policy and then, most recently, had expended more effort to defeat my opponents' watered-down alternative.

In the process I had cast my hopes, dreams, and convictions on the altar as Elijah had placed his sacrifice. I had gone out on a limb, casting my lot with the prophet's determination to stand for the truth—no matter what the cost—so that God's will would be represented faithfully and proclaimed purely in the church. Mt. Carmel felt like home. This citadel of truth was where I belonged.

Yet Caesarea, with its port opened wide to the sea, looked warm and welcoming, too—albeit in a different way. Here was the place from which God's good news had burst out of Israel's tribal monopoly. Here was the embarkation point for a gospel that ultimately welcomed into God's household my gentile Irish and German ancestors. Caesarea is the Ellis Island of Asian Christians, African Christians, European Christians, Australian Christians, et al. With its story of gentile inclusion, Caesarea had welcomed me and my friends to faith just as today it welcomed us to this holy land.

Well I knew that I was treading on dangerous ground, entertaining these thoughts. I certainly had been avoiding the Caesarea story for months. Throughout the amendment debates over the months earlier, my liberalizing opponents kept trying to make hay of this story, in the hope of convincing us to loosen our standards and broaden the church *to be a welcoming and affirming church,* as they so often urged.

Standing here on the terrace, I couldn't help myself. I had to ponder, "Perhaps God wants us to live both in Carmel *and* in Caesarea at the same time."

These were frightening thoughts, staggering thoughts. I could not think them without immediately identifying with the disappointment felt by Scott Anderson, the gay man in Sacramento who, years before, had demitted his ministerial ordination when outed by a member of his congregation. Several days before leaving for Israel, on the day we announced our amendment-vote victory, I had interrupted my celebration long enough to call Scott to express my sympathy over yet another setback for him and his allies. Now my thoughts moved beyond detached sympathy to a more attached empathy. I did not doubt that we conservatives were following an understanding of God's truth regarding sexual ethics that had stood uninterrupted for three thousand years. I felt no remorse for standing in line with so many great figures of Christian faith. I could not apologize for my efforts to proclaim Christ's liberating power from alternative sexual desires to live in heterosexual faithfulness. Yet I could not help but recognize that my opponents believed themselves to be following an understanding of God's love and grace that had wrestled against exclusivist trends ever since the days of the apostles. I surely could feel compassion for the way they felt shut out by the church's policy.

Looking out over such a vista and contemplating such thoughts forced one thing to become all too clear and too vivid to deny: the word "inclusion" belongs in my Christian vocabulary. In the past I would always shake my head in quiet derision when hearing that word uttered by denominational leaders or when coming across it while reading the *Christian Century* (yes, I subscribed to the *Christian Century*, but like other evangelicals I would carry it around inside my latest copy of the more conservative *Christianity Today*). The religion of inclusiveness had seemed to be nothing more than yet another step down the stairway into the bottomless pit of modernist and postmodernist relativism. Now, having seen Caesarea, I could no longer dismiss inclusivism as the buzzword of liberal foes. This port city burned an indelible mark in my mind's eye. It penetrated my theological lead shield. It commissioned me—at minimum—to take a whole new look at myself, asking, "If Jesus were here today, would I embrace him as did the Marys, Marthas, Matthews, and Marks . . . or would I be standing alongside the Pharisees, Sadducees, and scribes, opposing his inclusion of 'those people'?"

Not an easy question to ponder while visiting the Holy Land . . .

A couple of weeks after returning home from Israel, Stated Clerk Cliff Kirkpatrick called with a proposition. "Jack, these amendment votes are tearing up the church. We've got to find a way to stop the bloodletting. Would you be willing to meet with a small group of leaders to talk about finding a different way?" I could hardly say no to the senior constitutional officer of my denomination. Quickly he arranged a meeting to include Roberta Hestenes, John Galloway, Barry VanDeventer, John Buchanan, Laird Stuart, and me. The credentials of each were well-established. Roberta, one of the leading statespersons in American evangelicalism, and first woman to serve as president of an evangelical university, had chaired the General Assembly committee that forged the "Fidelity-Chastity" amendment, supported by the Presbyterian Coalition and adopted successfully a year before. Laird had chaired the General Assembly committee one year later that formed the alternative "Fidelity-Integrity" amendment, and John Buchanan, a former Moderator of General Assembly and present co-moderator of the Covenant Network of Presbyterians, had helped spearhead the unsuccessful efforts at adopting this liberalized policy. John Galloway had worked quietly behind the scenes from a neutral stance to bring warring parties together, and Cliff's overall love for and service to the church pleaded for peace and unity, and was epic in dimension and scope. Barry, a presbytery executive, had worked with me in supporting the traditional position and would have brought keen constitutional expertise to our discussions. Unfortunately, other obligations forced him to cancel the trip at the last minute.

Cliff asked me if I would prepare some thoughts to lead us in an opening worship. We met at a beautiful estate home in suburban San Diego, where a courtyard, supplied with backboard and basketballs, gave us an easy way to vent our competitive energies; a few airballs by us middle-aged pastors—all frustrated jocks at heart—served up enough humility to help break the ice. After a few embarrassed laughs we gathered in the living room, shared introductions, and I opened my Bible to Acts 10, the story of the conversion of Cornelius. I recounted my recent visit to Caesarea and Carmel, underlining the geographical irony I had encountered there and highlighting the tension of faithfulness that was challenging us here. After a song and a prayer, we began our discussions.

We shared both our hopes and fears for the larger church. No one held any illusions about the near future, given the relatively close votes that had ratified the one amendment and rejected the other. Cliff asked bluntly, "Is there another way to get through this?"

Roberta volunteered, "Well, I'm working on an article for the *Presbyterian Outlook* that calls for a time-out. What do you all think about that?" The conversation grew animated. Laird and John Buchanan acknowledged that the possibility of yet another defeat to their cause would be devastating. Roberta and I admitted that many evangelicals had made it clear that, if called to yet another denomination-wide amendment battle, they would refuse to participate; many of them were talking seriously about leaving the denomination; we knew we could lose by default. We all acknowledged that the recent debates and votes had polarized the church, had created many tensions within presbyteries, had promoted the use of diatribes while quashing attempts at thoughtful dialogue, and had drained so much energy from our own ministries and those of the whole church. We all wanted to take a break. John Buchanan offered the suggestion that we use more biblical language, like "sabbath." I proposed that we issue a "Call to Sabbatical."

The call urged taking a season (no specified time, but at least a couple of years was implied) to back away from writing new legislative proposals. We urged our fellow Presbyterians to refrain from provoking judicial actions, i.e., neither shining flashlights in bedroom windows to catch sinners "in the act" nor engaging in "ecclesiastical disobedience" that would require others to enforce church law. Of course such a call could carry no constitutional power. Neither could we presume to negotiate a commitment from our respective constituencies. If General Assembly commissioners wished to propose new legislation, they could. Judicial charges also could always be filed. We just hoped rather that moral suasion would hold sway.

After lots of group editing, Cliff published and circulated our Call from his office.

The initial response to the Call was disconcerting. *The Presbyterian Layman*,[1] a publication of the Presbyterian Lay Committee, decried it as a sellout, snatching defeat from the proverbial jaws of victory. They also charged that it grew out of a clandestine negotiation session engaged by individuals unauthorized to do so (of course a "call" to sabbatical does not equate to a sabbatical "treaty"; its only force being an appeal by the authors to the larger church to take a time out). Presbyterians for Lesbian and Gay Concerns also decried it as a sellout, insisting that their liberal

---

1. *The Presbyterian Layman* dissolved in 2018 after fifty-three years of publication.

allies were too willing to accept defeat against the villainous legalism of the conservatives.

Nevertheless, the Call was embraced at the broad center of the church. When the General Assembly convened a few weeks later, the "Call to Sabbatical" echoed through the halls. The Assembly, under the leadership of its newly elected moderator, Douglas Oldenberg, chose to follow the lead. The only related action taken was that of calling for a national conference to contemplate "The Nature of the Unity We Seek in the Midst of Our Diversity."

The weeks following the Assembly felt pretty rocky for this leader. I had already announced my resignation from serving as moderator of Presbyterian Coalition. Now it became clear that some were ready for me to step aside. Some board members felt betrayed by the Call. Others supported the idea, as expressed by Clayton Bell, pastor of Dallas' Highland Park Presbyterian Church and brother-in-law of Billy Graham, who said simply, "Folks I questioned the Call at first, but I'm now convinced that Jack has heard God in this."

Indeed, feedback over the next several months indicated that some evangelicals wanted to draw a hard line between "us" and "them." Others welcomed the prospect of finding a new way to deal with our conflicts in the church. While nobody seemed to know how to get there, many expressed the hope that those willing to extend the effort just might be able to forge a new model of relationships that would enable the church to stay together while reclaiming the central message of the gospel.

At the same time many liberal opponents added their voices to the call to seek a new path. Some of them began by striking up conversation with some of us evangelicals, startling us into discovering that they were not as wildly liberal as we had earlier perceived. Some acknowledged embarrassment over extremes taken by some of their liberal allies. Many made clear that their support of gay rights only extends to those engaged in monogamous relationships—that multiple partnering is off limits. Some articulated an understanding of the gospel that would have been scored an A+ by Billy Graham himself.

I had to admit my own embarrassment over having misinterpreted the intentions, the theology, and the ethics of these opponents. Face it, from where I sat it only stood to reason that all those supporting gay or-dination must also deny other uncomfortable biblical teachings, such as the uniqueness of Christ, Jesus' own virginal conception, his bodily res-urrection, the inspiration and authority of holy Scripture. They probably were okay, I supposed, with Re-Imagining God as Sophia (which in those days was a controversy of huge proportions). Like a long row of dominoes, anybody willing to compromise biblical teaching on marriage was setting in motion an unstoppable assault on all matters of the historic faith. So I had learned in earlier years, and so I had resolved to stand on the side of truth. Now I realized not only that my caricatures of them were wildly inaccurate; I also had to admit that even the expression *gay ordination* really misrepresented their point.

Many of us together recognized that we had stereotyped one another, had caricatured one another, and had demonized one another. Now we found ourselves becoming friends.

One early exchange of friendship came upon arrival at the General Assembly following the Call. After finding a seat in the back row of the Pre-Assembly conference—the price for arriving late—the next persons to arrive and sit in the lone empty seats next to me were John and Sue Buchanan. John introduced me to Sue. He and I exchanged a polite hug. "How goes it, John?" I asked.

"About the same as for you, Jack," he responded. "I'm just keeping busy pulling the arrows out of my back." We both smiled sheepishly; and I served ice water to the two of them.

The next day he reported to me that, after the event Sue asked, "Who was that nice man who gave us the glasses of water?"

John grinned and told me, "I straightened up and told her, 'That's no nice man. That's the czar of the Coalition!'"

In the midst of all these goings-on, it became increasingly clear—at least to a few of us—that we must find a new way to be the church together. Some clues also appeared, most notably the realization that most of us did not believe all the things that others had thought. Most of the liberals weren't radicals. Most of the conservatives weren't fundamentalists. We demonstrated that we really do love both the church and God, and don't want to drive away those with whom we differ. We all caught each other by surprise.

The one clearest conclusion that emerged for me was that the church is far too complex and that most believers far too complicated to continue to allow a simple, two-party theory to summarize the church's divisions. Us vs. them, lovers of God vs. fakes, liberals vs. conservatives . . . such categorizations provide a great way to run a war but they comprise a horrible way to be a church. While the term "diversity" may get misused, the church of Jesus Christ really does reflect a multiplicity of racial and ethnic origins, a diversity of affectional orientations, a variety of visions for mission, an assortment of theological emphases—all existing together around a core theology that gives substance to the expression, "Variety is the spice of life." Put metaphorically, living in both Carmel, the citadel of truth, and Caesarea, the port city of inclusiveness, requires us to embrace and affirm the ambiguities and complexities of our finite human existence as we try our best to comprehend and worship the infinite God.

Diagnostics Taken Seriously

We need to learn better how to diagnose just what's going on, to differentiate between dangerous heresies and nominal uniquenesses, to assess and reframe differences in terminology so as to find the commonality that really matters. In other words, we need to study the symptoms and diagnose the real problems.

In Kelly's case—yes, the case of our "advanced" five-year-old at the beach—she did develop diagnostic skills. A masters of physical therapy equipped her to implement programs of muscle development to help hundreds of patients to recover from accidents and to regain mobility after surgeries. However, while she can make her own assessments based on patients' presentation of their ailments, she can't make conclusive medical diagnoses. The proper chain of command in the field requires physicians' full panel of diagnostic tests to guide a therapist's plan of care for said ailments, toward full recovery and active mobility. Accurate diagnoses require professional skill sets, trustworthy diagnostic mechanisms, careful study of symptoms, and a thorough analysis of a person's medical history.

Have you ever arrived in a doctor's office only to be handed a clipboard with forms to fill out, including a long checklist of possible past ailments for which you must check "yes" or "no"? Medical history provides one of the most essential tools needed to diagnose present symptoms.

So, too, in order to assess the present symptoms of distress, conflict, and dysfunction in today's churches, we need to consider our ecclesiastical history. We need to take a close look at the matters of recent history, perhaps the past century, to identify and discern past ailments' lasting effects upon us. What injuries, what diseases, what poisons, what psychological disorders have collectively set us up for the maladies we are suffering today?

Might such diagnostics point a way for us to live in both Carmel and Caesarea at the same time, being at home, truly at home in the one body of Christ, the church universal?

— 2 —

The Best of Centuries, the Worst of Centuries

KELLY'S "I DIDN'T HEAR the shark" close encounter left her parents with every other parent's greatest fear: What she doesn't know could kill her!

Social scientists and communications professionals often tell us, "Perception is reality." That is to say, people perceive what you say or do, not so much by your saying or doing, but more by what they perceived to have happened to them in the past that informs and interprets your saying and doing. In Kelly's case, a movie did it to her. The *Jaws* theme song twisted her mind into thinking that that familiar tune is actually the singular and sufficient siren warning of an oncoming shark attack. Wrong.

Well, the same sort of "Wrong" has been rampant among Christians of our day. And that's because of an inaccurate memory of our recent past. By "recent" I mean the past century, the twentieth century, plus the two or so decades preceding and following. The forces shaping the early decades of the 2000s cannot be understood and addressed without connecting these more recent years to the context of the 1900s. Only with the insights of that collective, mostly unconscious memory can we begin to gain the guidance to see into our twenty-first-century future.

The Best of Centuries

The twentieth century was an incredibly amazing century for most brands of Christianity in America. Most of us can revel in the fact that, at least for a decade or two in some stretch of time, our own brand, denomination, or movement has flourished. But most of us can also mourn that, at least for some other decade or two, our brand, denomination, or movement has floundered. In summary ways, in the first sixty years, 1900–1960, the historic mainline Protestant and Roman Catholic churches dominated the American scene; in the next sixty years, 1960–2020, the Catholics dispensed with Latin masses and in Protestantism the fundapentacharisgelical[1] movement began to squeeze into, and eventually overwhelm, the traditional liturgical churches. Folk music and praise bands pushed out organs and choirs.

Now, let's pause for a moment. If this is sounding like the set-up for a bunch of boring history, do not give in to the temptation to skip this part of our conversation. You need—we all need—to learn every one of our histories and contexts in order for us to escape the black hole of the red-and-blue divide. Only by "getting each other" can we connect with each other in a full-spectrum church experience and community. So, let's consider the century behind us, on whose shoulders we hope to march toward the twenty-second century, by briefly recapping some of its more remarkable highlights:

- The publication of *The Five Fundamentals*,[2] and the resulting launch of American fundamentalism. Who could have imagined back then what a force that would prove to be a hundred years later?

- The first publication in 1900 of *The Christian Century* magazine, as a rebranding of *The Christian Oracle* initially published in 1884 by the Christian Church (Disciples of Christ). It aimed to fuel the optimism felt by many Christians that in the coming twentieth century the "genuine Christian faith could live in mutual harmony with the

---

1. "Fundapentacharisgelical" is a label coined by yours truly. More to be said about it shortly.

2. The Five Fundamentals:
   - The inspiration and inerrancy of Scripture.
   - The deity of Jesus Christ.
   - The virgin birth of Christ.
   - The substitutionary, atoning work of Christ on the cross.
   - The physical resurrection and the personal bodily return of Christ to the earth.

modern developments in science, technology, immigration, communication and culture that were already under way."[3] The then-recent elimination of the system of chattel slavery sparked hopes for the expansion of rights and privileges for women, for racial minorities, for union workers, etc., all manifesting the universal command to "love thy neighbor as thyself."

- The launch of the Federal Council of Churches (1908) formed to bring together thirty-two denominations to carry out the Social Creed[4]—written and adopted by the Methodist Episcopal Church (precursor to the United Methodists)—to guide their social and political advocacy, especially on matters of temperance, Prohibition, and industrial democracy. In 1950 it expanded to thirty-eight denominations and was renamed the National Council of Churches.

- The beginnings of women's ordination initiated by the African Methodist Episcopal Zion Church in 1898 (after a few short-lived attempts earlier in that century; more later about this). Soon Pentecostal churches of various ethnicities were empowering women to preach, such as Aimee Semple McPherson, who founded the Four Square Pentecostal denomination and pioneered radio preaching. By the mid-twentieth century, the Christian Methodist Episcopal and African Methodist Episcopal churches were ordaining women as well. Historically white mainline denominations followed suit,

---

3. *Christian Century,* "Mission."

4. "The Methodist Episcopal Church stands—

For equal rights and complete justice for all (people) in all stations of life.

For the principle of conciliation and arbitration in industrial dissensions.

For the protection of the worker from dangerous machinery, occupational diseases, injuries and mortality.

For the abolition of child labor.

For such regulation of the conditions of labor for women as shall safeguard the physical and moral health of the community.

For the suppression of the "sweating system."

For the gradual and reasonable reduction of hours of labor to the lowest practical point, with work for all; and for that degree of leisure for all which is the condition of the highest human life.

For a release from employment one day in seven.

For a living wage in every industry.

For the highest wage that each industry can afford, and for the most equitable division of the products of industry that can ultimately be devised.

For the recognition of the Golden Rule and the mind of Christ as the supreme law of society and the sure remedy for all social ills." See "1908 Social Creed."

each one accomplished through perseverance triumphing over traditionalism.

- The Azusa Street Revival (1909) in Los Angeles and the launch of modern Pentecostalism lasted not just for a few years, as in past revivals or awakenings, but for a whole century of expansion around the world. Today, Pentecostals comprise 279 million adherents worldwide. Nobody could have imagined how massive and world-influential this movement would become.

- The Charismatic Renewal emerged spontaneously mid-century, like popcorn on a hot stove, as a form of neo-Pentecostalism. It grew rapidly within many traditional churches and launched many other nondenominational congregations and fellowships of churches to the level of 305 million adherents worldwide (making the Pentecostals plus Charismatics, at 584 million combined, to be 27 percent of world Christians—second only to the Roman Catholics, who comprise about 50 percent).[5] Speaking of massive and world influential!

- Vatican II. It occurred not in the US per se, but in the Holy See, Rome's Vatican. By way of reforms adopted under the leadership of Pope John XXIII, world Catholicism replaced Latin-only readings and prayers in favor of the familiar, vernacular languages of its members, wherever they might be. They also declared that Protestants, those whom they had been calling "infidels" and "apostates" for the past 450 years, would now be dubbed "separated brethren" (separated, but siblings in the faith).

- Rev. Billy Graham (1918–2018). That American evangelist, who is believed to have led more people worldwide to faith in Christ than anybody ever before, also helped spearhead the launch of the neo-evangelical movement, which retained the five fundamentals (see fundamentalists above) but eschewed the anti-intellectualism and separatism typical of that movement. Institutions like *Christianity Today* magazine, the National Association of Evangelicals, the Evangelical Theological Society, and Fuller Theological Seminary fueled the rapid growth of the neo-evangelicals.

- Mother Teresa (1910–97). Again, not an American, but the Albanian-Indian Catholic nun and founder of the Missionaries of

---

5. Pew Research Center's Forum on Religion & Public Life: *Global Christianity*, December, 2011.

Charity extended such radically sacrificial care to the poorest of the poor that she inspired Catholic and non-Catholic Christians worldwide, culminating in her becoming the 1979 Nobel Peace Prize winner, followed by her canonization as St. Teresa of Calcutta in 2016.

- Rev. Martin Luther King Jr. (1929–68) was the greatest catalyst and unstoppable force in advancing the causes of civil rights, racial justice, and integration, by way of nonviolent protests and brilliant oratory. He remains one of the most defining figures in America, from leading the 385-day Montgomery Bus Boycott in 1955 to Congress' adoption of the Voting Rights Act in 1965, from the 1964 presentation of the Nobel Peace Prize to his tragic 1968 assassination.

- The Jesus Movement (late 1960s . . .) of hippies turned into "Jesus People"—also known as "Jesus Freaks"—converged Christ-centered lyrics with rock music, which grew into Contemporary Christian music, which supplemented or totally replaced traditional hymns in many US churches. Hymnals have largely given way to projection screens, too.

- Megachurches combined the popularity of new worship music, dynamic preaching, and both TV and online broadcasting to generate a wave of churches with attendance in the tens of thousands, which inadvertently contributed to an exodus of worshipers away from many smaller churches.

- LGBTQ+ believers came out of the closet, paving the way to begin normalizing the lives and roles of LGBTQ+ individuals into "welcoming and affirming churches," leading to marriage ceremonies and ministerial ordinations in a few denominations. While supported by many Gen X and millennial believers, this change is not generally approved in most churches, denominations, and movements. Regardless, the very subject has launched many a denominational battle, including the 2020s Methodist split, the largest denomination division since the Civil War.

- Jimmy Carter (b. 1924) was, in 1976, the first presidential candidate to identify as a "born-again Christian" (specifically as Southern Baptist), and the first of several to court the conservative, evangelical vote. It was, however, in his reelection campaign that his competitor, Ronald Reagan, succeeded in courting the evangelicals, who carried him to victory. They also became the force for the election of

George H. W. and George W. Bush, and ultimately, Donald Trump. More of this to follow . . .

- Scandals . . . from the infidelities of sawdust trail revivalists and television preachers, to the discoveries of the sexual exploitation of children by priests, missionaries, youth directors, and pastors; few religious traditions have dodged the indictments of perpetrators nor avoided the accusations of hypocrisy and institutional cover-up.

While some of the above listed events and individuals may be universally seen as great or tragic, others receive mixed reactions. What you remember with fond sentiments, another remembers with horrified disappointment.

Of course, many more events and personalities could fill out the high and low points of the faiths once delivered and ultimately exhibited in the past century or so.

But two more events and their respective luminaries rise to the surface as being the most defining upon the faith commitments and practices of the twentieth century. One occurred in the century's first few decades. The other arose in the final few decades.

The War to Launch Many More Wars

The defining faith-related event of the first half of the twentieth century was the Scopes Monkey Trial. Immortalized in the 1960 movie *Inherit the Wind* (which has been re-filmed and re-released numerous times), it cast its shadow across every decade that has followed it. In fact, it may not be an exaggeration to say that every ideological split and schism of congregations and denominations over the following hundred years was an aftershock of the still-unresolved conflict that came into focus in that 1925 Tennessee courtroom.

The indictment of John T. Scopes for teaching evolution drew two of the most celebrated lawyers in the land, William Jennings Bryan and Clarence Darrow, to face off against one another. Darrow, an agnostic[6] known as a legal champion for the unfortunate and oppressed, defended the high school teacher. Bryan, the three-time unsuccessful Democratic nominee for president and two-time unsuccessful candidate for moderator of the Presbyterian Church, prosecuted the case. Although known for

---

6. Darrow, *Essential Words and Writings of Clarence Darrow*, 20.

his liberal political convictions, Bryan was a biblical literalist and fundamentalist. The American media, especially journalist H. L. Mencken, covered this case as had never been done before, providing salacious details of each day's proceedings, often mocking Bryan's passion as driven by simplistic narrow-mindedness. Bryan ultimately won the case, but he died just a fortnight later. And American-brand evangelical faith seemed to die with him.

That conservatism had been a defining mark of American Protestantism since the arrival of the first colonists from Europe. Although subsequent history brought ebbs and flows (for example, the Revolutionary era was more noted for its deism than an evangelical faith), a cyclical pattern of renewal and awakening had kept alive a passion for the gospel and a broad adherence to biblical ethics and morals.

That cycle burst into a flashpoint in the early decades of the twentieth century. The academic world was aflame with new ideas fomented by Charles Darwin, Sigmund Freud, and Karl Marx. Schools of biblical criticism not only were questioning the authorship of the Pentateuch (the first five books of the Hebrew Scriptures, i.e., the Christian Old Testament) and the historical accuracy of Gospel accounts of Jesus' life; but these ideas were breaking out of the academy to be read by the general population. For example, Albert Schweitzer's first theological work, *The Quest for the Historical Jesus,*[7] was read widely upon its release in 1906. A pervasive optimism in humanity's innate ability to improve its lot was surging as the new century burst forth. The Enlightenment was finally shining its light where regular people could see it.

For conservative Christians, worldliness was winning the war against biblical faith, and they were not about to abide such setbacks. They drew a line in the sand by defining the five fundamentals, as stated above, but that line became a wall of demarcation when the modernists pushed evolution, and with it, the apparent repudiation of the Genesis account of creation *ex nihilo* (from nothing) into public school classrooms.

Specifically, in 1923, two years prior to the Scopes trial, J. Gresham Machen, professor of Princeton Theological Seminary, published *Christianity and Liberalism,*[8] titled intentionally to draw an unambiguous distinction between what he considered to be two mutually exclusive sets of beliefs.

---

7. Schweitzer, *Quest for the Historical Jesus.*
8. Machen, *Christianity and Liberalism.*

Following the Scopes trial, the general population came on board with a resounding support of the open-minded ideas of the moderns, along with a shunning disapproval of the fundamentalism promoted by Bryan and Machen.

In the years that followed, Machen turned his sights to the purification of theology at Princeton Seminary, where he was teaching. Convinced that both the church and the seminary had crossed their orthodox theological boundaries and confident that the vast majority of Presbyterians supported his commitment to conservative, biblical faith, he called for the organization of Westminster Theological Seminary in Philadelphia and a new Independent Board of Presbyterian Foreign Missions. Conflicts and controversy soon engulfed the new board. Machen challenged the leadership of Robert Speer, the venerable statesman of Presbyterian missions, and at the Presbyterian Church US General Assembly of 1936 Machen and several other clergy were suspended.

They quickly realized their dreams of forming a new Presbyterian Church of America, at whose first General Assembly, Machen declared his thrill over the new beginning: "On Thursday, June 11, 1936, the hopes of many years were realized. We became members, at last, of a true Presbyterian Church; we recovered, at last, the blessing of a true Christian fellowship. What a joyous moment it was! How the long years of struggle seemed to sink into nothingness compared with the peace and joy that filled our hearts! . . . With that lively hope does our gaze turn now to the future! At last true evangelism can go forward without the shackle of compromising associations."[9]

Convinced that the vast majority of Presbyterians shared his biblical convictions, Machen became a grand marshal, leading a parade of faithful Presbyterians into a whole new church. But nobody showed up for the parade. Or more accurately, a scant few thousand communicants joined the new church. Also, "within six months Machen had been ousted as president of the Independent Board for Presbyterian Foreign Missions, and his infant church was torn by dissent over premillennialism and the use of alcoholic beverages."[10] He soon contracted pneumonia and died on January 1, 1937.

---

9. Quoted in Longfield, *Presbyterian Controversy*, 212.

10. Quoted in Longfield, *Presbyterian Controversy*, 212.

The Division You Have with You Always

The division between fundamentalism and liberalism, having been so clearly drawn by the Scopes trial and reinforced by the efforts of Machen and allies, was escalated by the unplanned alliance between liberalizing denominational institutions' protectiveness and secular news reporters' hostility. The formulating of that progressive alliance was matched on the other side by the fundamentalists' formulation of a separation ethic: a commitment to resist the leaven of the modernists and liberals; it drove them to withdraw into the caverns of isolationism. A forty-year wilderness journey thereafter kept them out of the national public eye.

Of course, particular fundamentalist churches in particular towns served as the center of community life, especially in the Deep South. And particularly stunning fundamentalist and Pentecostal preachers found audiences in revival tents and on radio broadcasts.

But, whenever the national press reported the leading ideas of Christian thinkers, it was the such avowedly liberal pastor-theologian superstars as Harry Emerson Fosdick, Paul Tillich, Karl Rahner, to whom they would turn (they also would turn to Reinhold and H. Richard Niebuhr, who would self-identify as moderates, but who taught at liberal Union Seminary, New York City, and Yale Divinity School respectively).

After the end of World War II, it was the mainline Protestant churches that grew, riding on the wave of the baby boom, along with Roman Catholics, whose prohibition against birth control did aid in producing large families.

But gradually, it was the Baptists, Pentecostals, the Restorationists (such as Churches of Christ), and other fundamentalists whose birth rates grew and whose converting recruits soared. By the late 1960s, Sunday schools were expanding in such churches—with major churches enjoying friendly attendance competitions against one another. Add to that the Billy Graham Crusades that were filling sports arenas and stadiums, bringing thousands to faith, and creating enough of a buzz to draw press attention to this new movement, as well as the seemingly spontaneous outburst of charismatic faith among Roman Catholics and some mainline churches, along with the hippie generation of the late 1960s and early seventies bursting forth with fervor in the Jesus movement (which was shunned by some, like Bob Jones, president of the Greenville, South Carolina, university bearing his name, but embraced by Graham and many others). All these movements also crisscrossed racial segregation lines as Andraé Crouch and the Disciples, the Brooklyn Gospel Tabernacle Choir, Mahalia Jackson, James Cleveland, Shirley Caesar, and other musicians of color stirred the souls of crowds of all ethnicities with their musical fervor. Add all that together, and a very diverse movement of conservative inclinations was busting out all over.

Lest we get too far ahead of ourselves, it is essential to note that the above paragraph probably sounds more united than it was. Five separate movements were all exploding with growth and enthusiasm, but doing so mostly independent of one another.

The fundamentalists—commonly Baptist, Church of Christ, or nondenominational—read their favorite magazine, *The Moody Monthly*. The Pentecostals—commonly Assemblies of God, the Apostolic Church, the Foursquare Church, Church of God (Cleveland, Tennessee), and Church of God in Christ—followed their revival preachers and authors. The neo-evangelicals—some of them Southern Baptist, the Evangelical Free Church, and countless nondenominational churches—loved Billy Graham and read *Christianity Today*. The charismatic fellowships read *Charisma* and *New Wine* magazines, bought and read Logos personal testimony books by the millions, and met in newly organized nondenominational churches and/or gathered in Bible studies and prayer groups in church halls and homes while attending different mainline and Catholic churches. Plus, charismatic Catholics accommodated the influx of enthusiasm into their sacramental faith, mixing with those of Protestant affiliations but still retaining their Roman DNA.

In the process, most of these groups distrusted and even shunned the others. The fundamentalists thought the others were either too fanatical (swinging from chandeliers) or compromised (worldly and/or intellectual). The Pentecostals thought those not speaking in tongues to be too stuffy and closed to the Holy Spirit; they considered the charismatics to be too worldly, too. The evangelicals saw the fundamentalists and Pentecostals as narrow and uneducated, and considered the charismatics as too flaky and flighty. The charismatics saw all the rest as old school, uptight, and unspiritual. And the Catholics, having been the first on the block (for the first 1,500 years), could claim to be the one (and only) holy, catholic, and apostolic church, while all the rest were rebels, schismatics, infidels.

But then came Jerry Falwell and Pat Robertson.

The First Half of the Second Monumental Event: the Fundapentacharisgelical Movement

As the fourth quarter of the twentieth century emerged on the calendar, Jerry Falwell the fundamentalist and Pat Robertson the Pentecostal-turned-charismatic both emerged from their respective Virginia head-quarters onto TV screens and into conservative Christians' hearts, minds, and polling places. What had become known as the Religious Right and the family values movement—noting that both titles lacked the sectarian labels that would favor or disfavor any particular faith convictions or affiliation—found in these two men and their organizations incredibly strategic skill sets with which to build a mega-empire.

In the mountains of western Virginia (east of West Virginia, to be clear), Lynchburg was the country town that reared Jerry Falwell (1933–2007). Raised in the Baptist church, he was both the captain of the high school football team and the valedictorian of his class. He accepted Christ as his Savior, studied at Baptist Bible College in Springfield, Missouri, returned to Lynchburg in 1956 to start a new church, named for its address: Thomas Road Baptist Church. He "fashioned a Christianity that was well suited to this local context—one that was anticommunist, pro-segregationist, and infused throughout with a militant masculinity."[11] The church grew rapidly to be one of the top attended Baptist Sunday schools in the nation (in good fun, pastors of these early megachurches liked to challenge each other to attendance duels, in the process challenging their own members to invite all their neighbors and friends to bring home the victory; and Falwell won many of them). In order to bus children from nonreligious homes to the classes, they bought enough school buses to fill a massive parking lot.

Aided by his radio and TV broadcasts, Falwell established an empire of influence. Long-standing political conservatives prodded him to organize a national organization driven by the religious fervor. In 1979, the efforts came to focus as he gave birth to the Moral Majority. While the term was codified and popularized a decade before by Richard Nixon as a way to minimize the influence of the radicals on the left, who were staging marches for all their causes, now it was Falwell who wasn't going to be silent. He was quickly becoming the hub pulling together many disparate and distrusting groups—generating the Fundapentacharisgelical movement (my term, not his).

11. Du Mez, *Jesus and John Wayne*, 96.

Drawing upon the already existing *Christian Voice*, which was torn by internal acrimony, Falwell utilized his large TV and radio mailing list to pioneer massive direct-mail campaigns in order to build a far-reaching network of support and financial funding. Aligning singly with Republican party platforms, especially ones reflecting traditional values, and speaking against what he considered to be any threat to those values (such as abortion, the Equal Rights Amendment, lesbian and gay rights, and court-ordered racial integration), the national elections over the next two decades repeatedly surprised voters and especially pollsters. The Moral Majority-supported candidates repeatedly outperformed the pundits' predictions—and election night news broadcasters kept saying, "The Religious Right has completely outperformed all of our predictions."

Indeed, in Falwell's success at changing the subject away from such internecine, conflicting and parochial issues as speaking in tongues, prohibitions against dancing, drinking, and moviegoing, to find common concerns, such as abortion, he pulled all those disparate movements into a mega-movement, a religious-sounding but more truly a powerful political force for national cultural change.

He shuttered the Moral Majority in 1987, less than a decade after its inception, but it sent out ripples of impact right up to the present, five decades later.

The Second Half of That Second Monumental Event: Coalition

Turning back to just a few years after Falwell's ordination in 1960–61, and two hundred miles east in Virginia Beach, Marion Gordon "Pat" Robertson was ordained, also by the Southern Baptist Convention. A Marine veteran of the Korean War and recent graduate of Yale School of Law and The Biblical Seminary of New York, he served neither as a lawyer (he failed his only attempt to pass the bar) nor as a pastor. Instead, he bought a defunct UHF television station to open the Christian Broadcasting Network (CBN) in nearby Portsmouth.

Featuring family-oriented entertainment at first (mostly syndicated reruns), in 1966 he launched his own show, not one for preaching but for conversations mixed with periodic musical performances. A talk show, modeled after *The Tonight Show*, as pioneered by Steve Allen, Jack Paar, and Johnny Carson, Robertson's *700 Club* featured personal testimonies of God's work in his guests' lives, especially reports of miraculous healings, visions, and answers to prayer. He slowly established an audience that was made to feel like members of the extended Robertson family.

As producer, director, and host, Robertson kept the tone positive and enthusiastic, putting God's best foot forward in all aspects of the presentation.

His popularity and the show's ratings grew so rapidly that he campaigned to become the 1988 Republican nominee for president. Failing in that attempt, he turned his now huge mailing list into the beginnings of his successor to the Moral Majority, namely, the Christian Coalition. Picking up where Falwell's network left off allowed Robertson to carry forward the visible role of leader of this massive religiopolitical movement.

And what happened there? Robertson wasn't just a Baptist minister with evangelical theology, as was Falwell. He was both of those plus a card-carrying Pentecostal, having showcased many on his show and by giving open expression to speaking in tongues, making predictive prophecies, and outside speaking engagements. He was the embodiment of a fundapentacharisgelical.

Also, like Falwell who filled two roles, pastor and founding president of a Virginia university, Liberty University, Robertson served as both broadcaster and founding president of his own Regent University and Law School in Virginia. Both men cast shadows from coast to coast.

Most especially, the two functioned as tag-team boxers, leading the battle on behalf of the fundapentacharisgelical conservative Christians against the other camp of the modernist, liberal, progressive, mainline pseudo-Christians (as they would have dubbed them). They drew and defined a clear ecclesiastical divide between their own red Christian allies and those other blue pseudo-Christian opponents. In the process, they married the Christians of theologically conservative instincts to a political party of traditionally conservative values, although not nearly as explicitly Christian as they would claim, and they drove away those nominal Christians of more progressive political instincts, whom they now were confident they outnumbered, thereby polarizing the one against the other.

The red-and-blue divide in the body politic had been fed by and formulated in the body of Christ. By the turn of the century—that is, the turn from second millennium to third (which is loaded language in the light of the biblical use of the term), national denominations, nationwide movements, particular church congregations, and outspoken pastors

soon had aligned themselves for or against the Falwell-Robertson pairing. They may not have hung red or blue flags outside their front doors,
but in their parking lots, especially in election years, you could see with
which camp they identified by glancing at the bumper stickers supporting their congregants' favorite political candidates. Red or blue. We had
become a divided people.

The Worst of Centuries

As a point of personal witness, please allow me to express my radical
ambivalence about this best and worst of centuries. Each and every one of
the labels used thus far in this book, and especially in the account of the
past one hundred-plus years, is one that I have worn boldly and gratefully
at some stage in my spiritual journey of faith. And I say that not conde-
scendingly nor patronizingly, not as a "before-and-after" transition, not
the bad-past-replaced-by-the-good present. I am deeply indebted to my
Roman Catholic childhood, especially to the priests, nuns, and others
there who helped my parents to form a prayerful devotion to the triune
God. I praise God for leading me to encounter Jesus in a fresh way in a
small Southern-Baptist-in-nondenominational-clothing congregation. I
give thanks for leaders of the local chapter of the Full Gospel Business
Men's Fellowship International for introducing me to the charismatic
experience of the Holy Spirit, including speaking in tongues, which
deepened my walk with Christ. I am thrilled to have been paired to sing
in the duo "Nick and Jack" in coffeehouses of the Jesus movement as a
teenager, which empowered me to find a boldness in giving witness to
the gospel. I'm amazed to have been able to begin my college education in
the Pentecostal Elim Bible Institute, which took my prayer life to a height
of joy I could not have imagined and which endowed me with a great
aptitude for the Scriptures. It also introduced me to a wonderful partner
for life, who married me a week after her graduation. I am grateful to my
professors and classmates at Roberts Wesleyan College, who taught me
how to think deeply, analytically, and integratively, shaped by the Wesleyan holiness passions yet informed by a wide breadth of liberal arts
brilliance—thereby helping me to see that "all truth is God's truth" (as
St. Augustine once said). I count it all joy that a fellow employee at UPS
told me about the only seminary he thought worth attending was the
multidenominational Gordon-Conwell Theological in Massachusetts,

which helped me realize how little I really knew about most everything related to Bible, theology, mission, and ministry, and whet my appetite to become a lifelong learner of the breadth of the Christian faith. And I'm amazed to have been hired into a denomination I thought too stoic and too boring for any live Christian to abide that turned into just the right place for me to flourish in all of the aspects of the faith that my previous years had absorbed. Forty years later I'm flabbergasted to think that all of these venues, institutions, affiliations, and mission fields have kept me thriving in the faith and loving to be one of its witnesses and servants.

However, all of these joys have been accompanied by the heartbreaks caused time and again when I have found myself pressed into the place of choosing sides. Us vs. them. Right vs. wrong. Right vs. Left. Red vs. blue.

That kind of choosing sides was fun when it played itself out on Little League baseball fields and in high school football games. But it has been no fun when pressed by colleagues and friends in the faith who have demanded that I choose sides with or against them. On top of that, it has generated a lot of stupid mistakes on my part, a lot of self-defeating efforts when, on my worst days, I have allowed myself to forget what I know to be true about opponents of any one of a thousand or more top-ics of disagreement and have fallen into simple left-right, home-team-versus-visiting-team, us-against-them binary divisions of the house, in which my team is exalting itself as right and true and wise and loving, while judging the other team as wrong and false and stupid and hateful.

Put simply, when you're convinced that "they" are really, really bad, you can be sure that they're not as bad as you fear. And when you're con-vinced that you are really, really good, you can be sure that you're not as good as you claim.

The division of the teams in this past "best of centuries and worst of centuries" has left those of us living in this new century the task of redrawing the sides, renegotiating our rules of engagement, reimagining what it is to be the body of Christ.

But lest we think that is easy, we need to dig deeper still into the bi-nary divide. There's a lot more reality that we need to face if we are going to be able to match our perceptions to the reality that is true and right. While it's one thing to demonize good people, it's another to realize that there really are some demons out there—and some demons in here. In order to discern the reality in which we find ourselves, if we are going to truly and accurately diagnose what is ailing us, we do need to dig deeper. Indeed, we need to span wider, too . . .

— 3 —

The Two-Party Church?

COMMON SENSE TELLS US that we Haberers should have suffered PTSD, post-traumatic stress disorder, after Kelly's close encounter with that shark. You would think we were cured of the "Florida beaches are *paradise on Earth*" fantasy. The *Jaws* movie, which became the highest grossing movie ever that summer of 1975, was blamed for causing a huge drop in beach attendance as millions of sun worshipers were paralyzed by fear over even dipping their toes into such danger-infested waters. As a result, beach-town businesses suffered their own financial perils, as well. If we Haberers were in our right minds we would have done the same: stayed out of the water for at least a year or three.

But being in a right mind always has always seemed to be overrated for us.

Accordingly, all PTSD symptoms disappeared almost as quickly as they had arrived. We had moved three hours north along the coast to Satellite Beach, just south of Cocoa Beach, with its Ron Jon's Surf Shop—the world's largest—setting the tone for the area. After settling into the parsonage just four blocks inland from one of the state's top surfing beaches, it wasn't long before we were spending days out in the waves. We all took up body boarding, and soon, we boys were setting our sights on the real thing: surfing standing up. We knew we'd never become stars of the sport, like Kelly Slater, a classmate of our kids who was and still is considered the greatest surfer of all time. ("Perhaps only the swimmer Michael Phelps has so dominated an individual sport the way Slater has.")[1]

Not only was the location the right place for such recreation, but both kids had shown the talent. In their elementary and middle school years they had become accomplished gymnasts. In addition, David leveraged his gymnastics agility to compete as a diver on the high school swim team.

But the waves were begging for attention . . . and not just from the four of us, but also from his best gymnastics friend, Mike Herman, and their gym coach, Mark Peters, who also was a great friend of mine and an active member of our church. Mark taught us guys how to surf.

We became a regular foursome in the waves together. A few early mornings a week, we would head out our doors to the predicted best wave break of the day, in time to be in the water just as the sun was beginning to peer over the eastern horizon. On many of those days the whole surface of the water would sparkle like a bed of diamonds, at least for a few blindingly spectacular minutes.

The three of them would paddle out to the waves. I'd try to do so, too, but if the waves were taller than four feet, I didn't have the endurance. Then again, if the waves were smaller than three feet, I couldn't stand up on the board. I was the pathetically hopeless "kook" in the group (but that's beside the point).

Early that October, I took a two-day trip out of town. While flying back home Saturday evening, I had a layover in Atlanta. I called home to confirm with Barbie the pick-up time at the local airport. But she spoke first. "We had an incident today."

"What was that?"

"I'll let Dave tell you," she answered. "Dave," she called out, "Dad's on the phone." She paused to listen to his response, which was inaudible to me, and then returned with this message: "He wants to tell you in person after you get home." That didn't sound good, but I didn't have the nerve to press the point.

"Okay. I'll see you at the airport."

Of course, my imagination went in every direction on that final flight, mostly to the vision of a car wrapped around a tree. But at least I knew he was alive and speaking.

After landing, it was a short fifteen-minute drive before I stepped through the front door of our home to see David lying on the family

---

1. Lazzeretti, "30 Greatest Surfers."

room couch, his right foot wrapped in bandages. And somehow those visions of the car wrapped around the tree faded from view as reality dawned. "David. It happened, didn't it? You got bit by a shark."

"No, Dad. I got *attacked* by a shark." Oddly, he grinned from ear to ear.

Yes, he confirmed, that morning the threesome had gone out to Melbourne Beach and took some rides. Dave caught a wave, got a good ride, and fell off . . . appropriately. Inappropriately, he wasn't wearing his ankle leash, as usual. *"How many times have I told you . . . ?"* I squelched my dad-scolding voice to let him finish the story.

"As I swam to get the board, a huge school of fish swam around me . . ." (he paused to let me come to the obvious interpretation: they were fleeing from a big fish on the hunt for a meal) . . . then hit me with the punch line: "He chomped down on my foot."

"Did you kick him with other foot?" Mark had taught us to do that if we ever get bit, but in the moment that's not the first thing you think to do.

"No, I yanked back, which really tore up my foot. But the shark did let go and swam away." He elaborated, "I wasn't sure I was actually bit. I didn't feel much. But when I lifted my foot above the water it was gushing blood all over."

Mark and Mike quickly caught up with him and carried him to Mark's truck. An ambulance soon showed up thanks to another observant beachgoer who saw it all and called the EMTs. But Mark, who as a phys ed teacher knew how to wrap up his foot, drove him to the hospital emergency room. There the nurses got to cleaning spoonfuls of sand out of the wounds, accompanied by lots of grimaces from the patient despite the novocaine.

Then the doctor asked, "Do you want me to use small stitches or large?"

"Which ones will leave the bigger scar?" David asked.

"The larger stitches."

"Give me the big stitches," the teenage boy said.

Twenty-seven large stitches later, David headed home with a new nickname, "Shark Bait." He also took "Tiburon" (Spanish for shark) for his email handle.

Good News, Bad News

So, I've got good news and bad news for you. The good news is that not all of the fish in the sea are sharks. The vast majority are simply called fish. In fact, even most sharks rarely, if ever, attack humans. They pose no real threat, more often than not. But the bad news is that there are some sharks out there that can bite you, can kill you, can eat you. To clarify, Molly Edwards of the World Wildlife Fund summarizes: "Let's face it—sharks have a bad rap. Thanks to sensationalized stories and stereotyping, sharks have become feared rather than revered. They're labeled as dangerous, indiscriminate killers that eat anything in sight. But in fact, sharks are most often the victims. They're killed by the millions annually to supply demand for their fins, which are made into soup and eaten as a status symbol. Such demand for fins has led to overfishing and illegal fishing, depleting shark populations worldwide."[2]

To be specific, out of more than three hundred species, only about a dozen of them attack and/or try to bite humans. Most human-shark encounters result from their hunting for bite-sized fish when a swimmer or surfer (as in David's case) just happens to get in the way. In a typical year about a half-dozen humans may be killed by a shark, whereas humans kill tens of millions of sharks in the same year.

Still, there *are* real threats "out thar in them waters."

So What Does Marine Biology Have to Do with the Church?

Likewise, there are real threats here in America's body politic, as well . . . and specifically, for our purposes, in the body of Christ whose members are part of this body politic that regular characterizes itself in two comparably sized species: red fish and blue fish.

In spite of what we've heard, and even characterized so far in this book, most professing Christians are not sharks, and the Christian world isn't evenly divided between friendly, nonthreatening fish and monstrous, malevolent sharks. But that same spirit of division manifesting itself in America's two-party system appears also to be evident in the deepening divisions between rival sports teams, between dueling jousters, between competing gangs, between divorcing spouses, between jealous siblings,

2. Edmonds, "Shark Facts vs. Shark Myths."

and, most especially, between vote-gathering political parties—and unfortunately, also seems to be carrying over into dueling rival denominations, rival Christian movements, and rival theologies. Further, it has cut deeply between rival factions within particular denominations, within particular Christian movements, and within particular theological camps.

But the division of rivals is, in large part, the product of simplistic, motivational recruiting of an ends-justifying-means competition for the testosterone- and adrenaline-inducing possibility of achieving the thrill of victory, even at the risk of suffering the agony of defeat. There's something inherent in most of us that simply loves the fight.

Two Sides: Never Again

Please repeat after me. Yes, please read out loud after me—even if that threatens you being evicted from your seat in the library:

"I will never again say . . ."

"That there are two sides to every story . . ."

Now say the whole promise, the same oath, the same vow out loud: "I will never, ever again say that there are two sides to every story."

Yes, say it again, from memory, for extra good measure. Now, with your eyes closed say it again and again repeatedly until you have it fully memorized it and can say it with force, with conviction.

The reason for reciting this vow is to save you from embarrassing yourself by sounding like a blockhead. Anybody saying, "There are two sides to every story" hasn't done the math. Yes, there are two sides to some stories. But many stories have only one side, when all competing alternatives are flat-out wrong. Think: the world is round with an equivalently "valid" alternative: the world is flat. Or try the claims of Holocaust deniers or moon landing deniers or those reassuring you that if you swallow your chewing gum it won't stay in your stomach for seven years. Those offering the antithesis to the thesis, at least in these cases, are flat-out wrong. Yes, many stories have only one side.

Then again, many, many more—indeed, most—stories have three sides, or seven sides, or thirty-seven sides, or seventy-three sides. They may even have 3,737 sides. You get the point. Binary thinking—breaking all issues down to a two-choice debate or dichotomy—may make for fun rivalries, but it seldom leads to serious questions in order to find intelligent answers.

Deborah Tannen, professor of linguistics at Georgetown University, addresses the problem of such binary thinking in her monumental book *The Argument Culture*. She summarizes the challenge this way: "Our determination to pursue truth by setting up a fight between two sides leads us to believe that every issue has two sides—no more, no less: If both sides are given a forum to confront each other, all the relevant information will emerge, and the best case will be made for each side. But opposition does not lead to truth when an issue is not composed of two opposing sides but is a crystal of many sides. Often the truth is in the complex middle, not the oversimplified extremes."[3]

She goes on to say: "We love using the word 'debate' as a way of representing issues: the abortion debate, the health care debate, the affirmative action debate—even 'the great backpacking vs. car camping debate.' The ubiquity of this word in itself shows our tendency to conceptualize issues in a way that predisposes public discussion to be polarized, framed as two opposing sides that give each other no ground. There are many problems with this approach. If you begin with the assumption that there *must* be an 'other side' you may end up scouring the margins of science or the fringes of lunacy to find it."[4]

A Hard Habit to Shake

Being realistic, if any point in this book is fighting against all odds for your adoption, it's this one. The tendency to divide into two parties is deeply dyed into the fabric of human relationships. Think Democrats and Republicans. Think Hatfields and McCoys. Think Yankees and Rebels. Think Federalists (led by Alexander Hamilton) and Anti-Federalists (led by Thomas Jefferson). Think royals and commoners.

In fact, go back in history to 1789. It was the year when America's first Constitutional Congress stepped up to service, the year when George Washington took the oath of office to serve as the first elected president, and the year when that Congress established the first federal judiciary. Moreover, across the ocean, our Revolutionary allies, the French, were making headlines. On July 14 that year, crowds stormed Paris's Bastille, the symbol of royal tyranny. Within weeks peasants overpowered the nobles and bourgeois, the feudal regime was abolished, and the Declaration

3. Tannen, *Argument Culture*, 10.
4. Tannen, *Argument Culture*, 10–11.

of the Rights of Man and of the Citizen proclaimed liberty, equality, the inviolability of property, and the right to resist oppression. What resulted? A two-party democracy.

Prior to that revolution, that French National Assembly (Estates-General) had been dominated by that certain royal, King Louis XVI. As Glenn McDonald explains, "Those who supported Louis and his 'stay-the-course policies' sat on the monarch's right. Those who believed that the times were ripe for radical change sat on the king's left."[5] After the revolution—during which the king and queen were guillotined—the seating power remained. To this day, "the Left has represented change, while the Right aligns with the status quo."[6] It has continued to be so here on the west side of the Atlantic, too.

Yes, the divide in our country didn't begin with the nicknaming of our states as Republican-voting states as red and Democrat-voting states as blue. That regular practice began just in the year 2000. It goes much further back, before the formation of the American experiment.

Indeed, it goes back (minus the "R" and "D" designations) to the ancients. Think Jews and gentiles. Think David and Goliath. Think Spartans and Trojans. Think all the way back to brothers Cain and Abel. These first offspring of the first couple fought a zero-sum, winner-take-all game with only one surviving.

Then again, Cain and Abel's binary relationship was preceded in time and exceeded in breadth by their parents' rivalry. When caught with the half-eaten fruit in his hands, Adam blamed Eve for tempting him. He also blamed God for giving him the woman who tempted him. But Eve was wise enough to avoid the binary or even triangulated competition; she hearkened to a fourth option: "The devil made me do it." Or, literally from the text, "'The serpent tricked me, and I ate'" (Gen 3:13). That very first human story in the Jewish and Christian Scriptures starts out with four options, four suspects, four possible agents of initiative, even if tainted by trying to pass the buck, to place blame on another.

Indeed, given the juxtaposition of this story right after God's creation of these agents, the perceptive reader naturally will pose the question whether the ultimate blame for their actions should really fall upon the Creator. The God introduced in chapter one, verse one, was exercising agency over their action by creating and placing these humans in this

5. McDonald, *Glenn's Reflections*.

6. McDonald, *Glenn's Reflections*.

environment at this time, arguably setting up the likely conclusion. The assigning of cause for the effect is stunning in complexity in this most rudimentary prehistoric account.

In the here and now of the twenty-first century, we humans hardly consider ourselves to be "rudimentary." But when we in a rudimentary, simplistic, even ignorant way stereotype one another into caricatures of "red or blue," "left or right," or even "us or them," our oversimplification demonizes them and beatifies us. In the process, as warned above, we make all of us out to be blockheads.

The Ways Forward

If anything can be said at this point in time, if this writer can convince you my reader of one thing, it's that you would aim to stop boiling matters down to two things. Real life in the real world requires us to see beyond us and them, the red and the blue, the good fish and the bad sharks, and resist the urgings to do so, as the serpent would suggest.

Or if I dare to stretch our metaphor a bit further, we need to swim with the sharks, no matter which species, which label or shark we may designate them to be. Only as we swim with them, get to know them, wrestle with them, can we learn many lessons we would otherwise miss.

It was my teenage kids, David and Kelly, who helped me to do that very thing.

There Really Are Dangerous Sharks in the Waters

So yes, David really did get bit by a real, honest-to-goodness shark. You would think we would have learned our lesson by now, right? After all, nobody in their right mind is going to go swimming again in ocean waters after facing that threat. We did stay away from the sand and the sea for a month or two (as most Floridians do anyway in October when the afternoon highs drop below 80 degrees, so it wasn't too tempting).

In fact, doctor's orders kept David out of all water deeper than a bathtub for three weeks, thereby causing him to miss three swim meets. But he did return just in time for the district swim teams' championship meet. Having taken second place in every dual meet all season, odds were in favor of his losing to all those first-place winners and landing in about sixth place. Instead, he beat them all. The shark-bite victim took first place on his first time back in the water. That made for a great headline in the local newspaper—and a family keepsake to this day.

What's more, when the winter temperatures abated the following April, all of us were splashing in the shark-infested waters all over again. Nothing, not even the confirmed presence of sharks, was going to keep us away.

And, for all Christ-followers, nothing should be countenanced that will keep us away from the shark-infested waters of the church, of almost any church. We must cultivate the partnerships and prayer supports, the learning opportunities and worshiping encounters and mission projects, the conversations and dialogues that can present us with the opportunity to extend and receive the "speaking the truth in love" via the mutual affirmation and mutual admonition available to us amid the dysfunctional community of faith as it helps us "to grow up in every way into him who is the head, into Christ, from whom the whole body, joined and knit together by every ligament with which it is equipped, as each part is working properly, promotes the body's growth in building itself up in love" (Eph 4:15, 16).

So, who's up for a swim?

— 4 —

The Wheat and the Sharks

Diagnosing an Ailing Church

THE 1950S BABY BOOM brought a huge influx of new members into churches, and with them, a burgeoning industry of church development analysts. The task at hand was fun at first.

- Visit fast-growing churches.

- Interview the pastors of those churches.

- Compare the feedback that multiple pastors provide, extracting common denominators that seem to be fueling the results.

- Write books to be used in Bible colleges and seminaries, and sell them to on-the-job pastors and other church leaders hoping to follow the patterns of success.

- Provide consulting to churches at a premium price to help new clients grow like the rest.

Of course, actual growth of particular churches has ebbed and flowed due to innumerable local factors, right down to the most obvious: the popularity of a pastor, the economic strength of the congregation, the location of the church building, etc. However, most how-to books minimized those particular differences. They wanted to provide the tried-and-true rules of thumb to guide all pastors in all churches of all faith traditions and all ethnicities in all regions of the good ol' USA.

Then, in the late 1960s, historic mainline denominational churches were wakening to the fact that the 1950s baby boom and their corresponding church growth had peaked a few years before, and that the more conservative, nondenominational churches seemed to be soaring. The National Council of Churches set out to diagnose the difference. They contracted the services of sociologist Dean M. Kelley, who brought his research to focus in the book *Why Conservative Churches are Growing: A Study in Sociology of Religion*.[1] In sociological terms (not theological terms per se), he said that the mainline churches had set their goal on being respectful, dignified, and intellectually astute without being sectarian, which had effectively made commitment to the faith less convinced and rigorous. In contrast, he said, conservative churches promoted more certainty, greater demands, more missional urgency, and an unapologetic denominational movement loyalty, which in turn had made their faith commitments more determined, energetic, and contagious.

That diagnosis carried huge credibility, given that it was handed down not by self-serving conservatives but by their natural competitors— indeed, the major voice of the liberal, ecumenical, mainline churches. It soared to the top of church leaders' reading lists. And it stood as the gold standard of comparative Christian religion studies all the way through the second printing twenty-four years later, and even for another decade into the new millennium. By then its thesis had been validated and magnified by the fact that at the turn of the century, twice as many Americans identified as "white evangelical protestant" than those identifying as "white mainline protestant."[2] (Note: I am referencing trends in white churches not to the diminishment of congregations of color, but because the white groupings have shifted so radically; in the same decades, in general, congregations of color have sustained a more stable presence and participation. Also, white groups, with the largest plurality of the population and a higher level of wealth, have commandeered much more media exposure and overall influence.)

But gradually in the new millennium, in that first decade of the 2000s, the Kelley paradigm began to crumble. The conservative churches were slow to publish the statistics, but gradually the demographers began

1. Kelley, *Why Conservative Churches Are Growing*.
2. "2022 PRRI Census of American Religion."

to publish the news: conservative churches were growing no more. In fact, they were shrinking. And shrinking at an annual rate exceeding that of the worst slumping years of mainline churches. In fact, whereas in 2006, when the percentage of Americans identifying as white evangelical outnumbered the percent of white Protestant mainliners 23 to 17.8, by 2022, the Protestant mainline had slipped to 13.9, but the evangelical had crashed to 13.6.[3] For the first time in decades the white mainline churches commanded a higher percentage of adherents than the white evangelical churches.

This is not good news. There is no joy in republishing the above statistics and trends. Indeed, to brag, "We're shrinking slower than they are," is the most pathetic form of binary competition. Losses to any churches are losses to the whole body of Christ.

The only worst news to report is fact, it is bad news, the worst news being the fact that the only group gaining ground in the first quarter of the twenty-first century has been the unaffiliated, those in the white national population who have eschewed association with any faith: having expanded from 16 percent in 2006 to 26.8 percent in 2022.[4]

Which leads us back to the question of diagnosis. Who's to blame? On whose shoulders can we place the blame for the overall shrinkage of participation in the churches?

- Can we blame it on the COVID-19 virus? Well, that surely played a part for the years of 2020–22 for the Protestants, although the Roman Catholic churches did record an increase over those two years combined.

- Can we blame the secularists for stealing our children from us, when in fact, as a common truism glibly declares, "Well-fed sheep don't wander away"?

- Can we blame those sharks among us . . . some special interest groups that keep stirring up controversies in the congregation—for disparaging the leadership we have and deterring us from accomplishing our mission?

3. "2022 PRRI Census of American Religion."
4. "2022 PRRI Census of American Religion."

Their Fault . . . and Ours

Yes, that must be it. It's *their* fault—those others, the sharks as we have defined them. They have broken the church.

But, truth be told, all of us have to own the blame. We have to share the blame. It's the fault of us all.

First and foremost, we're not making enough babies. Yes, I'm kidding about that . . . but not totally. Ever since the end of the baby boom our population growth rate has slowed, and that's mostly caused by the ease of access to birth control. The growth rate has been slowed also by an overall increase in higher education, driven by the labor market being powered much more by technological careers than manufacturing and labor, all of which have delayed the beginning of childbearing years and decreased the number of children per family.

Second, the streak of very public scandals has damaged the churches' collective witness terribly. We can't quantify the number of predatory relationships between clergy and laity, between adult pastors/priests and innocent children, but we can certainly face the fact that the ubiquitous, omnipresent publication of news across all twenty-first-century media has not only put those scandals out in the public eye; it has exposed countless churches' efforts to cover up such sins, such crimes. And, it has pumped high-test fuel into the MeToo movement and other comparable movements demanding justice on behalf of abuse and harassment victims. In turn, their voices have brought shame upon the priests and ministers in the pulpits, whose efforts to carry out justice among colleagues have too often given way to insider advantage. Our actions have silenced our words.

All of which really complicates our attempts to break through the two-party categorizations we've been addressing. For indeed, we could say there are really two parties after all: those who have committed terrible sins, and those who have not. But, well, "all have sinned and fallen short of the glory of God" (Rom 3:23). And, while some sins are more heinous and more destructive than others, still none of us is exempt from sinning nor immune from being tempted to sin. We share a basic solidarity with the sins of all.

Is there some other way to redress the two-party categorizations?

Take Me Back to the Mediterranean, Take Me Back to Carmel and Caesarea

Go back with me to chapter 1, as we took in the seaside of the Mediterranean Sea's east coast. The eye-opening aha moment that staggered my imagination that day gave me a way to reevaluate the two-party system I'd known and taken as a given. The ranking of those two parties suddenly shifted from us good conservatives against those bad liberals to a pairing of two truth-telling and faith-promoting peers who simply had two sets of biblically based ideals: ours focusing on maintaining the truth once delivered, as did Elijah on Mount Carmel, the citadel of truth, and theirs focusing on welcoming sinners of all stripes into the body of the church, as the apostles did in Caesarea, the port city of inclusiveness.

In telling of that revelatory discovery, I shared how it redirected my thoughts back to the USA, back to a denomination divided over a few policy issues. I came to see that many of my opponents on those issues were and are Christians of genuine faith in the Savior, a faith comparable to mine. But I saw us as two parties nevertheless.

Now that you've gotten this far, I have to admit to one flaw with my shark narrative. Jesus never mentions sharks. It might have been possible for Jesus to make reference to sharks, given that his itinerating ministry through Galilee, Samaria, and Judea bordered the coast of the fish-rich, salty Mediterranean Sea, which is home to a moderate shark population. But, no mention of sharks by Jesus. One contemporary version of one psalm mentions them: "Oh, look—the deep, wide sea, brimming with fish past counting, sardines and sharks and salmon" (Ps 104:25, *The Message*), but that's it. Still, Jesus did tell a story that may parallel the thrust of our story, and which could be adapted to our use of the shark analogy.

Now Take Me Further Back, Back to the Farm

While Jesus did spend much of his time hanging around the fishing business, sailing over the sea, even walking on the water, most of his time was spent on terra firma, solid ground. And while he probably wasn't a farmer, he understood a few things about the challenges of the agrarian life, among them being the wheat farmers' never-ending battle against weeds.

When Matthew the tax collector set about to tell Jesus' story, he brought up the problem of weeds growing among the wheat. Though much of his Gospel parallels Mark and Luke, he alone reported Jesus' parable about weeds. He also wrote much more about Jesus' detractors, his critics, his opponents. In all likelihood, at the time of writing a few decades after Jesus' ascension, Matthew's churches were awash in theological controversies, factionalism, lawsuits, disruptions in worship, and careless disregard for the poor.

On one level it wasn't hard for Matthew to address the messiness in his community, given the messiness that had followed Jesus decades before. You will recall that in those earlier days other religious leaders were trying to build "holy communities." The Pharisees were pursuing disciplines of legalistic purity. The Essenes in Qumran promoted monastic idealism. John the Baptist preached repentant revivalism. In contrast Jesus was known for hanging around boisterous drunks, saucy prostitutes, and embezzling tax collectors (fingers point right at Matthew).

So this Gospel writer told story after story of Jesus' engagement with such unsavory characters. He also published clusters of stories Jesus told which and pulled back the veil off church messiness by way of the parable of the wheat and the weeds. Taken from the world of agriculture, it speaks of a farmer planting seeds for a wheat crop, and of an enemy under the cloak of darkness planting, in the same fields, seeds of weeds. Given the discovery, investigation, and determination of cause, what does the farmer tell his servants to do, pull the weeds? "No, for in gathering the weeds you would uproot the wheat along with them." He says. "Let both of them grow together until the harvest, and at harvest time I will tell the reapers, 'Collect the weeds first and bring them in bunches to be burned but gather the wheat into my barn'" (Matt 13:24–30).

Lest Matthew's audience not make the connection, this is one of only two of Jesus' parables wherein Matthew quotes Jesus' explanation of the story. The parable is about the kingdom of God, that is, the inhabitants living under the reign and within the particular realm of God. God's loyal farmhands brought together the children of the kingdom, but an enemy, the devil, brought in children of darkness. Ultimately, at the end of time, the angels will divide them, sending them to glory or to banishment, but in the meantime, the farmer tells his servants, do not try to separate them on your own (Matt.13:37–43).

Hmmm. Perhaps sharks among fish offers a comparable analogy to weeds among wheat. Who's to say which of those in my church who seem a bit aggressive aren't really tame, loving, caring fish? Not all nine-inch-high dorsal fins cutting through the waters' surface are attached to three hundred razor-sharp teeth ready to shred human flesh, break human bones, and swallow human organs. Some of those fins are attached to Flipper or one of her cousins.

And even among those labeled sharks, which of them are violent killers and which of them—the vast majority—have the disposition of a bunny rabbit or Shetland pony?

The point of the parable is comparable to the point of my aha moment by the Mediterranean: Living in the body of Christ, the family of God, the temple of the Holy Spirit requires us to live together with people—at least some of whom we would not have chosen as friends. We are not afforded the luxury of banishing those we don't like. And, indeed, most of those who are rubbing us wrong have been put here to help us as iron sharpening iron (Prov 27:17).

Even John Calvin, who wasn't always patient with church members' misdeeds, chided those who, in their zeal for righteousness, would separate themselves from the less holy. He responded with his judgment upon the judgers:

> Let them hear the parable from Christ's lips that compares the church to a net in which all kinds of fish are gathered and are not sorted until laid out on the shore (Matt. 13:47–58). Let them hear that it is like a field sown with good seed which is, through the enemy's deceit, scattered with tares and is not purged of them until the harvest is brought into the threshing floor (Matt. 13:24–30). Let them hear finally that it is like a threshing floor on which grain is so collected that it lies hidden under the chaff until, winnowed by fan and sieve, it is at last stored in the granary (Matt. 3:12). But if the Lord declares that the church is to labor under this evil—to be weighed down with the mixture of the wicked—until the Day of Judgment, they are vainly seeking a church besmirched with no blemish.[5]

Yes, Jesus' words to Matthew's congregation, reinforced by John Calvin, and illuminated by the juxtaposition of Mt. Carmel—the citadel of truth—and Caesarea—the port city of inclusiveness—all point to the need for us to stick together, even while having doubts about one another's beliefs and practices, and even when taking offense to those differences.

But that leads us to push further through the binary divide.

---

5. Calvin, *Institutes of the Christian Religion*, IV.I.13, p. 1028.

Purple?

Some are pressing us to simply bring the blues and reds together to blend into a tolerable purple state of being. Then again, where are the examples of purple actually succeeding as a viable option? To suggest purple as the answer is to press us to a Golden Mean (Aristotle's idealized virtuous state of living in the middle ground between extremes).[6] It's supposed to provide us a happy state of mutuality. But it really produces compromises, a mushy middle, a tasteless refreshment, a milquetoast meal. Add that all up and you get boredom. There is a reason that the voice of God says: "I know your deeds, that you are neither cold nor hot. I wish you were either one or the other! So, because you are lukewarm—neither hot nor cold—I am about to spit you out of my mouth" (Rev 3:15–16).

Instead, we are talking about being a full-spectrum church, a place where reds, blues, and purples all live and engage with yellows, greens, and oranges, and indeed all are given microphones to be free to express their hopes and fears, their passions and oppositions at full voice, so that all are free to fulfill God's diverse callings upon their lives, to advocate for others to join with them, and to listen to each other's issues and ideas so as to be better informed to do better what God is calling them to do. More about this later on . . .

Two Is as Lonely as One

How can we find some way to understand each other, to communicate with each other, be family together with each other? We need to do some translation, some delineation, some serious analysis, even exegesis of why it is that we in the body of Christ do differ as we do on so many matters. I offer the term "exegesis" because, while it is used most often as a process of biblical study, it fits equally well when it comes to interpreting the meanings of contemporary believers of all kinds and categories. *The Interpreter's Dictionary of the Bible* defines exegesis as: "An interpretive method that establishes the meaning of a biblical text or passage by studying its historical context and making application of that study to the contemporary situation and environment. Described as being derived from the Gk. *exagein*, 'to lead out,' this hermeneutical approach to biblical literature assumes an essential meaning within the text that can

---

6. Maden, "Golden Mean."

be isolated and explained through philological and historical methods that establish a literary contemporaneity between the community that produced the text and the reading community."[7]

To put that more simply, the simple goal of the exegetical method is to answer the question, "What were the original writers intending their original recipients to know, understand, believe, and/or do?" Put really simply, "What were they intending to say then and there?"

The equivalent endeavor of present-day exegesis of one another living our faith and beliefs today, is for us—you and me—to hear, discern, understand and, when possible, appreciate the intended meaning of what each other knows, understands, believes, and/or does. In order for us to faithfully, accurately, responsibly, and respectfully understand each other, we need to exegete each other's thoughts, mindsets, convictions, hopes, and fears, and to be able to articulate them out loud so clearly and accurately that they can say back to us, "You got it! You understand me better than I understand myself. You truly get where I'm coming from."

After having had that aha! moment near the Mediterranean coast, I continued to serve and engage in debates and dialogues across my particular denomination. Increasingly I got to know a much broader range of folks, in ethnicities, in theologies, in ideologies, even in food tastes (we had lots of meals together, especially one-on-one).

In the process, such travels led to unguarded conversations. They happened in unplanned ways. You see, when taking speaking engagements, especially debates on major issues, both my opponents (there were many of them) and I would showcase our points of view in a regional gathering of church leaders. The hosts of such debates would put us up in a hotel to give us a good night's sleep. A funny thing happened in the midst of that. Both speakers would make our way to the hotel's restaurant for a bit of late-night refreshment and, naturally, we'd sit at the same table. We would have typical conversations asking typical questions: about significant others, about family members, home churches, leisure activities. Before long, we would dig beyond surface topics to personal faith sharing, telling about our sense of call into ministry, about our educations, favorite professors, influential mentors. We shared about our greatest moments of achievement. In some cases, we even told about some of our worst failings, most painful church conflicts, greatest regrets. Eventually one of us might say something like, "Funny, but we haven't

7. McCormick, "Exegesis," 366.

said anything about human sexuality or life-and-death ethics," the topics about which we had flown hundreds of miles to debate.

Finally, I would ask what became my ultimate question of choice, "So what's God up to? What's God up to in your life and ministry?" Amazingly, my conversation partners then kicked into high gear, telling about one or two matters that filled their hearts with joy, about great things going on or soon to be launched. The excitement made no reference to some "liberal agenda," and, when they reciprocated the question (as most did), asking, "So what's God up to in your life and ministry?" my responses didn't blurt out some "conservative agenda." We weren't spouting party platforms.

In fact, we were sharing hopes and dreams that the other could embrace. We smiled a lot. And we often were the last hotel guests still snacking and drinking as the restaurant closed.

Unexpected Friendships: An Unanticipated Paradigm

Friendships were birthed in those late-night conversations. And new hypotheses were born in my imagination. As those conversations multiplied, I did notice some patterns that emerged from the comments of my conversation partners.

For one thing, their responses came quickly. They did not simply stare at me, muttering, "Hmm, hmm, hmm, let me think about that." No. Their responses jumped out of their mouths immediately. It was as if I'd turned open the spout on a fire hydrant. God was doing stuff in their lives that was begging to be reported. They spoke on impulse.

A second pattern emerged: what they were reporting or were hoping for was big. It was something burning within them with passion, excitement, verve. It was animated with broad vision, with high ideals, with deep thought. For all the ideology that seemed to be debated before the crowd an hour or so earlier, I was now hearing something truly idealistic, visionary, aspirational.

A third pattern emerged: what they spoke of most of all was God. Yes, God. You know, when pastors or priests get together we notoriously talk little about God. Like the invisible guest in Elijah's seat at a Passover dinner, we tend to avoid God-talk (if only to avoid sounding holier-than-thou or, conversely, sacrilegious). But, in these discussions, there was no hesitation to address and give credit to God.

I pondered within myself, "Are we on to something here? Dare I talk about these topics as theo-idealistic impulses?" . . . idealistic passions, blurting out of our mouths on impulse, and driven by a genuine faith in God as the author, impetus, and guide?

One other pattern emerged, namely, that there was some repetition among the topics of these visions and dreams. As one who always carries a notebook/journal to track all my work, including all my conversations, I wrote them down, and over time would refer back to these conversations. I found that the passions ignited in our conversations seemed to arise from a few broad categories. Given a penchant for analysis, I sorted out those theo-idealistic impulses into five categories, not carefully and exactingly differentiated, but like five magnetic force fields.

Visualize these as a five fence-post perimeter of a horse pen or sheep pen.

Imagine five admissions directors appealing to high school students to apply to their respective universities at a college fair.

Or think about five marketers of high energy protein shakes promoting their products to competitors in the lobbies of physical fitness competitions.

Cataloging these five impulses in the light of church life, mission, and ministry, I suddenly wasn't thinking about Carmel and Caesarea any more. I wasn't just thinking about two options, binary polar opposites, even ones that felt somewhat equalized in validity, living in an equivalent paradox, while visiting those two locations in Palestine. I was now thinking in a multivalent set of missional goals (as in Webster's definition of "multivalence: the quality or state of having many values, meanings or appeals").[8]

Each of the theo-idealistic impulses was driven by a nuclear-fusing potency of power. Each one was noble in its intentions. And each was fueled by a love for God and for people that mirrored the lifestyles of Moses and David, Hannah and Esther, Isaiah and Daniel, Mary and Joseph, the other Mary and Martha, Peter and Paul.

I soon was whispering to others what I imagined to be five theo-idealistic impulses. Dare I go public with them?

---

8. *Webster's Ninth New Collegiate Dictionary* (1985), s.v. "multivalence," 780.

They Who Write Are They Who Set the Agenda

The public came calling. Dubuque Seminary theology professor Mark Achtemeier called me with a proposition. "Jack, the folks at Presbyterian Publishing have asked Andrew Purves [a Pittsburgh Seminary theology professor] and me to put together a book, an anthology of articles about the conservative evangelical branch of Presbyterianism. They plan to call it, *A Passion for the Gospel: Confessing Jesus Christ for the 21st Century.*[9] We want you to write an article for it." He explained that Geneva Press (a division, alongside Westminster John Knox Press, of the Presbyterian Publishing House) was putting together a comparable anthology for the progressive liberal branch, *Renewing the Vision: Reformed Faith for the 21st Century,* being edited by McCormick Seminary president Cynthia Campbell.[10]

Then he added, "We want you to write from an evangelical conservative perspective on church unity and diversity."

"Great idea, Mark," I said. "But we evangelical conservatives have no perspective on unity and diversity. We're too busy splitting churches to care about that"—words uttered with a tinge of sarcastic shame.

"Yeah, we know that," he replied with his own guilty laugh. "But we've been hearing you talk about that, and even if you're the only one, we want you to write about it to help the rest of us to get onboard."

I did. I wrote the essay about theo-idealistic impulses, to which they attached the title, "The Unity We See in the Midst of our Diversity: An Evangelical Perspective." I also scheduled a few get-togethers of colleague pastors to discuss the substance of my emerging theory, suggesting that maybe there is a paradigm here that could help us understand better just where each of us is coming from. And how much we really do need each other. The responses were heartening.

So, a few months after submitting it, I called Tom Long, former preaching professor at Princeton Seminary, at the time serving as editor of Geneva Press. He immediately said how much he appreciated my essay.

"Did you really?"

"One of the best in the book." Of course, he probably said the same to all of the other writers. But I didn't mind hearing it nonetheless.

I posed a thought. "What would you think about me expanding that to a book? I think I can fill it out that much."

9. Achtemeier and Purves, eds., *Passion for the Gospel.*

10. Campbell, ed., *Renewing the Vision.*

"I like the idea, Jack." He paused. "But you may want to find another way to say, 'theo-idealistic impulses.' It's eminently forgettable."

"Yeah, I know," I laughed. "How about GodViews? One word, both the G and the V are capitalized. Not as views about God but as varying views of God's mission in the world."

"Now you're talking."

So I turned the talking into writing, and then they published *God-Views: The Convictions that Drive Us and Divide Us*. It became my best-selling book. And yes, that book became a diagnostic tool for folks to figure out where each other is coming from. At least, in my own, particular denomination. But, apart from a few smatterings of purchases, it did not find a following elsewhere. It was speaking to a very small slice of the American church pie that is so much larger and so much more diverse than my own tribe.

Fast-forward to a time that looks very different than it did when the book was published. In fact, just six months after its publication the worst international tragedy on American soil occurred, simply remembered as 9/11. The whole state of American life in general and American church life exploded with grief, with anger, with fear, with horror. And a different America slowly emerged from it, a cultural shape and form that was almost unrecognizable—more harsh, more reactionary, more hateful, more prejudicial, more insecure than most of us had ever encountered.

Oh, to be sure, for those of you who had known the horrors of minority status, of racist prejudice, or sexist predatory aggression, of sexual minority shaming—this new era did follow some of the patterns you had suffered. To those who had been displaced out of land, out of home, out of their place in society, this wasn't so new. But for the majority who had experienced the ease that majority status, those advanced educations, those multiple vocational options, and the sheer confidence of safety, security, and habitation—they were shocked into uncertainties never imagined.

September 11 was the wake-up call of wake-up calls. And for many it brought the worst out of us. And while the GodViews thesis was providing some help for this small slice of our own tribe, it was begging for a retranslation, a reimagination, a reformulation for all of us Christians of all colors, ethnicities, denominations, traditions, and movements.

So here we go . . . into the retranslation, reimagination, reformulation of GodViews into Jesus' Passions for Us . . . five passions for us to embrace, to experience and to emulate . . .

— Part II —

The Jesus We Adore,
the Jesus We Ignore

— 5 —

Jesus' Passions for Us in the Full-Spectrum Church

GODVIEWS HAD ITS DAY for Presbyterians in the early 2000s, but it fell short of my highest hopes for it. My ultimate hope was that that book could introduce a new vocabulary to reboot the conversations of a few million Presbyterians in the way that H. Richard Niebuhr did across denominational lines in 1950. In that year, he delivered a set of lectures at Austin Theological Seminary to address issues similar to the ones we are discussing today: How should the church relate to the world around it? Those lectures were adapted into the book *Christ and Culture*,[1] which reshaped how Christians around the world understood their connection to their national and international context. In the process it also explained the real divide between modernists and fundamentalists that the Scopes trial had catalyzed. It also added nuance. It was understandable. Niebuhr put the differences not in two categories but five, yet they were clear. The first three are differentiated simply by prepositions:

- Christ against Culture
- Christ of Culture
- Christ above Culture

1. H. Richard Niebuhr, *Christ and Culture*.

The other two are just a bit more complicated, yet memorable:

- Christ and Culture in Paradox
- Christ Transforming Culture

In the process of reading *Christ and Culture*, readers could locate themselves.

- Most obviously, fundamentalists, being separatists by intention, could identify themselves as *against* the culture.

- Modernists and academics could identify themselves as having a Christ *of* culture, comfortably blending the two frameworks into one.

- In between, those folks neither resisting culture nor assimilating to it, simply saw culture to be the context for Christ's work, and when they clashed Christ would be accorded the final answer.

- Some who are comfortable bringing contradictory claims together (like quantum physics' claim that light is both wave and particle at the same time), would see the contrariness between faith claims and cultural beliefs as dance partners, stepping on each other's feet, but *vive la différence* and bring on the adventure.

- Still others, those most given to the promotion of social righteousness, would tilt toward Christ transforming culture, fully expecting an ever-increasing pace of improvement.

Niebuhr's system worked well, and *Christ and Culture* became one of the most influential books of Christian thought of the century. His categories continue to inform Christian thinkers to this day.

As I said above, when putting forward my categories of differentiation, I hoped my terms would work better in the new century, but the terms were less familiar and less comprehensible.

- The Confessionalist GodView
- The Devotionalist GodView
- The Ecclesiast GodView
- The Altruist GodView
- The Activist GodView

The question being asked by Niebuhr was, "How should I relate to my culture?" In *GodViews*, the question was, "What aspect or two of God's global mission most inspires me, and conversely, which aspect or two of God's mission ticks me off?" Hopefully, we would also find clues on how to answer, "And why would so-and-so seem to think that *'that* mission' is so important?"

However, the five categories bulleted above and even the overall term *GodViews* did not show up in any new dictionaries. Nobody wrote a PhD dissertation on the subject. This paradigm and these particular categories did not make their way into typical church Bible study discussions. In fact, not even my best friends and closest family members would introduce themselves as an Altruist or a Confessionalist, etc. Indeed, when trying to interpret their mindsets they would more likely reference their Myers-Briggs Personality Type[2] or Enneagram[3] score.

In the two decades since writing *GodViews*, I have been digging more deeply into finding a new language. In Niebuhr's case the paradigm succeeded not just because the terms were self-explanatory. It worked also because it was all about Jesus. Instead of addressing "*my*" perception of God's mission, it sought to address Jesus' actual interactions with his culture. What was Jesus' relationship to the world around him? The Christ-centered approach won the day.

Accordingly, in the hope of helping our churches make a lasting, positive impact—this world needs our churches to make a positive impact for sure—I want us to turn our eyes upon Jesus. Let's ask more specifically than before, "What was Jesus doing in the world?" And then we can ask, "How should we imitate, or better yet, emulate him in this world?"

We are not the first ones to ask these questions. In the early 1400s, a full century prior to the beginning of Protestant Reformation, a monk by the name of Thomas wrote about Jesus and of his life's dream to emulate him. Having come from Kempen, in the Rhineland, and dubbed "Thomas of Kempen," i.e., "Thomas à Kempis," his book *The Imitation of Christ*[4] may be history's most widely read Christian devotional book next to the Bible. It addresses four topics: a) "Helpful Counsels of the Spiritual Life," (b) "Directives for the Interior Life," (c) "On Interior Consolation," and (d) "On the Blessed Sacrament."

2. See MyersBriggs.org.

3. See EnneagramInstitute.com.

4. Thomas á Kempis, *Imitation of Christ*.

On matters of personal prayer, contemplation of God's holiness, and the cultivation of a life of devotion, it is unsurpassed. It reads like a book of proverbs, statements of spiritual and moral counsel to help us live as imitators of Christ. But it won't help us to understand how to live with persons of different orientations in ideology, in lifestyle, in gender, in culture or ethnicity. It doesn't provide insights into the differences that divide us theologically, idealistically, or even politically.

And, speaking of the *imitation* of our Savior, that very word "imitation" is problematic. In the present era we place a high value on authenticity and genuineness. What do we call persons who are imitating some superstar? We call them "imitators," not a flattering label to wear. Worse, we also call them "copycats," "wannabes," "impersonators," "parrots," "pretenders," even "plagiarists." If Thomas were alive today, I think he would come up with a more acceptable, but still inspiring title to his book.

Thomas à Kempis isn't the only one to lift up Jesus as an exemplar to emulate. Charles Sheldon's 1895 novel *In His Steps: What Would Jesus Do?*[5] doesn't rank as the second-best seller in world history after the Bible, but it did sell about 50 million copies, so you can be sure it left a mark. At the time, Sheldon was a Church of Christ minister in Topeka, Kansas. He wrote the book one chapter per week and presented it to the congregation in every Sunday evening service until finished. The story traced the inspiration of a fictional pastor, Henry Maxwell, who presents a challenge to his congregation: "Do not do anything without first asking, 'What would Jesus do?'" Good behavior bursts forth, attitudes turn from hateful to loving, tempers are cooled, affections warmed, and a whole community transformed.

There is just one problem that always nagged some of us readers. Why did the good Pastor Maxwell ask, "What would Jesus do?" instead of asking the more obvious, "What *did* Jesus do?" I mean, we have a whole lot of data on what Jesus did, given the four different news networks that published his breaking news (Mark, Matthew, Luke, and John). But, no, Pastor Maxwell posed the question in a hypothetical way. Why? Well, maybe because when asked in a generalized hypothetical way, the answer would be self-evident: Jesus would do the nice thing. He would be, and always would be nice. It was plain and simple. But if he had asked, "What *did* Jesus do?" the answer would not be so simple. Jesus was gracious and empathetic on some occasions. But he was confrontational and

5. Sheldon, *In His Steps.*

judgmental on other occasions. There are reasons for the difference, as we will see shortly, but we really to need to ask, "What *did* Jesus do?"

I encountered this problem when, as a naïve eighteen-year-old, and a freshman at the Elim Bible Institute (think Moody Bible Institute for Pentecostals), I wrote a term paper about Jesus. To be specific, I was taking an introductory course on the Gospel of Mark, and I chose to do an analysis of "The Emotions of Jesus as Reported in the Gospel of Mark." Tapping into my background as the son of a psychology professor, I read verse by verse through the Gospel, underlining every word or phrase that indicated some expression of emotion by Jesus.

My faith fell apart. It didn't help that the movie *Jesus Christ Superstar* had just been released and I viewed it just days before going to Bible college. I'd enjoyed listening to the recorded album and then seeing the fantastic production of it on Broadway. But the vivid movie presentation of Jesus being explicitly confused, befuddled, second-guessing, and spiritually doubting ended up as co-conspirator with my Mark study to shake out all confidence in Jesus' divinity. I felt my faith dissolving like the Wicked Witch of the West did when Dorothy threw water on her. Fortunately, being the faith-fueled Pentecostal that I was, I asked my three roommates to surround me, to lay hands on me and cast out the unbelief that was trying to steal my faith. I recovered quickly.

But I never forgot how incredibly complicated Jesus was, as presented by his allies, those who announced the good news of the Savior and his love.

Today, I want to invite us to be reintroduced to Jesus as he was, as his original biographers presented him to us. I want us to look at the tangible, God-in-the-flesh Jesus of Nazareth. Not merely the proverbial fountain of sage advice. Not the perpetual picture of niceness. But the real Jesus. Let's talk about him who is the embodiment of God's mission, which is to say that *he is the incarnate mission itself*, and he is, through the Holy Spirit, the empowering agent for the church to participate in God's mission to the world.

Let me put it this way: Let's talk about the passions of Jesus.

The Passions of Jesus

Yes, the passions of Jesus. What comes to mind when you hear that phrase? The sufferings of the Christ? Do you visualize a bloody scene from that major motion picture, the one released on Ash Wednesday, 2004, directed by Mel Gibson and starring Jim Caviezel? It depicted in gruesome detail the last twelve hours of suffering of the Savior's death on the cross. It's consistent with the historic, Latin meaning of the root word, *passio*, meaning suffering. Leading Christian thinkers landed on that expression all the way back to Origen of Alexandria (c. 185–c.253 CE), one of the early Christian scholars of the faith. St. Augustine (354–430 CE) also spoke of the Passion of the Christ, and so that label stuck.

I don't want to pretend to improve upon the brilliance of mind or depth of faith of such leaders of the ancient church. But I do want to expand on their thinking. In modern English usage, when we speak of passion we usually mean something other than suffering. It can speak of romantic feelings for a significant other. More generally than that, it speaks of intense feelings of belief, of hopes, of goals, of callings, of endeavors.

You may not have contemplated before the passions expressed in Jesus' ministry. The same people who have painted Jesus with white face and blue eyes have also depicted him as blithely bland, emotionless, even to the point of being stoic. But, no offense intended, Jesus was not born with northern European DNA (as this author was). He was born into a fiery, passionate people-group living in an extroverted, demonstrative, expressive, and outgoing culture. He simply did not live his human life in the state of boring, tepid niceness implied and expected by many of those wearing WWJD wristbands.

When we read about Jesus' life in the Gospels, his beliefs, hopes, and goals, his proclamations, callings, and endeavors—all those bursts of energy rush out of this man of many passions. The sounds of his sermons and conversations, the touch of his hands, the gaze of his eyes all exude such intensity of feeling, of compassion, of joy. And those passions come through in his inaugural address in the Nazareth synagogue as well as around the Last Supper seder, on the mountain and on the plain, along the river and on the temple steps. They begin right after John's baptism (if not before, but we don't know much about those earlier years). They continue through the crucifying passion, right through the resurrected celebration, through the intimate fish fry on Galilee's north shore, right through his ascent to heaven's right hand.

Will you consider the full range of Jesus' passions?

As the Word of God made flesh, that is, the incarnate God-Man that he was, Jesus was, exhibited, and continues to showcase a breadth of emotion that is passionate at its core.

"Jesus Christ is the gracious mission of God to and for the world."[6] As such, Jesus was driven with a passion to fulfill that mission wherever he went, in whatever circumstances he found himself, and with whomever he made an acquaintance. Accordingly, he operated in a multiplicity of ways. Not simply evangelizing sinners, not simply advocating for justice, not simply organizing a movement, not simply delivering sermons, not simply performing miracles, but doing all of the above. With passion, focus, and determination. And treating each person and need as if it was the only thing on his mind.

As Benjamin Tomczak reports, this all hit home to Martin Luther as he was wrestling with the God he saw as severe and frightening. He even hated that God. That all changed after leaving law school, and enrolling in the monastic life with Augustinian monks. That order emphasized the reading of Scripture on a level far exceeding what he had ever known. One of the senior friars who prompted his Scripture studies advised him "to hope in God" and to have "a 'little bit' of faith in the absolution of sin." This friar pointed Luther to the Creed, "I believe in the forgiveness of sins" and a powerful quotation from the French monk Bernard of Clairvaux: "But add to this that you also believe this: that through him [Christ] your sins are forgiven you." From there, Luther dug into Augustine and then into the Scriptures, until finally everything changed for him.

Tomczak wrote of Luther's discovery, "Go back to the Bernard quote . . . . It was the Latin word *tibi*—'to you' or 'for you'—that was so powerful for Luther." What ensued in his mind were some basic thesis statements he presented in an academic debate in the 1535 school year, among them:

18. But true faith says, "I certainly believe that the Son of God suffered and arose, but he did this all for me, for my sins, of that I am certain.

19. For he died for the sins of the whole world. But it is most certain that I am some part of the world, therefore, it is most certain that he died also for my sins . . .

24. Accordingly, that "for me" or "for us," if it is believed, creates that true faith and distinguishes it from all other faith, which merely hears the things done.

---

6. Purves and Achtemeier, *Union in Christ*, xiii.

25. This is the faith which alone justifies us without law and works through the mercy of God shown in Christ.[7]

Tomczak concludes: "For you. Without the 'for you,' the death of Jesus is just a historical fact. But it was for you. Given for you. Shed for you. This is the righteousness of God, the righteousness made known through the Scriptures, the righteousness that comes through faith in Jesus Christ to all who believe."[8]

It is in that spirit of that same "for you," "for us" that we are laying out "Jesus' passions for us."

So what specific passions did Jesus showcase in his public ministry in the Middle East two millennia ago that continue to carry a universal, global reach two thousand years after his ascension? What were the passions of Jesus as initially introduced in the opening pages of the Gospels, the passions that resurfaced again and again as he itinerated around Galilee and Lebanon to the north, in Judea in the south and in Samaria and Jordan in between?

And how do these passions of the Christ surface in the lives of Christ-followers today? How might they empower Christ-followers to engage in Jesus' mission today?

How might our particular missional passions grate upon one another, whether intentionally or not, in ways that initially may be off-putting? In fact, some of those folks we don't really like—you know, those people you don't like, the ones we may consider to be the sharks in the pool of our church—just may be enamored, inspired, thrilled with one of the passions of Jesus that pushes all the wrong buttons in us.

Let me press the question to the point of getting personal. We all have a Jesus we adore and a Jesus we ignore.

Trusting you to be a sincere follower of Jesus, I am not saying that you intentionally ignore part of who Jesus is. I am saying that when you read biblical texts about Jesus, some words, phrases, sayings, or stories jump off the page. And some words, phrases, sayings, or stories are just there. They get garbled in the background noise. Your attentiveness slips as your eyes glide over the words.

The words that arrest your attention may be ones that affirm who you are, reassuring you that you are totally okay. Then again, the words that grab you may be the ones that convict you of your failings, your guilt,

---

7. Luther, *Luther's Works* vol. 34, 110–11.
8. Tomczak, "Luther Found the 'For You' for You."

your unresolved shame. The inspiring words may buttress your side of an argument you've been having with somebody else. They may provide the comfort you will quote to a friend or a child going through hard times.

Then again, the words you don't notice may be ones in which Jesus does the opposite of the above: words that bring you down, that indulge others' behavior you find reprehensible, that refute your position in an argument, that don't offer consoling words to share. Or, simply, his words, actions, or story simply will not ring your bell.

This disparity comes to mind when folks on their way out of a worship service express such different responses to the same sermon:

- "I feel so much closer to God now—the pastor had me in tears."

- "I now know God is calling me to teach a Sunday school class."

- "I felt so excluded by his constant references to God as a man."

- "She played fast and loose with the Scriptures."

- "I'm going right home to call my mother to tell her how much I love her."

This disparity also comes to the surface when sitting in a Bible study circle in which participants are invited to share what strikes them, what speaks to them. Or, in the practice of Lectio Divina, dating back to second-century church father Origen, and two hundred years later taught by Ambrose to Augustine, participants are invited to read or listen to a verse or passage of Scripture, to meditate on it, to hear it again, and—rather than doing formal exegetical interpretation of it—simply asking the Holy Spirit to speak the text's message to the heart.

In such instances, when the participants share their insights and learnings, they may be strikingly divergent. In my most guileless moments I will find those sharings to be cause for rejoicing over God meeting each one in the circle. But in my more critical moments I may find those responses to be colored by each one's neuroses—the ever-guilty participant getting guilt-tripped again, the flighty optimist hearing yet another flighty optimistic message. Oh well. Forgive me (and yes, my own guilt button is always ready to be pushed, even now).

With all these comments in mind, our attempts to emulate Jesus' passions depend first of all upon our perception of the Jesus we aim to emulate. And our vision of that Jesus is shaped by the Jesus we have come to know.

In the Eyes of the Beholder

The categories of perception earlier introduced as GodViews were based upon a long-researched hypothesis that people tend to perceive God's mission in the world to be focused on one or two mindsets, goals, visions. Listening to many church leaders, I theorized that those mindsets boiled down to five from which we choose. This choice also is an unconscious decision, but it does form a set of assumptions, presuppositions upon which all of our day-by-day decisions are based.

It wasn't hard to surmise that those assumptions, presuppositions, even postulates have been formed within each of us by a host of influences:

- our respective temperaments,
- our education (from Sunday school to postgraduate studies),
- our family systems,
- our key influencers such as teachers, coaches, and preachers,
- our spiritual giftings,
- our fears and wounds (we tend to become most ideologically passionate about things we fear can be or have been lost or stolen),
- our triumphs and our defeats,
- our association with an ideologically driven affinity group, such as the National Rifle Association, Greenpeace, Mothers Against Drunk Driving, etc.
- our spiritual formation: journeys, awakenings, backslidings, re-awakenings, dark nights of the soul,
- and our DNA.

An individual's favorite, most inspiring passion of the Christ is founded upon one's own psychological make-up. Miroslav Volf, one of the premier theologians of the faith, summarizes his analysis of the foundations of the core values of our being:

> Psychologists tell us that humans produce and reconfigure themselves by a process of identifying with others and rejecting them, by repressing drives and desires, by interjecting and projecting images of the self and the other, by externalizing fears, by fabricating enemies and suffering animosities, by forming allegiances and breaking them up, by loving and hating, by seeking

to dominate and letting themselves be dominated—and all this not neatly divided but all mixed up, with "virtues" often riding on hidden "vices," and "vices" seeking compensatory redemption in contrived "virtues." Through this convoluted process the center of the self is always reproducing itself, sometimes by asserting itself over against the other . . . , at other times by cleaving too closely to the other . . . , sometimes pulled by the lure of throbbing and restless pleasures, at other times pushed by the rule of a rigid and implacable law.[9]

When the psalmist says, "I am fearfully and wonderfully made" (Ps 139:14), those words only scratch the surface of how complicated we are. Fortunately, they imply that the loving Creator of the universe is the one who has made us, but my oh my, we are hard to figure out.

In fact, it would be easy to suggest that our mindsets are so varied that there is no way to find any common denominators, no way to form alliances, no way to break out of our own isolation. But the fact that, throughout history, friendships, partnerships, support groups, and affinity groups of all kinds have emerged within the human community, that persons of conviction have gravitated into enclaves of agreement, suggests that community does develop around a few common denominators.

Accordingly, we as individual, separate Christians of varying stripes are prone to latch on to one of Jesus' passions as central, as energizing, as inspirational, and even as vocational for us to be emulating and partnering with him. But our own simplifications of Jesus to our own mindsets strips us of the full-breadth mission of God that is as profound and complex as life itself, indeed, it is infinitely so.

Our best chance of resisting our own simplistic summations of Jesus is to read the Bible with others, listening to what speaks to them as their voices challenge our biases. We just may discover that their contrarian impressions are inspired by the Spirit.

In that light, let us consider Jesus' passions and the ways they help us to become a full-spectrum church in a red-and-blue world.

---

9. Volf, *Exclusion and Embrace*, 69–70.

— 6 —

Truth Be Told

Jesus' Passion for Us to Know the Truth

REMEMBER THAT SCHOOL OF fish that swam around my son David that were immediately followed by an open-mouthed shark? Sharks in the sea feast on smaller fish. Likewise, sharks in churches feed on a different kind of fish: those who they think are not as smart as they are. Or, as it were, those smaller fish are not completely sure about what they believe, which serves them up as a great main course for a large shark's Thanksgiving feast. Not all such sharks are as ferocious as the great whites, but many are as intense as the hammerheads.

They come upon such ferocity and intensity honestly. That's because they have adopted Jesus' Passion for Us to Know the Truth, as introduced by the Gospel writers.

The Jesus Teacher

It may be placed in the New Testament as the second Gospel, but most biblical scholars agree that Mark's Gospel was the first one written. And right from the start, Mark introduces Jesus as a teacher of the Truth with a capital T. The first words out of Jesus' mouth arrest us: "The time is fulfilled, and the kingdom of God has come near; repent, and believe in the good news" (Mark 1:15). The skeptical reader can be forgiven for taking those words as the brash brags of a narcissistic megalomaniac. The receptive reader may read it as a mission statement of the messiah. But nobody can simply shrug off those words.

In fact, as we continue to read that Gospel, we follow Jesus as an itinerant preacher-teacher, presenting insights of wisdom almost non-stop. When we read through the longer Synoptic Gospels of Matthew and Luke, we hear much more of what Jesus said and did. And then the Gospel of John gives a whole body of other narratives, teachings, and dialogues of Jesus.

Jesus was that favorite teacher whose enthusiasm for the subject piqued your curiosity, driving you to pursue that field of study that ultimately defined the career you would pursue. That's who he was for his disciples and other followers, back then and out there. That's who he is for so many readers of his teachings, narratives, and sayings, here and now.

On one occasion, when Jesus spoke of people eating his flesh and drinking his blood—sounding like he was expecting them to act like cannibals, which provoked many of his followers to take offense to the point of abandoning him—he asked the Twelve, "Do you also wish to go away?" Well, as off-putting, even gross, as Jesus' words were, Simon Peter blurted back at him, "Lord, to whom can we go? You have the words of eternal life. We have come to believe and know that you are the Holy One of God" (John 6:66–69). Jesus' teaching had an irresistible grip on his audience, and all the more upon those who knew him best.

When the apostle John set out to write the fourth Gospel,[1] he started not by reporting the story of Jesus' birth, nor by reciting his family ancestry. He began at the beginnings of creation, referencing the opening words of Genesis, "In the beginning . . ." But then, he shifted from the creation of the heavens and the earth to talk about the creation of communication: "[Jesus] was the Word, and the word was with God and the word was God" (John 1:1). He elaborated, "He was in the beginning with God. All things came into being through him, and without him not one thing came into being. What has come into being in him was life, and the

---

1. To the avid student of the Gospels, I want to acknowledge that nobody alive today knows for certain who wrote the four Gospels, and for one simple reason: the earliest manuscripts of the New Testament have no title, no signature, no name associated with them. The traditional identifications of authorship stand as the best options, and for clarity's sake most of us continue to identify them accordingly. No matter who actually wrote them, their "ring of truth" makes the content compelling to the receptive reader, and as your guide to full-spectrum church leading, I will honor that traditional understanding.

life was the light of all people. The light shines in the darkness, and the darkness did not overtake it" (1:2–5).

After two brief sidebars—the first introducing John the Baptist, the second offering a foreshadowing of the ultimate division between those receiving him and those not—he returns to the initial theme: "And the Word became flesh and lived among us, and we have seen his glory, the glory as of a father's only son, full of grace and truth. (John testified to him and cried out, 'This was he of whom I said, "He who comes after me ranks ahead of me because he was before me."') From his fullness we have all received, grace upon grace. The law indeed was given through Moses; grace and truth came through Jesus Christ. No one has ever seen God. It is the only Son, himself God, who is close to the Father's heart, who has made him known" (1:14–18).

Those first and fourth paragraphs together tie Jesus' appearance to God, distinctively and boldly communicating and connecting with humans, with the fourth paragraph emphatically stating twice that he brought "grace and truth" to the people. In other words, this communication of truth through Jesus was the top headline of the year—God come to be with us (another way of speaking of Jesus as "Emmanuel"—God-with-us—as he was introduced in Matthew's birth account—1:23).

Growing out of that remarkable beginning, one of the central tasks of the Gospel writers, as well as the epistle interpreters, throughout all of their writing was to transmit Jesus' truth-telling to as many people as possible, so that unbelievers would come to believe, and that believers in turn could follow Jesus, the living Word, faithfully. Accordingly, the writers quote Jesus at length.

- From his simple metaphors: "You are the light of the world, . . . the salt of the earth";[2]

- To his elaborate parables: the sower, the good Samaritan, the prodigal son;[3]

- From his massive questions: "Who do the people say that I am? . . . Who do you say that I am?";[4]

---

2. Matt 5:13, 14.

3. Matt 13:1–23; Luke 10:29–37; Luke 15:11–32.

4. Mark 8:27, 29.

- To his summary propositions: "You shall know the truth and the truth shall make you free;"[5]

- From his promises: "Ask and you shall receive, seek and you shall find, knock and the door shall be opened to you;"[6]

- To his predictions of the future: "For as the days of Noah were, so will be the days of the coming of the Son of Man."[7]

Put that all together and, quite frankly, Jesus was a prolific teacher of wisdom, faith, inspiration, and truth.

We Hold These Truths . . .

Thomas Jefferson recognized much wisdom in Jesus' teaching, but he did not hold the Bible to be absolutely essential or definitive.[8] Nevertheless, he did hold to some truths taught in the Scriptures. It was he who penned the words, "We hold these truths to be self-evident." Upon those lofty words a nation was born. As he penned, some values are so essential and foundational that every person in every place and in every time ought to know them, believe them, subscribe to them, submit to them, and promote them. The values of human equality, life, liberty, and the pursuit of happiness—inalienable rights endowed by the Creator—were proclaimed by Jefferson and the others signing the Declaration of Independence.

Behind all of these self-evident truths, Jefferson was making an even more essential claim—two claims, to be exact. First, he was claiming that there are truths and, by implication, they will match thoughts to reality, will make sense out of life itself. Second, he was claiming that specific truths, at least some specific truths, are knowable. They are not lost in the fog of unsolvable mysteries.

In 1788, just twelve years after Jefferson penned the Declaration of Independence, a body of Christians in the Synod of New York and Philadelphia of the Presbyterian Church in United States of America penned

5. John 8:32.

6. Matt 7:7.

7. Matt 24:37.

8. The Jefferson Bible, compiled by Thomas Jefferson, included an abridged version of the New Testament. In it he "rearranged the text of the Gospels into an account of the life and ministry of Jesus that eschews mention of any supernatural or miraculous elements. Jefferson exemplified the rationalistic bent of many Enlightenment intellectuals and also quietly professed a form of Deistic Christianity." See Stefon, "Jefferson Bible."

what would eventually be dubbed the Historic Principles of Church Order. The fourth of the seven principles is titled *Truth and Goodness*: "That truth is in order to goodness; and the great touchstone of truth, its tendency to promote holiness, according to our Savior's rule, 'By their fruits ye shall know them.' And that no opinion can either be more pernicious or more absurd than that which brings truth and falsehood upon a level, and represents it as of no consequence what a [person's] opinions are. On the contrary, we are persuaded that there is an inseparable connection between faith and practice, truth and duty. Otherwise, it would be of no consequence either to discover truth or to embrace it."[9]

Jefferson's list of self-evident truths was brief and compact, as was the Bible he drastically edited and read. Those New York and Philadelphia Christians proceeded to spell out many more truths held to be biblically evident, spiritually true, and God inspired. But in both cases, truth was being extolled to be essential for practical living, both for individuals and for those living in effective communities, be they small-town congregations of Jesus-followers or the body politic of religiously diverse citizens in the thirteen colonies, in order to operate together as a new organized nation.

We Hold His Truths

In recent decades we have seen an upsurge in the fascination with which American Christians are focusing on Jesus. Many are those who speak of themselves as "Sermon on the Mount" Christians. Rather than getting embroiled in others' interpretations of Jesus' teachings, they lay hold of the beauty and poetry of his words delivered to the crowds overlooking the north shore of the Sea of Galilee. They find more than enough substance in those three chapters, Matthew 5–7, to provide a fullness of understanding to guide their living.

Others have aligned themselves with Tony Campolo, a leading (and often humorous) Christian thinker of recent decades. His book *Red-Letter Christians*[10] prods students of the faith to focus on the quoted words of Jesus found in the four Gospels, which some Bible editions print in red.

While each of these selective approaches to Bible reading is fraught with other problems (like the dismissive ways other Scriptures, especially

---

9. *PCUSA Book of Order*, F-3.0104, p. 12.

10. Campolo, *Red Letter Christians*.

the Hebrew Scriptures, get treated, and how such claims of following Jesus' teachings alone require much more of us than we imagine), each approach's popularity does highlight the fact that Jesus still has a compelling impact on seekers of truth.

Speaking of recent trends, one of the gifts of *The Chosen*, the remarkable movie series launched initially on Christmas Eve of 2017, is the title expressed so affectionately by the Twelve when addressing Jesus: "Rabbi." That title never appears in the Hebrew Scriptures, as it came into use during the synagogue movement which began after the death of the final author of that body of Scripture, Malachi. When the singularity of Herod's temple in Jerusalem proved impractical due to an ever-widening spread of Jewish migrations, local synagogues were organized, each with an appointed rabbi to lead it. The title rabbi literally means "my master" or "my teacher." In those years, most rabbis were not provided the formal training that the priests of Jerusalem's temple had. Nevertheless, they were recognized by their fellow synagogue members to be excellent students of the Law and Prophets, and were ordained to the office by three other rabbis who were affirming the new candidate's scholarship in study and faithfulness in life.

The School of Jesus

Like the Greek and Roman scholars teaching by way of the Socratic method—each having a band of academic apprentices as constant traveling partners, ever engaging the deepest and profoundest questions of life—the leading rabbis of Jesus' day had their own apprentices, whom they called disciples.

Those rabbinic scholars taught their accompanying students according to similar patterns and purposes as the Pharisees (who served the community of faith, similarly to that of deacons or lay pastors do today, as an avocation). Modern theologian Joseph Small says of the Pharisees:

> They maintained that it was necessary to be a member of the covenant people in order to be a beneficiary of God's righteousness. Inclusion within the covenant necessitated comprehensive observance of the law, particularly those regulations that marked out the Jews in their distinctiveness as the people of the one God. Among these, food and Sabbath laws were particularly prominent, both in Jewish self-understanding and in Roman perception of the Jews as a people. The Pharisees, as that group

especially concerned to maintain Jewish identity and faithfulness, called for observance of the law that went beyond the
merely "religious." What was required within the Temple should
be observed in all of life.[11]

Yes, the rabbis were pursuing comparable purposes and goals.

Jesus, who taught his disciples through similar methods as rabbinic
scholars taught theirs also was challenging the conventional wisdom of
these rabbis and Pharisees. For example, in his Sermon on the Mount, he
declared his dogmatic commitment to biblical adherence: "Do not think
that I have come to abolish the Law or the Prophets; I have come not
to abolish but to fulfill. For truly I tell you, until heaven and earth pass
away, not one letter, not one stroke of a letter, will pass from the law until
all is accomplished. Therefore, whoever breaks one of the least of these
commandments and teaches others to do the same will be called least in
the kingdom of heaven, but whoever does them and teaches them will be
called great in the kingdom of heaven."[12]

However, immediately after extolling the existing Scriptures, he
added, "For I tell you, unless your righteousness exceeds that of the
scribes and Pharisees, you will never enter the kingdom of heaven."[13]

But the scribes and Pharisees were no slouchers. Not only did they
scrupulously carry out the behavioral requirement of the Law. They
fulfilled the general requirement of all Jewish men to memorize the five
books of the Torah (Genesis through Deuteronomy), and as Pharisees
they memorized the whole body of those Scriptures from Joshua through
Malachi. How could the disciples possibly exceed the scribes and Pharisees in any category of the faith and practice?

Well, the answer comes from Jesus. His command of the texts was
evident. He quoted the Hebrew Scriptures often, whether it was while
preaching to the crowds or responding to questions from his disciples
or to the challenging temptations in the wilderness. He knew the text.
But he also knew the spirit of the text, the spirit of the Law. Unlike those
protectors and defenders of Scripture's accuracy and authority, and often
with a judgmentalism that was quick to condemn those violating the Law
or disregarding it out of ignorance, Jesus explained the Scriptures with

11. Small, "Who's In, Who's Out?," 60–61.

12. Matt 5:17–19.

13. Matt 5:20.

a bent toward the spirit of the Law, the heart intention of what God inspired in the Law and Prophets to lovingly guide the lives of God's people.

The Letter and the Spirit

True to the promises of Jeremiah (31:31–33), Ezekiel, and other prophets, the writer of Hebrews (8:10–12) proclaims those promises are now being fulfilled by Jesus in and through his followers: "The days are surely coming, says the Lord, when I will make a new covenant with the house of Israel and the house of Judah. It will not be like the covenant that I made with their ancestors when I took them by the hand to bring them out of the land of Egypt—a covenant that they broke, though I was their husband, says the Lord. But this is the covenant that I will make with the house of Israel after those days, says the Lord: I will put my law within them, and I will write it on their hearts, and I will be their God, and they shall be my people."

In effect, Jesus was not doing away with the Law but intensifying it, sharpening its focus on the sins not just outward but inward, and teaching the necessity of an exacting faithfulness to its demands. Thankfully he fulfills its demands by way of his sinlessness, and offers his perfect human obedience on behalf of sinful human beings as our divinely commissioned Representative and High Priest. The Holy Spirit then unites us to Christ the Mediator, so that we then participate in his sacrificial holiness to Abba, Father on our behalf. In the process the Holy Spirit also grants us healing of our brokenness. All of the convicting teaching and the redemptive presentation of Jesus was a reflection of his passion to bring the full Truth to bear on our lives—especially the truth about his forgiving, redeeming, healing love (about which we will say more in the next chapter).

As a result, he was fending off the sharks of rigid, rules-based, stonehearted, "prove your worthiness" legalistic living—a kind of shark that we have had with us always, in every brand of Judaism and Christianity, if only as a way for parents to get better behavior out of their children—and gifting to us forgiving grace and soft, heart-of-flesh tenderness.

To use a contemporary verb, Jesus was *reframing* the truth, so that his students, not just the Twelve but all of his family, friends, and followers, could now live in a new covenant (Luke 22:20), as a new temple

(John 2:18–21) and a new people of God which now includes the gentiles (1 Pet 2:9).

To clarify, Jesus was not replacing Judaism nor reinventing it. But he was reframing it, recasting its essence in such a way as to cause many to do double-takes on things he said:

"Did he really say that?"

"I've never heard that before."

"But what about . . . ?"

Brain-twisting questions and puzzlements buzzed around the crowds. And yet, so many people could answer their own queries by whispering to themselves and to one another, "That really caught me by surprise. But it's so biblical, and it makes so much sense; in fact, it's so obviously true. How come I've never heard that before?"

Jesus had a passion to reframe the truth, and in the process, to reframe people's faith, their lifestyles, their relationships, their communities, their world. He was a rabbi like no other. Head and shoulders above the scribes and Pharisees. More, what is not to be missed in the translation of the word "rabbi," as mentioned earlier, is the single letter suffix, "i." It is the pronoun, "my." In their traveling, the students grew close to their rabbi. Hence, the apostles' term of endearment when addressing Jesus, speaking of him as rabbi, suggested a closeness, a trust, an embrace (at least in spirit) between them. Most certainly, the embrace between Jesus and the Twelve was deep.

Put this all together, and it became apparent years later that, when followers of Jesus sent letters to faraway places to explain his teachings or sat down to record his parables, proclamations, promises, and predictions or chronicle his journeys and his miracles, his encounters with admirers and his arguments with opponents, as well as other noteworthy events, they were aiming to proclaim his good news and to preserve it for future generations. They were following the implied assignments of all disciples. And having been explicitly commissioned to make disciples (literally "students" or "apprentices") of all nations, they did so with in earnest.

From Jesus' Passion to Our Pulpits, Bible Studies, and Life Groups

We, the students of Scripture reading the texts 1,900 years after their completion continue to learn from them, being confident that their writings arose not just by their own volition, but also by Jesus' direction and instructing, with the added help of the Holy Spirit's inspiration.

Accordingly, these fonts of wisdom and truth stand as the primary source of all that we learn and teach, of all that we say and do. And some of us do so with earnest effort that aligns with that of those original writers.

That's not an easy job. Not only do biblical scholars need to learn to read in the original languages in which the inspired scriptures were written—Hebrew for the Hebrew Scriptures (the Christian Old Testament), Greek for the New Testament—but they also need to pore over those Scriptures and other ancient writings, maps, archaeological digs, and artifacts in order best to reconstruct the original contexts of the writers and their recipients. As they do so, they need to compare multiple writings of multiple writers throughout the Scriptures to see how their communications about Jesus and the other figures converge, complement, enlarge, add nuance, and offer multiple angles from which best to discern the original intended meanings of those writers to their original audiences, with the goal of then bridging responsibly and faithfully to our audiences in our present contexts, two thousand years and six thousand (or so) miles away.

Jesus' Passion for Us to Know the Truth set into motion in his time and place models the appropriate passion of biblical students and scholars to do the same in our own times and places.

Which presents a dilemma. All biblical scholars, all theologians, all authors, all preachers and teachers are flawed. Oh, most are devout students of Scripture. But still, they have their flaws. First and foremost, they have a tendency to sin. And sin has a tendency to twist one's thinking. Scholars ranging from Augustine to Aquinas and Calvin to Edwards, right up to S. K. Moroney have long expounded on the "noetic effects of sin."[14] Drawn from the Greek word "nous," meaning "the mind, the intellect," it suggests the fact that sinful behavior is generated and reinforced by sinful thoughts, which in turn tarnish, twist, and corrupt our reasoning powers. Not that we are incapable of reasoning clearly, logically, or artistically. We simply cannot maintain the full knowledge and wisdom of the wise without it going awry at least from time to time.[15]

---

14. Moroney, "Noetic Effects of Sin," esp. appendix 3.

15. "For the wrath of God is revealed from heaven against all ungodliness and injustice of those who by their injustice suppress the truth. For what can be known about God is plain to them, because God has made it plain to them. Ever since the creation of the world God's eternal power and divine nature, invisible though they are, have been

Most theologians can affirm, at least sheepishly, that all of our best works are tainted by self-interest.

Which leads to the great calling and challenge of believers embracing and emulating this first passion of the Christ: how might we follow Jesus' Passion for Us to Know the Truth, and specifically to follow his example of reframing the truth, in order to faithfully proclaim and preserve that truth?[16]

Historically, we have fallen short not just by the tarnishing of our ability to live and explain the truth, but also by our militancy in defending what we believe to be the truth. As church historian Bradley Longfield says, Christians fight so intensely among themselves because of their very confession that Jesus Christ is Lord. Making such a confession immediately obligates a person to do the will of Christ, no matter how much opposition one encounters, no matter how nontraditional one's convictions may be, or even no matter how much one may be accused of heresy, ignorance, or bigotry. "If Jesus is Lord, and Christians believe that faithfulness to Christ calls them to a certain position on particular issues, then they are compelled to respond. Jesus is Lord. Not just over part of life but all of life, and this will, sooner or later, tend to push individuals and groups to conflict."[17]

So, given that the Bible says pastors and Bible scholars are saints who still sin, and given that they can become entrenched in convictions whose defense they clasp onto in harsh, judgmental, and argumentative ways, and, I will add, given that our communicating skills often lag far behind our theological training, the Bible and its truths often incite riots of disagreement and contention among us.

That's certainly is not what Jesus had in mind when promising "You will know the truth and the truth shall make you free" (John 8:32). Yes, truth has sufficient power to liberate from enslavement. That's a power

---

seen and understood through the things God has made. So they are without excuse, for though they knew God, they did not honor him as God or give thanks to him, but they became futile in their thinking, and their senseless hearts were darkened. Claiming to be wise, they became fools, and they exchanged the glory of the immortal God for images resembling a mortal human or birds or four-footed animals or reptiles. Therefore, God gave them over in the desires of their hearts to impurity, to the dishonoring of their bodies among themselves. They exchanged the truth about God for a lie and worshiped and served the creature rather than the Creator, who is blessed forever! Amen" (Rom 1:18–25).

16. For further in-depth discussion on Jesus' reframing of the truth, see my *It's Complicated*.

17. Longfield, "Presbyterian Conflict."

worth fighting for! But the sheer variety of life experiences, of geographic settings, of cultural varieties, of ethnicities, genders, and orientations among us all drive us not just to proclaim the truth but also to protect it as we understand it and to preserve it from being distorted.

Accordingly, when considering Jesus' passion for telling the truth and for training his students to spread the good news of his mercy, grace, and love, many of us have sought in the past, and will continue to seek into the foreseeable future, to continue his preaching and teaching ministry. Which segment of worship in most churches takes up the largest portion of the service on most Sundays? The reading and exposition of Scripture. In some churches worshipers are even taking notes, whether on a notepad or in the margins of their print or digital Bible. As the pastors are trained, the congregations expect to hear inspired learnings about one or more biblical passages in that worship service, and many worshipers talk about those sermons after they depart from the church sanctuary or worship center.

Unfortunately, too often pastors grow stale in their faith, predictable in their preaching, secular in their thinking, and partisan in their advocacy. They forget the power of Christ's proclamation and substitute other matters in its place. Theologian John Leith elaborates:

> The primary source of the malaise of the church . . . is the loss of a distinctive Christian message and of the theological and biblical competence that made its preaching effective. Sermons fail to mediate the presence and grace of God. Many sermons are moral exhortations, which can be heard delivered with greater skill at the Rotary or Kiwanis Club. Many sermons are political and economic judgments on society, which have been presented with greater wisdom and passion at political conventions. Many sermons offer personal therapies, which can be better provided by well-trained psychiatrists. The only skill the preacher has— or the church, for that matter—which is not found with greater excellence somewhere else, is theology, in particular the skill to interpret and apply the Word of God in sermon, teaching, and pastoral care. This is the great service which the minister and the church can render the world. Why should anyone come to church for what can be better found somewhere else?[18]

18. Leith, *Crisis in the Church*, 22.

Where pastors keep on track in the exposition of the text, focusing on the teaching gift Jesus delivered and modeled, folks will find good reason to come to church.

A passion for us to know the truth. Jesus felt it, he modeled it, promoted it, and commissioned his disciples—who, in turn, commissioned their own disciples generation after generation—so that the truth would continue to set people free.

The truth is that important. The teaching of it is that central.

Then again, this passion of Jesus did not end with simply the passing of ideas from one person's daily journal to another person's daily journal. Jesus proclaimed the truth so it would not just set free, but also so it would unite us to God, turn walls into bridges, turn strangers into friends, catalyze service to neighbors near and far, and change the world.

Accordingly, for those of us so entrusted, the endeavor to know, to reframe and to proclaim God's word holds forth the prospect to transform lives, to reframe goals and to reframe the connection to the living God in our congregants' very human lives. It may be carried out by taking stands on issues of justice. It will manifest itself in acts of generous care for the hurting. It will integrate the individual within the community of faith. And it will lead the person into a deepening, expanding, vital relationship with God.

On the other hand, those inclined with passion toward truth may not be the ones others of us would want to call our friends. What is it about them who share Jesus' passion' for the truth?

- They can be pretty opinionated.
- They are always ready to stage a debate.
- Many of them have an obnoxious attitude of certitude.
- Others of them may revel in the pursuit of truth, but actually they resist it.
- They can come across as just too smart to accept anything you say to them.
- They often get really judgmental, even like the Pharisees.

Still, they came by it honestly. They got that passion from Jesus.

— 7 —

The Ebb and Flow of the God-Connection

Jesus' Passion for Us to Love God

"Now as they went on their way, he entered a certain village, where a woman named Martha welcomed him into her home. She had a sister named Mary, who sat at the Lord's feet and listened to what he was saying. But Martha was distracted by her many tasks; so she came to him and asked, 'Lord, do you not care that my sister has left me to do all the work by myself? Tell her then to help me.' But the Lord answered her, 'Martha, Martha, you are worried and distracted by many things; there is need of only one thing. Mary has chosen the better part, which will not be taken away from her'" (Luke 10:38–42).

The church has had a running argument with Jesus about Mary and Martha. We take him at his words when he says, "Mary has chosen the better thing," but we don't really believe him. Perhaps a few do. Like the nuns and monks that gather in their convents and monasteries, practicing the discipline of silence. Lacking televisions, stereos, and conversation, they have cultivated an ethos of awe-filled serenity. They appreciate the value of sitting and listening. Quakers, the Society of Friends, and pilgrims to Iona and Taize retreat centers also support Jesus' alignment with Mary against Martha. They gather in their unadorned meeting houses, and in silence they listen for the "inner light" to speak God's word and to guide their way. In so doing, they are emulating the example set by Mary and affirmed by Jesus.

In fact, most churches have a few members who are known as the prayer team or intercession team or, with vigor, the prayer warriors. Given that most are usually women, they may call themselves the Mary Society. They're usually respected and appreciated by their fellow church members. They may be the first ones to be called when a parent or spouse sits down in the hospital's emergency room waiting area. But, as I said, they usually number in the "few" category.

Most of us are not wired that way. We may well shrug with disgust when hearing the Mary and Martha story. Some even feel an acid-burning, gut-grinding repulsion when it is quoted. "Jesus was really unfair to Martha," they protest. Some try to help him interpret himself. "He obviously didn't really mean what he was saying," they explain apologetically. Others, looking to rationalize their own instincts, say with a shrug, "I guess I'm just more of a Martha than a Mary."

What's more, when the church is called to action, when new teachers are needed for classes, or caregivers are needed to manage the nursery, these super-saints are nowhere to be found. Nobody would outwardly call them sharks, but we Marthas may complain under our breath that they are not carrying their weight. They do no more than the inert clams or oysters along the sea bottom.

Here are these two sisters, who with their brother Lazarus were probably Jesus' closest friends outside the twelve disciples. Jesus stops by Martha's house—where Mary had already arrived for an afternoon visit—and Martha goes about the business of picking up the clutter, preparing tea and bread. In the meantime, sister Mary simply sits at Jesus' feet and, all awed, takes in his every word (in modern terms, the label "groupie" comes to mind). Martha, feeling miffed over her sister's apparent laziness, mutters her suggestion that maybe Jesus ought to hint to Mary that she should join in serving their famous friend.

Jesus turns the tables on the two sisters, and indeed on the modern reader. "Martha, Martha, you are worried and distracted by many things; there is need of only one thing. Mary has chosen the better part, which will not be taken away from her."

How could he say such a thing? How could he discount the servant spirit in Martha and endorse the truancy of Mary?

Why Such Difficulty?

Why do we have such a hard time accepting the import of this story? Why is it so hard to imagine that Jesus was more intent—indeed, passionately yearning—to cultivate in people their adoration of God than their service to humanity? Why is it hard to believe Jesus when he says, "I do not call you servants any longer, because the servant does not know what the master is doing; but I have called you friends" (John 15:15)? Why do we get squeamish when we stop and really ponder that first great commandment: "You shall love the Lord your God with all your heart, soul, mind and strength"—and that it is directing us not per se to give God our wholehearted service, or energetic obedience, or holy fear, but, rather, our wholehearted and whole-bodied love?

Jesus did not invent the idea of loving God. It goes all the way back at least as far as the days of Moses. One of the cornerstone faith statements of that day is called the "Shema Israel" (Hebrew for "Hear, Israel,") attributed to Moses himself:

> "Hear, O Israel: The Lord is our God, the Lord alone. You shall love the Lord your God with all your heart and with all your soul and with all your might. Keep these words that I am commanding you today in your heart. Recite them to your children and talk about them when you are at home and when you are away, when you lie down and when you rise. Bind them as a sign on your hand, fix them as an emblem on your forehead, and write them on the doorposts of your house and on your gates." (Deut 6:4–10)

When Jesus was questioned about his teachings he responded accordingly:

> When the Pharisees heard that he had silenced the Sadducees, they gathered together, and one of them, an expert in the law, asked him a question to test him. "Teacher, which commandment in the law is the greatest?" He said to him, "'You shall love the Lord your God with all your heart and with all your soul and with all your mind.' This is the greatest and first commandment. And a second is like it: 'You shall love your neighbor as yourself.' On these two commandments hang all the Law and the Prophets." (Matt 23:34–40)

But many of us today get squeamish over such sounds of sentimentality. Face it: as J. Mary Luti muses, "We know we are supposed to love God, but the idea can seem strange and a little flaky, In love with God?"[1] In fact, many of us are more comfortable thinking about loving neighbors—consistent with the second part of the Great Commandment, which we will take up shortly—and serving people, as did Martha, than doing all that sentimental spirituality of sister Mary.

The Reconciled, Relationalized Life

But Jesus preferred Mary's adoration over Martha's service, because he had a passion for both sisters—and, indeed, a passion for all of us to love God. Among all of the truths he was reframing in his preaching and teaching ministry, one of the most central was the truth that the sovereign, transcendent God, whom the children of Israel had been taught to obey, to honor, to worship and fear from afar, had come to visit them, to love them, to listen to them, to turn that visit into being continually with them. And that, as suggested above, the first commandment before and above all the others is that they love that God—not just obey, not just honor, nor fear, but L-O-V-E—LOVE!

As in the other truths Jesus was reframing, this was not a new truth. It simply was one that was getting short shrift among the religious elites of the day. And now that he—Emmanuel—was *God with us*, incarnated as one of us, he was teaching and modeling what it is like to be related to God as family around a table rather than as an emperor on a throne.

Throughout the three years of Jesus' public ministry, he kept encountering persons who felt separated from God, estranged from God. It came as no surprise. Long before the initiation of his ministry, launched by John's baptism, he had been schooled in the narratives and teachings of the Torah and the prophets. He knew that the human condition was one of having been created in the image of God, but also one of having rebelled against God, leading to a wholesale banishment from God's presence. He also knew that rebellion had become the prevailing pattern of human existence even among those specially chosen to live in a grace-filled, faith-generating covenant with God. Jesus' mission, born out of eternity past in the dance of the three members of the trinitarian God, included him serving as an atoning sacrifice for humans' sins past and future. That mission was driven not merely out of obligation nor even out of sympathy but, ultimately, out of that yearning to lift people up from their hopeless exile

1. Luti, "Whole World is Singing," 338.

to the joy of communion with God. He was born with an innate passion to raise them up, to raise us up, into the interpersonal relating to God on the level of that of a beloved child with its loving parent.

The story of Jesus' death, classically dubbed the Passion of the Christ, provided an atonement for our sins, which, in turn, extended forgiveness to all who seek it. Combined with his subsequent resurrection from the dead, those repenting and believing in Jesus as Savior and Lord were, and continue today to be, raised from spiritual death in order to enter into the eternal quality of life summarized in the words of prayer by Jesus as, "And this is eternal life, that they may know you, the only true God, and Jesus Christ, whom you have sent" (John 17:3). That existential knowing of God brings a quality of life, of relational life, into the experience of the believer, that equates to the "abundant life" (John 10:10) that Jesus promised to give his disciples.

The quality of such a connected life for the current believer is captured profoundly by the apostle Paul in his summary of the essential faith he wrote to the Roman church: "Therefore there is now no condemnation for those who are in Christ Jesus. For the law of the Spirit of life in Christ Jesus has set you free from the law of sin and of death" (Rom 8:1–2).

This in turn is reflected in those other words of Paul to the Romans: "But God proves his love for us in that while we still were sinners Christ died for us" (Rom 5:8).

These words are echoed by John: "God's love was revealed among us in this way: God sent his only Son into the world so that we might live through him. In this is love, not that we loved God but that he loved us and sent his Son to be the atoning sacrifice for our sins. . . . No one has ever seen God; if we love one another, God abides in us, and his love is perfected in us. . . . We love because he first loved us" (1 John 4, excerpts).

And That's Not All of It: Love-Driven Worship . . .

The love-of-God relationalizing of life extended through Jesus to the new believer extends to the chief end of our own existence—here on earth, not just postponed until the eternal future. As stated in response to the opening question of the Larger Catechism of the Westminster Confession, "[Humanity's] chief and highest end is to glorify God, and fully to enjoy [God] forever."[2]

---

2. "Larger Catechism," Q. 1.

This, in fact, is an experience embraced and embodied by Mary's choice of "the better thing" (Luke 10:42b). By expressing herself with Jesus not as a worker nor as a table server (as noble as are those vocations) but as an attentive listener, she was expressing a kind of worship and adoration that is measured not by productivity but by affectional honor, worship, and love. She was worshiping Jesus.

Compare her experience to that of the woman at the well, whom Jesus met in the middle of Samaria. Although she and her people were dread enemies of Israel, and although she was simply a woman who any self-respecting man of local traditions and chauvinist inclinations would ignore in that time and public place, she was approached by, and invited into conversation with, Jesus. Then, when she perceived him to be a prophet, she posed a controversial theological question to him, asking which mountain is the right mountain on which to worship. He responded, "Woman, believe me, the hour is coming when you will worship the Father[3] neither on this mountain nor in Jerusalem. You worship what you do not know; we worship what we know, for salvation is from the Jews. But the hour is coming and is now here when the true worshipers will worship the Father in spirit and truth, for the Father seeks such as these to worship him. God is spirit, and those who worship him must worship in spirit and truth" (John 4:21–24). You can call that "love-driven worship": worship animated by the life-giving Holy Spirit and truth.

Still More: Prayer

The love-driven life also offers the animating power of prayer. The Jewish experience of prayer had heretofore been amazing. Remarkable stories of God's intervention in people's lives were as epic as the parting of the seas for the exodus of the newly liberated slaves from Egypt, and as powerful as Elijah calling down fire from heaven to humiliate the priests of pagan gods. God's ability to bring success in a time of war was exemplified by Moses's upraised hands bringing the defeat of the Amalekites during the wilderness wanderings. Fast-forward to the prophets' days to see such epic interventions as displayed by the three boys, Meshach, Shadrach and Abednego, surviving a fiery furnace, followed by Daniel surviving a lion's den.

---

3. We will discuss in chapter 12 the meaning attached to Jesus' naming of God as "Abba, Father."

The amazement of Israel's praying wasn't just that of seeing miracles through the power of unique prophets. It also amazed in its candor, its heart-felt adoration and anguish, its praise and complaints. In fact it took the longest book in the Bible to provide sufficient guidance for Israel's praying—the 150 poetic prayers in the book of the Psalms. We don't hear a lot of prayers from Jesus' mouth, but his comprehensive collection of praise and petitions in the Lord's Prayer, the yearnings expressed in his high priestly prayer (John 17), and the anguished petitions on the cross evidence the same kinds of intensity.

Jesus didn't have to invent intimacy in praying. He simply show-cased all over again what it is like to talk with the God who is knowable, available, listening.

Put this all together and Jesus' Passion for Us to Love God provides a complete package of activities and impacts upon those engaging in them. It begins with Jesus' life, death, and resurrection, together provid-ing the tools for humans to be connected to God, fully forgiven for sins past and in anticipation of sins yet to be committed. It invites the believ-ers to engage in worship with the God of the universe, doing so not out of duty but out of sheer joy and gratitude for the indescribable gifts of God's grace, mercy, and love. And it provides the spiritual networking connections to pray to God, confident of God's attending to and tuning in to those prayers of thanks and of petition, those of personal supplication and, for others' sakes, those prayers of intercession. All together this gen-erates a relationalized experience to be lived in this life day by day. The someday-in-eternity glory in heaven gets experienced in the present here and now—even if experientially interrupted intermittently by competing interests and necessary tasks.

Living in God's Love

Through the ages believers have waxed and waned in their experience of the interactive intimacy with God that Jesus encouraged. Compet-ing interests and necessary tasks have been compounded by times of apostasy and immorality, of scandal and betrayal, especially ecclesiasti-cal betrayal—along with waves of intellectual incredulity and theologi-cal suspicion of faith-claims—to give birth to seasons of secularity and backsliding. Most recently, the swell of "dechurching"[4] trends have been

4. David, Graham, and Burge, *Great Dechurching*.

compounded by the worldwide COVID-19 pandemic that intensified to tsunami—even "Sharknado"[5]—proportions. As this book goes to press, it remains to be seen which sectors of the faith will rebound with the spiritual vitality that arose in past seasons of awakening, revival, and renewal, such as have been studied at length by Richard Lovelace.[6]

Alive in the churches in the past century have been leaders and movements aiming for this very spirit of renewal and awakening. The highest profile movements of energetic and intimate faith have come through the phenomenal growth of Pentecostalism and Neo-Pentecostalism (the charismatic movement), whose stories we allude to at various points of this book, so I won't elaborate again here.

Another movement that, by design, flies under the radar is that of Cursillo, birthed on the Spanish island of Majorca during World War II, under the leadership of Father Eduardo Bonnín Aguiló. A small but growing youth movement in Spain gave impetus to Aguiló to organize a group of men in his parish to prompt others to re-engage the faith introduced in their baptisms. They organized a weekend-long retreat, titled "A Little Course in Living What is Fundamental for Being a Christian," or dubbed simply, "Cursillo," literally, "little course." While its actual outline and script are pretty much kept secret (the suspense of unknowing is part of its appeal), the simple summary that can be told is that the participants get to discuss and respond to summaries of the core beliefs of the faith, taught mostly by lay members of the parish, all the while they are being blessed with great food and fellowship, quiet worship services and boisterous singing, belly laughs and sweet tears. Many of the participants connect with God as they never have before, and agree to join a reunion group, a handful of co-participants who then meet for an hour once a week to share about their ongoing learnings and "close moments" with Jesus. The net effect of such retreats has produced a relationalizing of spiritual vitality in the Roman Catholic Church.[7]

After several years of development on Majorca, the movement spread slowly, until Vatican II promoted it. Then it spread worldwide. Soon, what had begun as a men's movement (the Catholic women in Majorca were already actively practicing their faith) generated an equivalent women's Cursillo movement. Today comparable retreats are led by the

---

5. See series of movies by this name, directed by Anthony Ferrante.

6. Lovelace, *Dynamics of Spiritual Life.*

7. "History of the Cursillo Movement."

Episcopal, Lutheran (Via de Christo), Methodist (Walk to Emmaus), Presbyterian (Great Banquet), and other churches.

While I have served on a dozen or more such weekends (sponsored by Lutherans, Methodists, and Presbyterians), Glenn McDonald, my great friend, covenant brother, and side-by-side coach in the writing of this manuscript, sponsored over one hundred Great Banquet weekends. He shared with me, "The Great Banquet is hands-down the most transforming ministry I've ever experienced as a pastor—a retreat setting in which countless men and women have come alive, many for the first time, to the reality of God's gracious invitation to a Spirit-empowered way of life."[8]

Alongside such retreats, churches and nondenominational movements have organized a plethora of learning and growth opportunities, national conferences, specialized magazines, revivals, retreats, websites, podcasts, and blogs to incite spiritual fervor, beautiful expressions of worship, prayer meetings, prayer vigils, prayer groups, prayer chains, prayer mountains, prayer towers, prayer institutes, prayer labyrinths, and prayerful silent retreats.

Movements all about worshipful music, ranging from the AGO (the classical sounds of American Guild of Organists) to CCM (the rock reverberations of contemporary Christian music), have evolved their genres of Christ-exalting and God-honoring music into entire industries and associations of colleagues in partnership to bring whole congregations into the practice of glorifying and enjoying God here and now in anticipation of doing so forever, at the ultimate resurrection—and in the ultimate fulfillment of Jesus' Passion for Us to Love God. And then they will "know that they know that they know" that, indeed, Mary has chosen the better thing.

On the other hand, those who have caught Jesus' passion for us to love God may not be the ones others of us would want to call our friends. What is it about them who share Jesus' passion' for God?

- They may act so super spiritual.
- Sometimes they come off as "holier than thou."
- They can make you feel guilty for not praying enough.
- They can throw a wet blanket on simply having innocent fun.

Still, they came by it honestly. They got that passion from Jesus.

8. Glenn McDonald, personal correspondence, February 16, 2024.

— 8 —

To Build, to Fish, to Shepherd

Jesus' Passion for Us to Love One Another

So, SOME OF US are captivated by and are seeking to emulate Jesus' Passion for Us to Know the Truth. The Israel of his day had its share of scholarly rabbis, but Jesus the Teacher excelled above the rest in his ability to reframe those texts to the intentions of the original God-inspired writers and to the current lifestyles, contexts, and understandings of his apprentices. As his twenty-first-century disciples, many of us are regularly stretching our minds to interpret and enflesh the spirit of his thinking in the hope of forming the next generation of faithful disciples.

Others of us are captivated by Jesus' Passion for Us to Love God: i.e., to embrace his redeeming, reconciling work of dying for the sins of the world, forgiving all of our sins, and tearing down the veil of separation that had kept people away from God's presence, and entering into the full experience of God's incredible agape love. That whole work of redemption has led into a connection with God by which our prayers can be carried to heaven's throne, with promises of God hearing and responding to them. Growing from all of those gifts, Jesus has drawn us into expressions of worship, whether liturgical or informal or sheer silence, whether expressed in ancient chants, medieval classics, or contemporary praise songs, any one of which on any occasion can raise us, resurrect us into worshiping God in Spirit and truth.

Some of us have been granted the privilege to ascend into pulpits to proclaim the news of such divine, agape, perfect love, while others of us have been gifted to write poetic prayers, singable melodies, complex harmonies, or add rhythms to help many others experience the joy such worship prompts.

This second passion of Jesus could be summarized as his first response to a lawyer's question, "Teacher, which commandment in the law is the greatest?"

Jesus responded, "'You shall love the Lord your God with all your heart and with all your soul and with all your mind.' This is the greatest and first commandment. And a second is like it: 'You shall love your neighbor as yourself.' On these two commandments hang all the Law and the Prophets" (Matt 26:36–40).

Yes, having expounded on Jesus' first passion as relating to the truth, and then suggesting that the second passion matches the first half of the greatest law, it would stand to reason that I would say that the third passion of Jesus would address the second half of the greatest commandment, "You shall love your neighbor as yourself." The commands to love God and neighbor date all the way back to Moses's day. But for our purposes the neighbor-love command will come forward in the fourth passion and will then be expanded in the fifth. For a simple sequence that will be obvious shortly, we have another passion to come as our third. This third passion does not date back to Moses but begins with Jesus himself.

Passion Number Three: One Anothering

The third step in this sequence is Jesus' Passion for Us to Love One Another. It is what Jesus introduced as "'A new commandment I give to you, that you love one another; even as I have loved you, that you also love one another. By this everyone will know that you are my disciples, if you have love for one another (RSV).'"

As emphatic and repetitive as Jesus was throughout his three-years-long preaching about loving God and neighbors, this commandment seems to have come as a last-minute thought, or to be exact, a Last Supper thought. The gathering in the upper room began with Jesus washing the disciples' feet, then challenging the disciples to continue to do so for one another, and then his introduction to this brand new commandment.

Pause a moment with me. "Every text has a context"—so I heard in every Bible class I ever took: from home Bible studies to Baptist Sunday school classes, from Serendipity groups to Life Groups, from Elim Bible

Institute to Roberts Wesleyan College, from Gordon-Conwell Theological Seminary to Columbia Theological Seminary. Every one of those learning venues had its own biases and traditions, but they all knew that serious Bible study requires the reader to ask, "What's going on here?" Well, that's exactly the question to be asked when reading about the new commandment from Jesus.

What's more, there are two contexts to consider: the context of Jesus and the disciples when they gathered for that Passover supper, and decades later, the context in which John wrote his Gospel account of Jesus' life.

For Jesus, the primary context was all the buildup to what he knew was going to be the longest twenty-four hours of his life in human flesh, the "Passio Christi": his suffering and death. This was the time for him to express his last words to his disciples, extending to them his last directives for their future. How did he begin that meal? As host of the meal he moved from the seat of authority to the knees of a servant: humbling himself by washing the guests' feet. He explained himself: "'Do you understand what I have done to you? You call me Teacher and Lord, and you are right, for so I am. If I then, your Lord and Teacher, have washed your feet, you also ought to wash one another's feet. For I have given you an example, that you also should do just as I have done to you. Truly, truly, I say to you, a servant is not greater than his master, nor is a messenger greater than the one who sent him. If you know these things, blessed are you if you do them'" (John 13:12–17).

Jesus was putting a radical challenge before the disciples. They repeatedly picked sides among themselves, trying to assert their insider status against each other. Jesus was definitively saying, "No more!" . . . "Enough of this!" . . . "Love one another as I have loved you!"

For John writing the Gospel decades later,[1] long after all of the other apostles had died, his approach to Jesus' story ended similarly to the Synoptic Gospels' accounts of Jesus' death, but most all of the earlier years covered very different material. To read his account compared to the others would be like reading accounts of American's first moon landing in three American news reports (e.g., in *The Washington Post*, *The New York Times*, and *The Chicago Tribune*) and then reading the account of *Pravda*

---

1. To reiterate an earlier footnote, the actual authorship of John's gospel is not a proven fact. But the regular belief in his authorship emerged in the early Christian centuries and persisted through nearly two millennia. If not John, then most likely, the writers would have been "Johanine," his own disciples reporting their understanding of his teachings. The same goes for additional comments about his leadership of the church in Ephesus.

(the former USSR's premier daily). The facts may be similar, but the rest of the story would have reflected a different point of view.

Specifically, John took up pen to write Jesus' Gospel late in the first century. His audience was a group of churches located mostly in Ephesus and the region around it, i.e., Asia Minor (today's Turkey). A case in point features the seven churches in the early part of the book of Revelation—every one is in that region. In the year 52 CE, the apostle Paul had traveled from Corinth in southern Greece to Ephesus, near the eastern shore of the Aegean Sea. He preached in synagogues, led many to Christ, and planted the church there (Acts 18:19). He remained two to three years (Acts 19:8–10). In the process, the church became a model congregation in its ability to unite Jew and gentile together (see the first two chapters of Ephesians).

Sometime later John returned there until exiled to Patmos. According to second-century theologian Irenaeus, John's friend Polycarp reported that John become pastor of the Ephesians' church, and wrote his Gospel and three epistles there—with that congregation being the primary recipients of them. However, the Ephesians had become a contentious lot, suffering great rivalries and conflicts, especially between those of Jewish roots and those not so. Accordingly, John's Gospel repeats virtually none of the Synoptics' teachings about behavior, about neighbors, about the Law. Instead, John's Gospel focuses on the identity of Jesus, his pronouncements about his identity, the call to believe in him, and, finally, the one moral command: love one another.

In fact, when comparing Jesus' new commandment to Moses's and others' Great Commandment to love neighbors, there are two differences. First, they set a different standard. Moses says "Love the other *as yourself*" and Jesus says "Love the other *as I have loved you.*" Certainly, Jesus raises the bar to a higher height.

But a second difference stands between the objects of the two commands. Whereas Moses directs the people to "Love *your neighbor,*" Jesus directs his disciples to "Love *one another.*" There is a difference here. These are not two different ways to say the same thing. As we will explain further in the next chapter, the neighbor is defined repeatedly in the Hebrew Scriptures as the alien, the outsider, the foreigner—as is also the case when Jesus speaks of loving the neighbor in Matthew, Mark, and Luke. But for Jesus in John's Gospel, "one another" is referring to us, that is, our people, our tribe, our fellowship, our friends and family. When introducing the term in his upper room discourse, Jesus is turning his attention to the gathered disciples, the gathered congregation, the gathered tribe. Or, dare I say, "the us"—indeed, *the us that is among us."*

In fact, the term Jesus uses here isn't just a combined pronoun, like the two words in English, "one another." In Greek those pronouns come together to be a singular composite noun, "allelon," pronounced, "ah-LAY-loan." It is, so to speak, a proper noun. It has specific meaning, the closest term being "our tribe," or "our people." Now, in segregated societies, it could be used as a tool of exclusion, i.e., loving our own and shunning the rest. Not so for Jesus, whose repeated teachings about loving those outside the tribe are ubiquitous in the Synoptic Gospels. But for him at the Last Supper, being surrounded by his dozen closest friends who are so predisposed toward rivalries and contentiousness, he pleads "Love one another! Love *the us that is among us!*" And for John writing the church he has served for years, and doing so at a time when he is nearing the end of a long life, he too is pleading, "Love one another! Love one another! Love *the us that is among us!*"

That allelon term is used repeatedly through John and the remainder of the New Testament, and in every context it deals with the need to the believers to love their fellow believers.

Where He Began . . .

Jesus' Passion for Us to Love One Another in fellowshipping communities did not just begin at the Last Supper. It showed forth initially in his gathering of a band of disciples. The bigger version of his passion and vision emerged from the first words of his preaching/teaching ministry in his painting a picture of the kingdom of God. On top of all that, Jesus also provided us a collection of metaphorical labels for himself that together get close to its enormity. Let's consider three other labels used for Jesus in his day that translate directly to ours today: Carpenter, Fisherman, and Shepherd.

A Carpenter Building a House

The Gospels quote Jesus speaking very little about the church. Although that would become the primary label for the community of his followers after the first Christian Pentecost, the Gospel writers quote Jesus mentioning the word just three times. The second and third times he utters

the word are found in the same sentence, in the exercise of spiritual discipline in the church (Matt 18:17). The first instance comes two chapters
earlier when he renames Simon and commissions him to lead.

> Now when Jesus came into the district of Caesarea Philippi, he
> asked his disciples, "Who do people say that the Son of Man is?"
> And they said, "Some say John the Baptist but others Elijah and
> still others Jeremiah or one of the prophets." He said to them,
> "But who do you say that I am?" Simon Peter answered, "You
> are the Messiah, the Son of the living God." And Jesus answered
> him, "Blessed are you, Simon son of Jonah! For flesh and blood
> has not revealed this to you but my Father in heaven. And I tell
> you, you are Peter, and on this rock I will build my church, and
> the gates of Hades will not prevail against it. I will give you the
> keys of the kingdom of heaven, and whatever you bind on earth
> will be bound in heaven, and whatever you loose on earth will
> be loosed in heaven. Then he sternly ordered the disciples not to
> tell anyone that he was the Messiah. (Matt 16:13–20)

Here, Jesus is putting on the toolbelt of a carpenter, which, as the
firstborn son of the carpenter Joseph, he would have donned daily as an
apprentice in order to build homes out of rocks and logs. (Carpenters of
that day worked with both materials, especially squaring off the sand-
stone rocks from which most homes' main structure was constructed.)
In all likelihood Jesus and Joseph did much construction in the village of
Sepphoris near Nazareth, around which Herod built a wall and declared
it to be the center of Galilee.[2]

Ironically, the capital-C Church has spent so much energy arguing
about the meaning of the phrase *upon this rock* ("It was Peter who was
the rock!" "No, it was Peter's confession which was his rock!" "No, it was
Peter's faith which is our rock!"), that Jesus' passion has usually gone un-
noticed. "Upon this rock" was just an introductory prepositional phrase.
The center of the sentence (subject, verb, object of the verb), i.e., the
thesis of the sentence, is, "I will build my church." And lest we interpret
that act as a passing thought or a short-term, provisional suggestion, his
second "independent clause" guarantees the outcome and permanence of
it, ". . . and the gates of Hades"—hell itself—"will not prevail against it."

Yes, while the term "church" isn't quoted on Jesus' lips often, his intention to create a movement that would last long after his ascension is clear.
All those promises he made about the coming Holy Spirit indicate the

2. Josephus, *Antiquities of the Jews*, XVIII, II, 1, p. 377.

existence of an ongoing, organically connected, communified company of the faithful. And the first days of that post-ascension movement demonstrate that that is exactly what did arise (more on this in a few pages).

Further, years later, when the apostles are assembling together heretofore enemies—Jews vs. gentiles—they hearken back to the construction language to characterize what's going on.

> So then, remember that at one time you gentiles by birth, called "the uncircumcision" by those who are called "the circumcision"—a circumcision made in the flesh by human hands—remember that you were at that time without Christ, being aliens from the commonwealth of Israel and strangers to the covenants of promise, having no hope and without God in the world. But now in Christ Jesus you who once were far off have been brought near by the blood of Christ. For he is our peace; in his flesh he has made both into one and has *broken down the dividing wall, that is, the hostility between us*, abolishing the law with its commandments and ordinances, that he might create in himself *one new humanity* in place of the two, thus making peace, and might reconcile both to God in one body through the cross, thus putting to death that hostility through it. So he came and proclaimed peace to you who were far off and peace to those who were near, for through him both of us have access in one Spirit to the Father. *So then, you are no longer strangers and aliens, but you are fellow citizens with the saints and also members of the household of God, built upon the foundation of the apostles and prophets, with Christ Jesus himself as the cornerstone; in him the whole structure is joined together and grows into a holy temple in the Lord, in whom you also are built together spiritually into a dwelling place for God.* (Ephesians 2:11–22; emphasis added)

The metaphor of a carpenter's construction also parallels the language of "body of Christ," which we will consider later in a different context. But in both metaphors, the interdependency, the strength of interlocking but different kinds of parts (body parts or construction elements) gives the church a breadth of abilities and a multiplicity of flexibilities and tensile strength to be able to withstand inclement weather, oppositional forces, and worrisome strains within and without. Jesus' Passion for Us to Love One Another reflects the work of a master carpenter.

The Fishers Bringing in a Netful

Jesus was multi-vocational. His skills weren't limited to saws and hammers and chisels. He also knew how to wield a fishing pole and a net to bring in big catches of fish.

His father's carpentry business was based in Nazareth, which was about eighteen miles due west of the southern tip of the Sea of Galilee. The ancient winding trail to the sea was twice the distance: about thirty-eight miles. Hence, fishing wasn't his regular vocation or even hobby. But after launching his public ministry in Nazareth, he relocated to the north shore of the sea, the town of Capernaum, which remained his home base until he relocated to Jerusalem about six months prior to his arrest and crucifixion. It was in Capernaum that he recruited his apprentices, several of whom made their living by netting fish from the sea. When he called them to follow, he tied their present vocation into a new one: "As he walked by the Sea of Galilee, he saw two brothers, Simon, who is called Peter, and Andrew his brother, casting a net into the sea—for they were fishermen. And he said to them, 'Follow me, and I will make you fish for people.' Immediately they left their nets and followed him. As he went from there, he saw two other brothers, James son of Zebedee and his brother John, in the boat with their father Zebedee, mending their nets, and he called them. Immediately they left the boat and their father, and followed him" (Matt 4:18–22).

One reason I use the word "apprentice" for disciple is that the twelve hand-picked disciples and then the thousands of others didn't simply listen to Jesus, putting as much to memory as possible, and taking notes on iPads. They also were carrying backpacks, collecting and counting offerings, managing crowds, providing security, distributing food, and carrying out other tasks that roadies (road crews) do for traveling Broadway shows or rock bands' concert tours. Midway through his public ministry Jesus sent the Twelve along with fifty-eight other unnamed disciples to spread the word, to preach his message, to heal and cast out demons wherever they could. They were component parts of the ministry machinery, the ministry team spreading the good news of Jesus' love. And in the process, they were extending the invitation to the many to join with them in a movement to change the world.

They were fishing for people.

This calling became their greatest calling after Jesus' ascension and sending of the Holy Spirit into their lives. They then saw in ever-expanding view the fulfillment of his earlier promise that the good works they had seen him do they would be doing all the more, since he had gone to heaven's throne room to intercede and to oversee that work.

Accordingly, to mix metaphors, they were fishing for the people, and then they were building them together into a house, a temple for the Holy Spirit's work in the world.

The mixed metaphors don't end there.

The Shepherd Keeping Watch

A third metaphor breaks into this discussion of loving one another, namely that of shepherding. We have no explicit evidence of Jesus doing shepherding, except for him calling himself the Good Shepherd—perhaps that is sufficient, unless he was just using the label as a metaphor, which still makes the intended point (John 10:1–19). Then again, he probably did spend some time away out in the fields far from home, watching his flocks by night. It was customary in those years for Israeli families to own at least a few sheep, and as soon as the firstborn male child was able to do so, he was given the responsibility to tend those sheep—until a second-born brother could take over. Since Jesus was the firstborn, he probably began shepherding at age six or eight until the next in line brother took over. Note: Shepherding was so boring that all of the boys would root for Mom to give birth to more boys to relieve them of the duty.) In Jesus' case, after delegating that responsibility to the second child (possibly James), he shifted his duties to carpentry, as suggested above.

So what about shepherding? What was the duty Jesus would have learned out in the fields? At first glance, the duties would seem to be straightforward. Take the flock out into fields where they can graze, sleep, and then move to another field—and on and on for a few weeks, and then return home. Simple.

But what wasn't so simple was the possibility of running short on grassy fields. Or foxes sneaking in to steal and feast themselves on your prized sheep. Or just as notorious, the habit of sheep to wander away. The shepherd needed to keep attentive, even during their sleep time. And when the inevitable did happen, the disappearance of a sheep, the shepherd would need to secure a safe habitation for the rest of the flock— maybe asking a nearby shepherd to manage both flocks for a time or, alternatively, setting up a bunch of broken-down tree branches to create a corral of containment for them—so he could take his rod and staff to capture the wandering sheep and bring her back home.

When Jesus spoke of himself as a Good Shepherd, he emphasized that aspect of the duties: bringing back the wandering, lost sheep.

A poet/hymn-writer penned his take on the shepherds who welcomed Jesus on that first Christmas:

> Shepherds, in the fields abiding, watching o'er your flocks by night, God with us is now residing, yonder shines the infant light: Come and worship, come and worship, worship Christ, the newborn king![3]

Jesus spoke of himself as a good shepherd, not like a hireling who cares nothing of the sheep and abandons them at the first sign of trouble, but as one so connected to and related to the sheep as family members—as moderns connect with their cats or dogs—that they know each sheep's distinctive timbre and pitch of voice. And the sheep, in turn, know the shepherd's voice; they bleat with delight when catching the shepherd's gaze, and they *usually* hang close to the shepherd's proximity. "My sheep know my voice," Jesus said.

> "I am the good shepherd. The good shepherd lays down his life for the sheep. The hired hand, who is not the shepherd and does not own the sheep, sees the wolf coming and leaves the sheep and runs away, and the wolf snatches them and scatters them. The hired hand runs away because a hired hand does not care for the sheep. I am the good shepherd. I know my own, and my own know me, just as the Father knows me, and I know the Father. And I lay down my life for the sheep. I have other sheep that do not belong to this fold. I must bring them also, and they will listen to my voice. So there will be one flock, one shepherd. For this reason the Father loves me, because I lay down my life in order to take it up again. No one takes it from me, but I lay it down of my own accord. I have power to lay it down, and I have power to take it up again. I have received this command from my Father" (John 10:11–18).

---

3. James Montgomery, "Angels, from the Realms of Glory," Sheffield, England, 1816.

The Composite Metaphor for Jesus' Passion for Us to Love One Another

Jesus spoke of these three vocations—Carpenter, Fisherman, Shepherd—as they, together, showcased his passion for us to love one another. Building the community like a carpenter brings together all the component parts needed to build a home, like a fisher throws out the net to pull all kinds of people into church family, like a shepherd nurturing, feeding, and rescuing wandering members.

But his best efforts to unify (dare I to make up a word, "communify"?) his twelve disciples were met with stunning cluelessness. Rivalries over who's closest to Jesus, who's going to sit at his right hand when he comes into his glory, who's going to sit at his left hand when he comes into his glory, who's the most loyal, who's his favorite? So, Jesus took them to school all over again. He pressed and pressed them to do one thing: Love one another. They did make good strides after he ascended to the heavens and sent the Holy Spirit to dwell within and among them. But it didn't all turn out well.

In fact, fast-forwarding several decades to John's time in Ephesus, it generated a sad ending. Those Ephesian Christians refused to give up their contentiousness. Squabbling among them, probably prompted by a renewed rift between Jewish Christians and gentile Christians, was pulling them down into a quicksand of division. John wrote his Gospel to stem the tide of quarrelling. But they didn't relent. Then he wrote the First Letter of John, repeatedly urging them to love one another (allelon), to push back against a tidal wave of conflict. Then he wrote the Second Letter to push back against a tsunami of factionalism. Then, finally, he wrote the Third Letter to excoriate the schismatics for blowing up the whole fellowship. Historians tell us that the church fell apart, never to be rebuilt again. The magnificent ruins of Ephesus, among the greatest of the ancient world, include a massive outdoor amphitheater where Paul once preached, prior to founding the church there, but there are no other signs of a Christian presence. Sad. And yes, it was the internal battles, the power struggles, the hatred of each other, the competing sub-tribes within the church, that proved to be its undoing.

Joining Jesus in the Calling to Love One Another

Many are the Christian believers who have poured their life's blood into loving one another in the communifying church of Jesus Christ. In most cases, the effort has been invested into their local small-c church congregation. Church surveys say that the average attendance of churches in America is something like sixty-five on any given Lord's Day. But a church of any size, like thirty or just thirteen (think of Jesus' last supper attendance, before one broke rank), or like three hundred or three thousand or thirty thousand, requires a company of workers, prayerful co-servants, to function in partnership to carry out the building, fishing and shepherding that congregations need. Thankfully, this is the cadre of members most ready to do the work, to do the educating, to do the visiting of the sick and grieving, to seek out those drifting away. And as we will cover in the third section of this book, vitality can then flourish through such efforts.

Amazingly, such interactive engagement was the first outgrowth of the gifting of the Holy Spirit upon that nascent church in Jerusalem. After Peter preached his explanatory sermon about this boisterous, jubilant gathering, we read:

> So those who welcomed his message were baptized, and that day about three thousand persons were added. They devoted themselves to the apostles' teaching and fellowship, to the breaking of bread and the prayers. Awe came upon everyone because many wonders and signs were being done through the apostles. All who believed were together and had all things in common; they would sell their possessions and goods and distribute the proceeds to all, as any had need. Day by day, as they spent much time together in the temple, they broke bread at home and ate their food with glad and generous hearts, praising God and having the goodwill of all the people. And day by day the Lord added to their number those who were being saved. (Acts 2:41–47)

Herein lies a mandate, then: a calling and commissioning to be making disciples who are integratively re-communifying the people of God into an expression of the body of Christ, the family of God and the temple of the Holy Spirit (to mix in other metaphors that further make the point of this passion of Jesus).

Three Down, Two to Go

So yes, many of us are impressed by Jesus' rabbinic work of reframing the truth for all to learn it. And many of us happily join with him in helping to frame our own and others' understandings of the truth.

And yes again, many of us are inspired by Jesus' work rescuing us from banishment and inviting us to experience God's love and inciting us to love God back. And many of us happily join him in proclaiming that good news and cultivating lifestyles in community of resurrecting worship, prayer, and contemplation.

And yes, many of us thrill to see how Jesus has enveloped us into communities of mutual support and nurture, re-communifying us along with others—including others we never would have chosen to be our friends—and inciting us to live in common, in mutual care, and in nurturing each other in the spirit of loving one another—allelon—with the perfect agape love with which Jesus has loved us.

Then again, those who have caught Jesus' passion for us to love one another may not be the ones others of us would want to call our friends. What is it about them and their never-ending passion to love one another?

- They are so wrapped up in caring for their own.

- They're always ready to organize events, teach classes, repair facilities.

- But they are also so resistant change, lest it be disruptive to the esprit de corps.

- They can be dismissive of mission or outreach projects.

- As friendly as they are toward their fellow members, they can shun outsiders, those who are "not our kind of people."

Still, they came by it honestly. They got that passion from Jesus.

—— 9 ——

To the Least of These

Jesus' Passion for Us to Love Our Neighbors

JESUS WAS NOT THE typical itinerating scholar of the ancient world. Whether we consider the rabbis of Israel or the philosophers of Greece and Rome or the magi of Syria, Iraq, and Iran, scholars' steps were shadowed by students who operated and co-itinerated as apprentices. But, such scholars' work focused on lecturing, discussing, debating, and reframing the thinking of their students. And, yes, the students assisted the life tasks of their teachers: learning to teach other students, promoting to the locals (at least by word of mouth) the professor's upcoming lectures, ushering and managing crowds who would gather to listen to the scholar. But the success of the scholars was measured by the aptitude and knowledge accumulated by their students. End of story. Their job was to teach.

But Jesus wasn't typical. From the start, as he taught in *reframing* ways, so he called people to worship and prayer. And as he worshiped and prayed in relational ways, he was delivering the love of God into the lives of his larger audiences as well as the Twelve. He also turned his teaching into community-building, communifying, cultivating interdependence and mutual support, mutual love among his followers.

He also extended his love beyond their cluster of friendships out to others: to the sick, to the wounded, to the deaf and blind, to the poor and outcast, to the eccentric and deranged. Those persons' lives were changed. Nothing remained as it had been. He was doctor, nurse, counselor, therapist, paramedic, social worker, advocate, speech therapist, community organizer all rolled into one. And he had no billing department. He practiced his therapeutic skills on those unable to pay for the services of those specializing in medical arts. In fact, most of his patients were strangers to him . . . indeed, rebels, outcasts, aliens to the tribe of Israel.

Which leads to Jesus' Passion for Us to Love Our Neighbors.

He Set the Stage from the Beginning

Jesus launched his public ministry by submitting to the baptism his cousin John was offering people in the Jordan River, and then by going out into the wilderness for forty days' testing and training. Then he returned to his hometown on a Friday just in time for the sunset Sabbath service. He had spent most of his past thirty years in this town, but at this moment he opted to reintroduce himself to them, through the reframing of words of the Prophet Isaiah, layering those words with a new, self-referential meaning. Luke presents it in this way:

> When he came to Nazareth, where he had been brought up, he went to the synagogue on the Sabbath day, as was his custom. He stood up to read, and the scroll of the prophet Isaiah was given to him. He unrolled the scroll and found the place where it was written: "The Spirit of the Lord is upon me, because he has anointed me to bring good news to the poor. He has sent me to proclaim release to the captives and recovery of sight to the blind, to set free those who are oppressed, to proclaim the year of the Lord's favor." And he rolled up the scroll, gave it back to the attendant, and sat down. The eyes of all in the synagogue were fixed on him. Then he began to say to them, "Today this scripture has been fulfilled in your hearing." All spoke well of him and were amazed at the gracious words that came from his mouth. They said, "Is this not Joseph's son?" (Luke 4:16–22)

These words, read quickly and strung together, sounded nice, like the exhortations one might deliver in a college valedictory address; or the promises strung together in a presidential candidate's stump speech, spelling out an agenda to generate stellar improvements in all aspects of national life. But if we read each phrase Jesus quoted from Isaiah, each related topic, visualize it and think about the highlight events of Jesus' ministry, we realize that they lay out a table of contents for the stories that are soon to follow in Luke's account of Jesus' rehabilitation ministry to the masses.

Jesus empathized with those suffering want. And he published good news to them—the literal poor, such as is captured in Luke's version of the first Beatitude: "Blessed are you who are poor, for yours is the kingdom of God" (Luke 6:20). Such empathy was extended to the masses when feeding the crowd of thousands (9:10–17).

He empathized with those held captive by all forces that enslave, from the slave owners out there to the addictive habits inside, from the mocking voices in the community to the inside voices of mental disorder—and the unrelenting pains of loss, grief, and torment ("Blessed are you who weep now, for you shall laugh"—9:21b).

He empathetically gave sight to the physically blind, the intellectually blind, the spiritually blind.

He empathetically freed those oppressed by bullies and oppressed by public scorn (like the woman about to be stoned to death by "religious" men—John 8:1–11).

He proclaimed the year of the Lord's favor, the Year of Jubilee, when old debts were canceled.

Yes, on that sabbath day and in the days to follow, Isaiah's promises would come true. And most especially they would come true for people considered the least deserving. In one or two cases, a petitioner of God's mercy uttered, "I am not worthy . . . ," but in general those receiving such blessings, such gifts and miracles, offered no repentance. Just about none asked in confidence, with an entitled attitude, as if they were offering a perfect, doubt-free faith as their ticket to get the golden healing. He just gave and they just received, many with amazed exhilaration.

The introductory announcement of his coming mission painted glistening smiles on the faces of his fellow synagogue sabbath worshipers. And those smiles turned into shouts of joy when, after handing the Isaiah scroll back to the attendant, he sat down and declared, "Today this scripture has been fulfilled in your hearing."

What? Fulfilled here and now? "Is this not Joseph's son?" they asked. And probably added, "Is the carpenter's son the messiah for whom we have longed all these years? Could that possibly be?" They were exuberant.

But for only a minute or two. Because Jesus didn't stop there. He launched into an odd, contrarian prediction of them turning against him. "He said to them, 'Doubtless you will quote to me this proverb, "Doctor, cure yourself!" And you will say, "Do here also in your hometown the things that we have heard you did at Capernaum."' He kept going: "'Truly I tell you, no prophet is accepted in his hometown.'"

They had to be perplexed by this projection of rejection upon them. "Surely," they thought, "we'll accept you here. Stop talking like that, Jesus! You're our favorite son." He didn't stop for a second. He gave no chance for them to try to correct his accusations of their predicted mis-accusations of him. He charged ahead, digging a deep hole for them and him.

In fact, he raised two examples of empathetic medical and social intervention from days of old, all the way back to the earliest days of the prophets of Israel.

"'But the truth is, there were many widows in Israel in the time of Elijah, when the heaven was shut up three years and six months and there was a severe famine over all the land, yet Elijah was sent to none of them except to a widow at Zarephath in Sidon'" (Luke 4:25–26).

Wait a minute. We love the father of the prophets—the hero Elijah, who humiliated the prophets of Baal when he called fire down from heaven—and we feel a special attachment to him, since he defeated those false prophets on Mt. Carmel, less than fifteen miles away from here in Nazareth. But why are you mentioning the woman from Sidon? Yes, Elijah miraculously provided her flour and oil to stay alive in a time of famine, and yes, he raised her deceased son from the dead. But why are you highlighting her background? She was from Lebanon to the north, an Arab, a gentile, a pagan, an outsider to the people of Israel! How dare you focus on her and her nationality, rather than on the miracles themselves!

Without pause, he goes on. "'There were also many with a skin disease in Israel in the time of the prophet Elisha, and none of them was cleansed except Naaman the Syrian'" (Luke 4:27). How dare you equate Elisha, the inheritor of Elijah's mantle, with a Syrian, another Arab, another gentile, another pagan, another outsider to the people of Israel, and a leper at that—those sinful sick people who brought that disease upon themselves! You're acting like God loves those people! In fact, you're saying that God favored them then . . . and, obviously, you're suggesting that you are going to favor them now. How dare you? How dare you!!!

Well, they may not have said those things out loud. Luke doesn't quote what they said, but no need: their actions shouted louder than any words. "When they heard this, all in the synagogue were filled with rage. They got up, drove him out of the town, and led him to the brow of the hill on which their town was built, so that they might hurl him off the cliff" (Luke 4:28,29). Whoa, that's a mood change if you've ever seen it.

Luke, the narrator, quickly assures the reader, "But he passed through the midst of them and went on his way" (v. 30). But Luke's report about those prophets of old cast the die, foreshadowing the violent end of Jesus' years in public ministry that lay ahead. Jesus' words, exhibiting his passion for the love of neighbors, also previewed the intervening years of his public ministry. Jesus will be empathizing with broken, diseased, abused, injured, impoverished, mentally wounded lives—especially those of outsiders, folks whom the insiders, the orthodox, the healthy, and the wealthy ignore or, worse, blame, or even attack . . . just like they attacked their town's favorite son when he dared to bring those others onto center stage of his future healing ministry.

Not an Original Idea

Jesus did not invent the idea of loving neighbors. As we heard about loving God, Jesus' teaching to love others goes back to Moses. And, in fact, when the Pharisees asked him what was the greatest commandment he referenced not just the Shema Israel's command to love God, he immediately added that other command of Moses: "You shall not take vengeance or bear a grudge against any of your people, but you shall love your neighbor as yourself: I am the Lord" (Lev 19:18). That final signature, "I am the Lord," puts an imprimatur, an exclamation point on the command.

What's more, there were other instances when Moses came out specifically focusing on that neighbor: "When an alien resides with you in your land, you shall not oppress the alien. The alien who resides with you shall be to you as the native-born among you; you shall love the alien as yourself, for you were aliens in the land of Egypt: I am the Lord your God" (Lev 19:33–34).

From Here to Empathy and Back

Jesus' healing ministry took on epic proportions. People carried their sick many miles in hope of seeing them restored. From the man lowered through the roof of a house who took up his mat to walk home (Matt 9:1–8), to the ten lepers who could now take up their lives to live free (Luke 17:11–19), the ministry took compassion and care to a level never before seen. That is spoken in superlative terms, but it is not an overstatement.

- The rapt attention given to an anemic and religiously ostracized, blood-hemorrhaging woman while he was being mobbed by hundreds of others (Mark 4:25–34) . . .

- The tender care he gave to a school-age girl to bring her dead body back to life (Luke 8:40–56) . . .

- The opening of the eyes of two blind men (Matt 9:27–31) . . .

- The healing of a gentile woman's demon-possessed daughter (Matt 15:21–28) . . .

. . . and about thirty other recorded cases of persons' lives forever transformed by his love of the neighbor—and miraculous healing—which redefined "top-skill-with-kind-bedside-manner" care to a level never seen before. And, yes, "love of the neighbor" is the operative term: Jesus did not sweep into town, do some quick incantations or mass-produce a new vaccine (as valuable as that has been done through the ages, as in the case of penicillin). He engaged with his patients, allowing no distractions to interrupt that rapt and therapeutic attention he was giving them.

Which leads to the long-term return on his investment of such empathetic care of strangers. When receiving Jesus' commission to make disciples of all nations, his disciples and their disciples translated that into both words and actions, as they saw him model.

Translating his words into their own, they picked up megaphones on the very first Pentecost, approximately ten days after Jesus' ascension (having just received the inbreaking presence of the Holy Spirit). Peter stood up, read a prophecy from Joel about that outpouring, and proceeded to tell the kerygma (i.e., "the apostolic proclamation of salvation through Jesus Christ").[1]

Those apostles then put words into action:

> One day Peter and John were going up to the temple at the hour of prayer, at three o'clock in the afternoon. And a man lame from birth was being carried in. People would lay him daily at the gate of the temple called the Beautiful Gate so that he could ask for alms from those entering the temple. When he saw Peter and John about to go into the temple, he asked them for alms. Peter looked intently at him, as did John, and said, "Look at us." And he fixed his attention on them, expecting to receive something from them. Peter said, "I have no silver or gold, but what I have I give you; in the name of Jesus Christ of Nazareth, stand up and

1. *Webster's Ninth New Collegiate Dictionary* (1985), s.v. "kerygma," 659.

walk." And he took him by the right hand and raised him up, and immediately his feet and ankles were made strong. Jumping up, he stood and began to walk, and he entered the temple with them, walking and leaping and praising God. All the people saw him walking and praising God, and they recognized him as the one who used to sit and ask for alms at the Beautiful Gate of the temple, and they were filled with wonder and astonishment at what had happened to him. (Acts 3:1–10)

The ministries of the apostles, extended through the churches they launched and the prayers and efforts of their congregants, emulated what they had seen and heard from and about Jesus. The Passion of Jesus to Love Neighbors poured into a contagion of ministry to the world in need of a savior, a physician, a counselor, a therapist, a nurse, a social worker.

In the process, there emerged a worldwide movement of a community of faith, the Church—subdivided into local communities of faith, the churches—which carried the good news of Jesus and his love wherever they went.

And that movement continues to this day, in the form of missionary doctors and church-sponsored hospitals, pastoral counselors and homeless shelters, children's protective services and Habitat for Humanity home builders. Then there are Catholic charities and Baptist charities, the United Methodist Committee on Relief and Lutheran World Relief, World Vision International and Compassion International . . . . The list goes on and on. Why? Because Jesus' pattern of loving neighbors has spread like a contagion of care and healing. Not only has it produced recipients, it also has generated whole vocations of service and a myriad of volunteers and organizations who are ready to put everything on the line to provide the lifesaving relief needed where it can be found. Jesus' Passion for Us to Love Our Neighbors. Catch it, if you've resisted it so far.

But Is That Enough?

Many are those who are ready to save the world one person, one victim, one patient, one sufferer at a time. But many of those suffering are there due to systems and structures in society that overrule or stampede or systemically exclude or inherently disfavor some persons in comparison to others. Insiders overrule outsiders, an entrenched wealthy class hoards resources to the detriment of the less privileged, managers override laborers, high school seniors bully freshmen. There's nothing new in all of this.

But Jesus wasn't one to let that go unaddressed. In addition to the one-on-one care extended to them, he spoke out as a voice of truth to power, as an advocate for the feeble and the ostracized. That's because he had a Passion for Us to Love Our Neighbors.

Then again, it's not always fun to sit and talk with folks caught up in loving outsiders and strangers. They may not be the ones you would seek out to be your friends.

- They are constantly starting new mission projects.
- They're always ready to spend money beyond the budget for new issues.
- Many of them don't show up for Bible studies, and fellowship gatherings.
- They keep inviting people into the church who make us feel uncomfortable; strangers who are not our kind of people.

But, they came by it honestly. They got that passion from Jesus.

$$—\ \ 10\ \ —$$

Breaking Chains of Injustice

Jesus' Passion for Us to Change the World

Out of the Mouths of Babes

FRESH OUT OF COLLEGE, she took her first job, a dream job: kindergarten teacher. Then came marriage, four babies, and a master's degree in child psychology. Thus equipped and earnestly determined to be the best she could be, it was quite the slap in the face when she landed an F on her parental report card—delivered by none other than her firstborn.

Allow me to explain. As a devout Roman Catholic, Mom attended parochial schools from kindergarten all the way through college, led by Jesuit priests in the multicultural borough of Queens, New York, from kindergarten all the way through college in New York. After meeting and marrying a World War II veteran, John Henry Haberer Sr., she delivered three children before their four-year anniversary. Just after their fifth anniversary, the family had moved out of Queens to the suburb of Ramsey, New Jersey, and child number four came along.

Fast-forward four more years: with hubby commuting by train daily to and from Manhattan, and baby number four heading to kindergarten, Mom accepted an invitation to serve as the first professor of psychology at the new Rockland Community College. She scheduled her classes between us kids' school bus pick-up and drop-off times.

To help handle the busyness, she found weekly assistance with the household duties from a cleaning lady, an African American who commuted a half-hour to our house from Paterson.

One day Mom drove the four of us to go see Bamma, our name for her mom, who still lived in her own Queens apartment. As we neared the apartment building, Tobi, the eldest of the four of us and the one most likely to blurt out whatever the rest of us were thinking, looked out the car window—first to the left, and then to the right—and exclaimed, "Mommy, Mommy, all these people are garbage men and cleaning ladies!"

"Oh, my gosh," Mom whispered to herself. "This is awful. I'm raising racial bigots!"

Not one to let such a revelation go unaddressed, Mom soon initiated a project. She searched around our lily-white community to find a neighborhood of persons of color to whom she could introduce her children. Sure enough, she discovered that Mahwah, the next town over, had just such a community on Stag Hill, among the Ramapo Mountains, just across the highway from the Mahwah Ford auto assembly plant. Then she—all five feet, one inch of her—with a slightly taller social worker friend, Helen Reed, drove up the hill, teeth on edge as they rounded life-threatening hairpin turns, found their way to the top, and then began knocking on doors to meet these people.

Commonly called "Jackson Whites," the people living there were local social outcasts, "alleged to be comprised of a mongrel hybrid of renegade Indians, escaped slaves, Hessian mercenary deserters, and West Indian prostitutes."[1] The "Jackson Whites" moniker she first learned was considered by them as a derogatory label, so soon Mom and Mrs. Reed were calling them by their preferred name, "Ramapo Mountain People."

They learned that their children were being bussed daily to Mahwah's public schools. That was good news to hear. But they surmised that those children were starting school at a great disadvantage: a lack of pre-school preparation. They proposed—and the mothers on the mountain agreed—to start a preschool together.

Soon we four Haberer kids were riding with Mom up the mountain every weekday that summer to neaten up and sweep out the small town hall, to move in kid-sized tables and chairs, and to bring in supplies for young learners. Best of all from our perspective, Geoff and I—whose labors were pretty weak at the ripe ages of six and seven—were mostly playing

---

1. Sceurman and Moran, "History and Legends of the Mysterious 'Jackson Whites.'"

with close-aged mountain kids. Billy Mann, the junior to Billy Mann Sr., the mayor of that small community, became one of our best friends.

Three years later, when President Lyndon Baines Johnson initiated the national Head Start program, Mom and Mrs. Reed helped their new friends apply to become part of the program. It became one of the first Head Start preschools in the country.

Mom's desire was to teach her own kids they could learn to love those ignored and marginalized, those born a different color and into a lower economic status, to see them as people, to even become their friends. Her vision for us mirrored what was unfolding in the larger culture.

Community Organizing

Little could we have known, and little did Mom even know, that such an initiative would someday be branded, "community organizing." As defined by the Center for Community Change,

> Community organizing is the process of building power through involving a constituency in identifying problems they share and the solutions to those problems that they desire; identifying the people and structures that can make those solutions possible; enlisting those targets in the effort through negotiation and using confrontation and pressure when needed; and building an institution that is democratically controlled by that constituency that can develop the capacity to take on further problems and that embodies the will and the power of that constituency.[2]

Little did any of us know that we were actively participating in a growing movement for cultural change, that was being fueled throughout the nation, a push against racial injustice. It was happening especially in the more segregated south by none other than the Reverend Doctor Martin Luther King Jr. It was he and his allies who were the defining figures of civil rights initiatives to take on systems and structures of oppression and hate.

For those of us alive at the time, MLK was the greatest American prophet we would ever encounter. A Christian minister, he took the cause of Christ, and the promotion of the kingdom of God on earth into the everyday functions of eating in luncheonettes and riding on buses.

2. Beckwith with Lopez, "Community Organizing."

He was following the lead of the greatest prophet of all time, the most revolutionary leader in the history of the world.

The Premier Prophet

Prophet. Priest. King. Those three titles were categorized by some of the Reformers as the three offices of the Christ. It was particularly John Calvin who brought this threefold title to the fore.[3] The three roles are joined together by the common thread of anointing. That is, in the Hebrew Scriptures, these three offices were conferred and consecrated by the anointing of oil on the head of the person of renown, hence the overall title "Christ," i.e., "Messiah," which means "anointed one." The three roles are different in scope and function, as the titles imply.

In this book we are categorizing not Jesus' offices per se but, instead, are looking at Jesus' Passions, which we have delineated as five in number. We now focus on the fifth of those passions, which coincides with the name of the first of Calvin's triad of offices. What he called Jesus' role as prophet, I label Jesus' Passion for Us to Change the World. But whereas Calvin's use of the term "prophet" really means a scholarly teacher-preacher (a teaching theologian), I am using the term as it is more commonly used, both in the ancient world of the Hebrew Scriptures and today's world that engages in protest events and movements. This kind of prophet speaks out in a way that exhorts people to take specific, culture-changing, justice-promoting, evil-defeating ways. In a word, revolutionizing.

The Radical Revolutionary

The word "revolution" suggests overthrowing systems and structures, defeating principalities and powers, standing up for the downtrodden by bringing down the power of the privileged. It challenges the status quo by waking up a slumbering populace to the ills afoot, aiming to create a new order of goodness, righteousness, and justice, as fitting within the reign and realm of God.

Compare two terms with me: "revolution" with "evolution." They both lead to change. But evolution changes gradually, even indiscernibly. Revolution aims to catalyze change boldly, abruptly, rapidly, even precipitously.

---

3. Calvin, *Institutes of the Christian Religion*, II.XV.2, 495–96.

Like Jesus' Passion for Us to Know the Truth, his Passion for Us to Change the World hearkens back to the two other commonly cited prophetic tasks of "foretelling" and "forthtelling." Some branches of the Christian faith stress a prophet's ability to predict the future. Others stress a prophet's ability to persuade masses of people to change the future. They all—that is, we all—see prophets as leaders to move people to rethink, to reimagine, to hope, and to work for major breakthroughs in church and society.

Both teaching and prophesying share the mechanism for implementation: public speech. Having leaned into the professorial, pedagogical teaching direction of Jesus' reframing of the truth in chapter 6, let us now look closely at his forthtelling, confrontational, revolutionary preaching, and efforts, through negotiation and confrontation when deemed necessary, that marked aspects of Jesus' public ministry—hence, his passion for us to join with him in changing the world.

The Galilean's Unique Style of Speech

What are we to say about the collection of prophecies uttered by Jesus himself? Let us state the obvious: Jesus' words and speaking style differed depending on the nature of the audience he was addressing. Of course, that's true about all of us. We talk differently to a police officer than to our sibling, differently to a teacher than to a classmate, differently to a stranger than to a friend.

Likewise, the Gospels' accounts of Jesus' speeches and conversations differed radically depending upon the audiences at hand.

Our understanding of this pattern of speech was advanced exponentially a generation ago, when a lone Gospel scholar took it upon himself to type the ancient (oldest available and certifiable) Greek version of the Synoptic Gospels into a University of Pittsburgh computer (back when a computer offering a fraction of the capacity of today's laptops would fill a gymnasium). J. Arthur Baird[4] did that typing, and then engaged in a linguistic and grammatical analysis of every word, every root word, every philological and syntactical phrase, and every sentence in each of the first three Gospels.

Then he cross-compared them. To the surprise of many Gospel scholar colleagues, he discovered that all aspects of Jesus' speech differed

4. See Baird, *Audience Criticism and the Historical Jesus.*

according to four different audience groups: 1) the Twelve, 2) the broader group of followers, 3) the oppositional crowd, and 4) the bitterly antagonistic officials who would ultimately plot his prosecution and crucifixion. When Baird compared Jesus' speech patterns among the three Synoptic Gospels, he discovered, contrary to commonly accepted "Form Critical" scholars who had been his scholarly mentors, that those writers did *not* inject their own distinctive styles; they reported Jesus' words in ways specific to him. That is, they didn't shape his message according to their bias or literary style.

Among those spoken words, Jesus waxed pastorally empathetic in comforting and hopeful ways when speaking with the Twelve and his other loyal followers, but waxed prophetically judgmental when challenging his opponents, and even more aggressively so when confronting those who were plotting his demise.

The Great Reversal: The Promise and the Threat

How might we summarize the collection of those prophetic utterances? To put it simply, as Jesus did, "So the last will be first, and the first will be last." This promise and threat of the great reversal, as these words have been dubbed through the years, is quoted twice in Matthew, twice in Mark and once in Luke.[5] That's pretty emphatic. So let us not just brush over them.

The first promise/prediction, "the last will be first," expresses a word of hope and comfort for the marginalized, i.e., those lacking in the blessings, assets, prestige, and power that the insiders of privilege enjoy.

In his seminal work *The Prophetic Imagination*, renowned Old Testament scholar Walter Brueggemann drifted into the New Testament to offer his analysis of Jesus' prophetic ministry according to his respective audiences, beginning with this first promise/prediction:

> Jesus in his solidarity with the marginal ones is moved to compassion. Compassion constitutes a radical form of criticism, for it announces that the hurt is to be taken seriously, that the hurt is not to be accepted as normal and natural but is an abnormal and unacceptable condition of humanness . . . . Thus the compassion of Jesus is to be understood not simply as a personal emotional reaction but as a public criticism in which he dares to

---

5. Matt 19:30; 20:16; Mark 9:35; 10:31; Luke 13:30.

act upon his concern against the entire numbness of his social context. Empires live by numbness. . . . Thus compassion that might be seen simply as generous goodwill is in fact criticism of the system, forces and ideologies that produced the hurt. Jesus enters into the hurt and finally comes to embody it.[6]

Repeatedly, Brueggemann points out how Jesus expressed compassion for and with individuals' suffering.

- In the case of the crowds following him, "When he went ashore, he saw a great crowd, and he had compassion for them and cured their sick" (Matt 14:14).

- When with the hungry, "As he went ashore, he saw a great crowd, and he had compassion for them, because they were like sheep without a shepherd, and he began to teach them many things" and he fed them (Mark 6:34).

- In the case of Mary's anguish over the death of her brother Lazarus, we read, "When Jesus saw her weeping and the Jews who came with her also weeping, he was greatly disturbed in spirit and deeply moved. He said, 'Where have you laid him?' They said to him, 'Lord, come and see.' Jesus began to weep" (John 11:33–35).

Brueggemann tied this compassion (cf., Jesus' Passion for Us to Love Our Neighbors) to "the radical prophetic tradition. The internalization of hurt for the marginal ones is especially faithful to the tradition of anguish in Hosea and Jeremiah . . . Both prophets and now Jesus after them bring to expression and embodiment all the hurt, human pain, and grief that the domination royal culture has tried so hard to repress, deny, and cover over."[7] He then adds, "The capacity to feel the hurt of the marginal people means an end to all social arrangements that nullified pain by a remarkable depth of numbness."[8]

Don't miss the point that expressions of compassion are not just ways to empathize. They also function as disruptors, challenges to the status quo, threats to the existing structures of oppression. "The imperial consciousness lives by its capacity to still the groans and to go on with business as usual as though none were hurting and there were no groans . . . Jesus had the capacity to give voice to the very hurt that

6. Brueggemann, *Prophetic Imagination*, 88–89.

7. Brueggemann, *Prophetic Imagination*, 90.

8. Brueggemann, *Prophetic Imagination*, 91.

had been muted, and therefore newness could break through. Newness comes precisely from expressed pain. Suffering made audible and visible produces hope, articulated grief is the gate of newness, and the history of Jesus is the history of entering into the pain and giving it voice."[9]

In effect, Jesus was starting a revolution of compassion against oppression.

He also was starting a revolution of conviction against oppressors. In their presence Jesus did not come across as the "What Would Jesus Do?" bracelets, a namby-pamby nice guy. As Baird outlines extensively, Jesus did things and said things to some people that were harsh, condemning, insulting. Having inherited the Hebrew prophets' determination to break chains of injustice (see Isa 58:6), the concept of justice "literally consumes the mind" of Jesus.[10]

> The opponent material [passages of Synoptic speeches] reveals Jesus setting himself in clear and aggressive opposition to his audience. Sixty-five percent of all [hard-core opponents'] teaching shows that Jesus was the aggressor. It is true that there are many apothegms [maxims, precepts] here containing questions showing aggressiveness: on the part of the religious officials. There are, however, many more sayings and parables where the origin of the denunciation is Jesus himself. The pattern seems to be that this was a two-sided battle, where Jesus himself provoked most of the opposition. There are eighty-seven logia [passages, sayings of Jesus] where this criticism is sharply evident. Whereas he criticized the Twelve for putting *themselves* before the Kingdom, Jesus criticized the opponents for putting *their religion* before the Kingdom of God. They put the traditions of the elders before justice and the mercy of God; they put ritual legalism before their concern for men; they put external purity before their own inner righteousness. In this stance, they were unable to understand the working of God in and through him; they did not enter the Kingdom themselves, and they hindered those who were entering. "You blind guides," he cries out in a characteristic summary, "straining out a gnat and swallowing a camel!" (Matt. 23:24). If [these passages] are any indication, Jesus was an intensely critical person, and one can perhaps see why not only the opponents, but at times his own disciples, were set against him.[11]

9. Brueggemann, *Prophetic Imagination*, 91

10. Baird, *Audience Criticism and the Historical Jesus*, 112.

11. Baird, *Audience Criticism and the Historical Jesus*, 132–33.

In other words, Jesus the prophet, the revolutionary, spoke out against the forces of public power—both those of temple and throne; and hence, to carry those words then and there to the here and now—in current contexts' equivalents, those of church and state—demanding justice for all and mercy most especially for the underprivileged, the maligned, the marginalized, the overlooked.

Lest we brush off the severity of his denunciations, consider the things he *said about his religio-political opponents*: "Then Jesus said to the crowds and to his disciples, 'The scribes and the Pharisees sit on Moses's seat; therefore, do whatever they teach you and follow it, but do not do as they do, for they do not practice what they teach. They tie up heavy burdens, hard to bear, and lay them on the shoulders of others, but they themselves are unwilling to lift a finger to move them. They do all their deeds to be seen by others, for they make their phylacteries broad and their fringes long. They love to have the place of honor at banquets and the best seats in the synagogues and to be greeted with respect in the marketplaces and to have people call them rabbi" (Matt 23:1–7).

Consider the things he said *to those religio-political opponents*:

- "But woe to you, scribes and Pharisees, hypocrites! For you lock people out of the kingdom of heaven. For you do not go in yourselves, and when others are going in you stop them. Woe to you, scribes and Pharisees, hypocrites! For you cross sea and land to make a single convert, and you make the new convert twice as much a child of hell as yourselves . . ." (Matt 23:13–15).

- "Woe to you, scribes and Pharisees, hypocrites! For you tithe mint, dill, and cumin and have neglected the weightier matters of the law: justice and mercy and faith. It is these you ought to have practiced without neglecting the others. You blind guides! You strain out a gnat but swallow a camel!" (Matt 23:23).

- "Woe to you, scribes and Pharisees, hypocrites! For you clean the outside of the cup and of the plate, but inside they are full of greed and self-indulgence. You blind Pharisees! First clean the inside of the cup and of the plate, so that the outside also may become clean" (Matt 23:25–26).

- "Woe to you, scribes and Pharisees, hypocrites! For you are like whitewashed tombs, which on the outside look beautiful but inside are full of the bones of the dead and of all kinds of uncleanness. So you also on the outside look righteous to others, but inside you are full of hypocrisy and lawlessness" (Matt 23:27–28).

- "Woe to you, scribes and Pharisees, hypocrites! For you build the tombs of the prophets and decorate the graves of the righteous, and you say, 'If we had lived in the days of our ancestors, we would not have taken part with them in shedding the blood of the prophets.' Thus you testify against yourselves that you are descendants of those who murdered the prophets. Fill up, then, the measure of your ancestors. *You snakes, you brood of vipers! How can you escape the judgment of hell?* For this reason I send you prophets, sages, and scribes, some of whom you will kill and crucify, and some you will flog in your synagogues and pursue from town to town, so that upon you may come all the righteous blood shed on earth, from the blood of righteous Abel to the blood of Zechariah son of Barachiah, whom you murdered between the sanctuary and the altar. Truly I tell you, all this will come upon this generation" (Matt 23:13–15, 23–36, emphasis added).

Jesus doesn't live up to the polite, pleasant, "What Would Jesus Do?" label in such confrontations with the religious elites of the day. And we moderns mentally tear these inconvenient pages out of our Bibles, just as Thomas Jefferson tore out the inconvenient pages about Jesus' miracles from his.

As we said earlier, "We all have a Jesus we adore and a Jesus we ignore."

Please turn back and read again those quotes from the mouth of Jesus. They are harsh. He felt anguish over the mistreatment of those suffering the injustices of those thriving, and he pinned the blame where it belonged. Visualize each one—he has given us vivid imagery with which to see them with the eyes of our hearts—and feel his pain for the hurts of those who have been suffering.

Ask yourself, "Where is my passion to change the world?"

From Reframing to Revolutionizing

While many of us believers find these words of Jesus to be unbecoming, even mean, many others of us find this Passion of Jesus to be compelling. It challenges us to the core of our being.

Some of us feel drawn to this passion because we have been hurt. Abused. Violated. Shunned. Penniless. Unsafe. And the perpetrators causing such injuries, anxieties, and estrangements have come from macroeconomic institutions and structures. Other perpetrators have been microcommunities of parents, spouses, siblings, neighborhoods, schools, clubs, workplaces, and churches. Some of the perpetrators glowingly lift themselves up as the ideals of care and compassion: church congregations, outreach programs, social service agencies, even children's protective centers, adoption agencies, and, to state it with intentional redundancy, the church.

Some feel drawn to this passion as ones not as much hurt directly as moved deeply and called to stand with and in the gap for those others who have been hurt, victimized, abused, shunned, diminished, violated, marginalized. You know who the people are that God has been calling you to help. You may well be actively pouring heart and soul into addressing such issues of injustice, and advocating, stumping, lobbying to break those chains of injustice.

When Jesus sent first the seventy-two followers to relay his message, to pass on his healing power, and to extend his compassion to many cities all directions, he was presenting a precursor to the commission that he would finally entrust to the Twelve at the close of his public ministry.

In Peter's Pentecost Day sermon, it is clear that he finally understood what Jesus had been speaking about through the previous three years. His words included the joyous proclamation of the newly available presence of God's Spirit. And they also challenged those who plotted Jesus' death. The "last" were being introduced to a future of joy unspeakable, and the "first" were being put in their place as those missing out.

The New Testament writers continued to communicate compassion by empathizing with the suffering believers along with the empathy of Jesus, by engendering hope and by prophetically challenging—revolutionizing—the hard-heartedness of those who would exclude, who would build unscalable walls of disqualification, who would create insider-outsider divides within the church and larger community.

And note, those words of condemnation were directed only seldom against nonbelievers. Mostly, they were directed at religious leaders within the church, such as the Galatians who were reinstituting the ritual of circumcision and heaping other ritual requirements upon gentile believers already baptized into Christ.

The Continuing Books of the Prophets

Sadly, the Passion of the Christ to Revolutionize has become marginalized by a relentless drive to change the subject from the kingdom, the reign and the realm of God, to the political categories of socialism, communism, capitalism, and democracy. Repeatedly, when prophetic voices speak out about justice for the poor, the immigrant, the women, the ethnic minorities, outspoken, Christ-following protectors of the status quo brand the prophets as socialists or communists or internationalists or anti-Semites, or a host of other labels. Such branding needs to be named for what it is: an excuse to ignore these aspects of Jesus' prophetic ministry—both his love for strangers and his work to change the world.

Let us set aside such dismissing brands and consider how our American forebears tackled these matters—on their best days—without pinning partisan brands on them.

So, starting with the assumption that Americans enjoy the fruits of a free-market economy, let us consider the following:

- Our independent businesses deliver their products in rail cars on railroads built by government funds.

- Those products also get delivered to free-market retail outlets on highways built by government funds.

- Such products get marketed through telephone lines strung between telephone poles, buried underground, and laid across oceans by government funds.

- Most of our children receive their primary and secondary education in public schools and colleges paid in large part by government funds.

This list can go on and on, but the point is already made. Our lives for at least 150 years have thrived best when our free market economy is supported by collective sharing of funds for the greater good, which of necessity has been managed by government leaders and agencies.

While human history is testament to amazing examples of good overcoming evil and to tragic examples of evil overcoming good—a string of events that have both enchanted and disenchanted—it often has been the prophetic voice of Jesus, his passion for folks like us to change the world, that has provided the impetus for the good to prevail. His overflowing Passion to Revolutionize a world gone bad, a culture consumed with economic stinginess, privilege hoarding, class dividing, outsider excluding, oppositional competing, predatory molesting, environmental exploiting, and cynical mocking has repeatedly had the final word.

Like the prophets of old, such as Jeremiah and Ezekiel, Amos and Hosea, Micah and Malachi . . . like the modern, prophetic revolutionaries such as Mahatma Gandhi, Martin Luther King Jr., Nelson Mandela, and Mother Theresa . . . and like all of those ancient and modern prophets, Jesus didn't always talk nice, he didn't always speak gently, he didn't always affirm the "good intentions" of those he knew were violating others' lives.

But his words turned darkness to light and brought creation out of chaos. His words, learned by my mom and shocked into relevance through the stunning observation by her daughter that resembled comments one might hear from bigots of any age drove Mom to take action, to face up to generations of prejudice and poverty, to engage in community organizing to address a major structure of society—public education—in order to challenge the sheer epidemic of academic denial of preschool children— and to partner with those children's mothers to make for a new beginning.

Those prophetic words of Jesus driven by his Passion for All of Us to Change His World made a difference in the world for a rising generation of mountain people. I say that that was a good start, a good Head Start.

Still, some of those who share Jesus' passion for us to change the world may not be the ones some of us would seek out to be out to be our friends.

- They are always getting wrapped up whatever protest is the cause of the month.
- They keep dropping everything to complain about the world as it is.
- They're insulting that way!
- They always ask hard questions, embarrassing us in public.
- They are so intense!

Then again, they came by it honestly. They got that passion from Jesus.

— 11 —

The Net Effect

Time for a Brief Recap

SO WHERE ARE WE now? We have made the case that while America may be served best by a two-party system of representative democracy, the American churches are terribly mis-served by the same. The labeling of churches or particular believers as red Republicans, blue Democrats, or even purple Independents or moderates damages the ministry and saps the power of the gospel. It allows political ideologies to override theological truths. It stereotypes and vilifies those of the other political party, while it stereotypes and hallows those of our own party.

Truth be told, those other folks are not as bad as we fear, and our folks are not as good as we claim.

Moving from political talk to biblical teaching, we all are a far more complicated mix of sinner and saint—actually: sinners all, but redeemed by Jesus and declared to be saints, hopefully walking mostly forward in our process of sanctification, but certainly falling backward along the way. Put differently, we have been created in the image of God but also conceived in the hearts and bodies of sinful parents.

From there we took a more detailed look at what makes Christians into persons of significance and value, namely, the person of Jesus Christ. We laid claim to the language of classical theologians like Origen and Augustine, Luther and Calvin, who spoke of the suffering and crucifixion of Jesus as "the Passion of the Christ" (from the Latin, "passio": suffering). We also suggested that, in the more typical use of the word ("intense, driving, overmastering feeling or conviction, . . . a strong liking or desire for or devotion to some activity, object or concept"),[1] Jesus was a self-avowed, practicing person of passion from the first time the crowds met him at his baptism by John. But his was not a singular passion. He was driven by multiple convictions which we have categorized as these five:

- Jesus' Passion for Us to Know the Truth;
- Jesus' Passion for Us to Love God;
- Jesus' Passion for Us to Love One Another;
- Jesus' Passion for Us to Love Our Neighbors;
- Jesus' Passion for Us to Change the World.

When considering these different passions of Jesus, we cannot help but ask ourselves,

- "Which of these passions most inspire us and which do not?"
- "Which of these passions have we been trying to emulate, and which have we been avoiding?
- "Which Jesus have we adored, and which Jesus have we ignored?"

Have you answered for yourself?

Given that "Therefore there is now no condemnation for those who are in Christ Jesus. For the law of the Spirit of life in Christ Jesus has set you free from the law of sin and of death" (Rom 8:1,2), we suggest no criticism for having our own preferences. A host of motivations, personal histories, mentor and peer influences, gifts and talents, heart yearnings, and especially "the hopes and fears of all [our] years" have led us in directions that bias each of us in our own individual perceptions of what matters most, even what matters most about Jesus of Nazareth.

What also matters is the fact that the host of conflicts between believers in our day, like the conflicts between believers of the first century CE, reflects our own personal biases about the relative importance of particular aspects of Jesus' teachings and actions as over and against others.

---

1. *Webster's Ninth New Collegiate Dictionary* (1985), s.v. "passion," 860.

The Questions at Hand

The bottom line challenge: We need to take a close look at each other's perceptions of God's work in our particular lives and contexts, so that we better can be the aggregated family of God, body of Christ, and temple of the Holy Spirit whose ideological diversity reflects every aspect of the radically diverse passions of the Jesus who brought us together.

How can our particular congregations embody those five passions in ways that strengthen the sinews that hold us together, by sharpening our understanding of God's Word and will for us together, and by elevating the glory of God and the enjoyment of the Spirit's presence among us in worship and prayer? How can we implement them to deepen the empathy expressed to one another and broaden the outreach to our neighbors near and far? How can we engage them to find our prophetic voices and organize our world-transforming efforts by unleashing our gifts and callings in all of those directions? And, how can we do all of the above not just in our own local congregations but also in concert with our siblings in Christ throughout the churches in our country, and ultimately, through the Church universal?

It is to those questions that we now turn our attention. And the first question—the prerequisite question—we turn to first.

But wait . . . is that the theme to *Jaws* I'm hearing again?

Those Darn Sharks among Us

What about those darn sharks among us? I know. The shark metaphor fits when it's pinned onto people who vote for the wrong candidates, watch the wrong TV news networks, and blurt mocking jokes about people we love or for whom we shed tears.

But having already talked about the weeds among the wheat in chapter 4, and about saints who are still sinners, it's appropriate to stretch this shark metaphor as an internal battle for each of us as well. Because while every one of us has a preference among the Passions of the Christ, each one of those passions, when emulated by us who are fully human but not fully God—indeed, not God at all (even with the Holy Spirit indwelling us)—ends up turning good things into bad, staining exalted aspirations with base appetites, and morphing virtues into vices. As the psalmist wrote while in a time of deep grief, "We have all become like one who is unclean, and all our righteous deeds are like a filthy cloth. We all fade like a leaf, and our iniquities, like the wind, take us away" (Ps 64:6). Accordingly let us consider the sharks among *and* within us—or, to mix metaphors, the filthy underclothes that our emulating best selves wear as we try to follow the Passions of the Christ that most define our best intentions.

Passion for Truth or a Penchant to Condemn?

A passion to learn and to teach the Truth with a capital T has long guided the work of many believers in particular, and churches in general. "You will know the truth, and the truth will make you free," Jesus said (John 8:32). And in fact, he went on to say, "So if the Son makes you free, you will be free indeed" (John 8:36). Countless believers have inscribed those verses into their memory banks, and have been motivated by such a promise to dig into the depths of understanding that await those who do as Timothy was directed: "continue in what you have learned and firmly believed, knowing from whom you learned it and how from childhood you have known sacred writings that are able to instruct you for salvation through faith in Christ Jesus. All scripture is inspired by God and is useful for teaching, for reproof, for correction, and for training in righteousness, so that the person of God may be proficient, equipped for every good work" (2 Tim 3:14–17).

However, love for the truth as revealed in Scripture can leads to battling about what is the Truth with a capital T, and in the process promoting the destruction of people who challenge that truth as we understand it. The church has picked many a fight with people, movements, and institutions that have opposed its current message or its memory of "the faith that was once and for all handed on to the saints" (Jude 13).

The phrases above, ". . . that truth as we understand it . . ." and ". . . its current message or its memory . . ." are used intentionally. In every era, many of the teachings of churches have remained faithful to the core messages of Scripture. In every era, some of the teachings have challenged our memory and even broken from the tradition due to fresh ideas and new discoveries—whether prompted by in-depth analysis of biblical texts, learnings from biblical archaeologists, or by new insights from the world of science or psychology or social movements, or by the prose of novelists or visions of poets, or shocked into awareness by the horrors of criminal misdeeds, especially ones perpetrated by governments, institutions, or church leaders. Some of those new ideas have faded away for their inability to persuade the church at large; others (like a theology of the environment) have taken hold.

How has the church at large responded to new teachings? Sometimes we have organized inquisitions and heresy trials. Hans Küng indicts his Roman Catholic Church for its history of exacting violent punishment against alleged heretics. "Few [things] have harmed the Church and its unity so much as the violent treatment of heretics, the evidence of a lack of love which made countless people doubt the truth and drove them out of the Church. The road to 'pure doctrine' cannot be driven over corpses. Zealous faith must not be perverted into doctrinaire intolerance."[2]

Lest Protestants take solace in that criticism of their Roman Catholic neighbors, Reinhold Niebuhr indicts his fellow Protestants: "In the long history of religious controversy in England from the reign of Elizabeth to that of Cromwell, Presbyterianism pursued a policy very similar to that of Catholicism. It pled for liberty of conscience when it was itself in danger of persecution; and threatened all other denominations with suppression when it had the authority to do so."[3]

As one who was raised as a Roman Catholic and ultimately was ordained as a Presbyterian, my faith was most shaped by the neo-evangelical movement. Guess what: such exclusivism and line-drawing around the claim to theological purity has been championed by that movement, too. Jon R. Stone's remarkable study of the early decades of that massive movement suggests that conservative evangelicals have obsessed over the dual questions, "Who's in?" and "Who's out?" In his book *On the Boundaries of American Evangelicalism,* wherein the operative term is "boundaries," he shows how since World War II, evangelicals have worked incessantly to differentiate themselves from other brands of Protestantism: "This is especially noticeable in the writings of postwar evangelicals whose flood of books and articles documents a sustained effort at defining the limits of evangelicalism by affirming and reaffirming its boundary differences with both fundamentalism and liberalism."[4]

In the end, the knowledge of the truth has often been weaponized into grounds for judging others, for excluding others, for banishing others. As Miroslav Volf says, "Rightful moral outrage has mutated into self-deceiving moral smugness."[5]

2. Küng, *Church*, 328–29.

3. Niebuhr, *Nature and Destiny of Man*, 227.

4. Stone, *On the Boundaries of American Evangelicalism*, 179.

5. Volf, *Exclusion and Embrace*, 58.

Such judgmentalism need not have the final word. One of the most remarkable public expressions of confession of guilty judgmentalism can be found in the center of Lima, Peru's national capital, at the Monumental Museum of the Inquisition and Congress. Here the Court of the Holy Office of the Inquisition was established in 1570 as an ecclesiastical court trying religious crimes. To walk through it today—it was established as a museum in 1968—is to see gruesome depictions via life-size wax figures suffering all kinds of torture, even waterboarding. It stands in center city so that all Peruvians and tourists will be shocked by the horrors that their self-righteous ancestors committed in the name of God, so that they, in this time and place, will never repeat such injustices. Horrifying as it is to see such a presentation, its lessons for us moderns scream for our attention, so that our love for the Truth not be allowed to deteriorate into the horrendous violence we all are capable of when fueled by religious zeal.

Behind these harsh reactions to new ideas have been truth-tellers' most basic flaw: the attitude of certitude—the conceits of dogmatists (whether fueled by protectionism of the tradition or by premature embrace of new data against the tradition)—which push churches into constant infighting. The impolite and impolitic battles neither redound to the glory of God nor to the preservation or promotion of the truth.

In other words, the beauty of the truth, so profoundly reframed by Rabbi Jesus, who kept pressing his disciples to see God's will in different ways, easily draws a school of sharks within and around us even as we seek to emulate and partner with his Passion for Us to Know the Truth.

God help us all to promote Jesus' reframed truth in such a way that the grace of our Lord Jesus Christ and the Spirit of the Law that together triumph over the legalisms that choke the life out of people, indeed, over the letter of the law that kills.[6]

---

6. I invite you to read my earlier text, *It's Complicated*, which posits the proposal that the nonnegotiable absolutes of our faith include the identity, character, and mission of our trinitarian God, the full humanity and divinity of Jesus Christ, the power of the cross and resurrection, the plan of redemption, etc. It then shows that the moral and ethical teachings found in the Decalogue and the other commandments provide specific ways to guide how we love God with heart, soul, mind and strength, and our neighbors as ourselves. Those commands are aspirational; they define benchmarks that point and draw us toward holiness, righteousness, mercy, and justice. However, the NT reports numerous times that Jesus and the apostles approximated or even adapted those aspirations/benchmarks to their particular times and places, which, in turn invites us to reason accordingly through the complicated options we face in life. The ultimate conclusion of the book is, "The letter kills. The Spirit gives life."

The Passion for Us to Love God or a Penchant to Withdraw?

Jesus' Passion for Us to Love God is animated by his central mission: to give his life as a ransom to free captives, to carry the weight of the sins of the world, to extend God's forgiveness, to raise us from darkness and death into light and life, to adopt us as children of God, and to grant us the privilege of communing with God by way of the indwelling Holy Spirit. That's one long sentence that could be quadrupled in length with other theologically pregnant expressions of the reconciled relationship with God that the crucified Savior has granted the children of God. Happily, all of those gifts of the grace of our Lord Jesus Christ tend to generate not smugness, but sheer joy and gratitude.

They also generate a lifestyle of devotion: one marked by raising hands in praise, singing out in worship, bowing heads in prayer, kneeling at an altar in hushed awe.

At various times in the ancient and medieval church, persons of highest devotion would withdraw into monasteries to live in the quiet presence of God and to dedicate themselves to contemplate the depth and wonder of God. Some did remarkable work, such as the monks who built St. Catherine's Monastery at the foot of Mt. Sinai in Egypt between 548 and 565. The monks collected an extraordinary library, containing the Codex Sinaiticus, one of the earliest manuscripts of the Bible, dating back to the fourth century, where it remained protected in hiding until the mid-nineteenth century (it found its way ironically through the hands of Stalin (!?) to London's British Library).

Most monasteries gained much less notoriety. But their goal was to provide a sacred space, a thin place, for pilgrims to turn their lives around from secular frivolities to holy devotion to God.

Jumping ahead to the seventeenth century, several waves of spiritual passion blew through Europe and the colonies. The revivalist Congregationalist pastor Jonathan Edwards, considered to be America's first great theologian, launched the first Great Awakening, beginning in New England and spreading outward. A similar commitment to devotion arose late in the seventeenth century in Germany, called Pietistic Lutheranism, under the impetus of Philipp Spener. It spread through much of northern Europe and finally to the colonies.

Likewise, the "strangely warmed" conversion of John Wesley in England led to a revival within the Anglican Church, which formed a movement of small groups who prompted earnest Bible study, prayer, and the pursuit of personal holiness. This revival spread to the colonies and soon after Wesley's death, its adherents split away from the Anglican Church to form the Methodist Church.

This seventeenth-century wave of spiritual passion also arose in the Roman Catholic Church, under the leadership of François Fénelon and his cousin Jeanne Marie Bouvier de la Motte Guyon, best known as Madame Guyon. She wrote, "Prayer is the key of perfection and of sovereign happiness; it is the efficacious means of getting rid of all vices and of acquiring all virtues; for the way to become perfect is to live in the presence of God. He tells us this Himself: 'walk before Me and be blameless' (Genesis 17:1). Prayer alone can bring you into His presence, and keep you there continually."[7]

However, she did not escape controversy. She was imprisoned by the church for promoting the "heresy" of quietism, the practice of quieting the soul in pursuit of divine interaction.

Quietism also came to the fore in nineteenth century European Protestant churches in ways that crossed denominational sectionalism. In 1875, a big tent was erected in Keswick, England, in order to gather for what became an annual, weeklong convention to promote the Higher Life in Christ. The Keswick Movement rose above denominational lines, aggregating—and bringing into close alliance—Anglicans, Quakers, Plymouth Brethren, Presbyterians, Methodists, Baptists, and others (think Oswald Chambers, Andrew Murray, Evan Henry Hopkins, Fred Meyer, D. L. Moody). They adopted the motto, "All One in Christ Jesus," which continues to this day. Its focus on consecration—dying to self to come alive in the Holy Spirit—has provided a framework for a panoply of devotional books promoting spiritual disciplines to this day. Early on, it gave impetus and a framework for the Pentecostal movement as it emerged around the beginning of the twentieth century.

All of these expressions of "quietism" seek to experience an inner serenity via spirituality through contemplation of the divine. The will and the intellect are perceived not as tools for spiritual growth but as impediments to the quest for a boundlessness of the soul.

In the process, such an experience of the exalted resurrection life, built upon the self-denying deeper life, has tended to generate a more passive disinterest toward the outer life.

---

7. Guyon, *Short and Easy Method of Prayer.*

Have you ever heard the criticism, "They're so heavenly minded that they're no earthly good"? Consider the words of the Letter of James: "What good is it, my brothers and sisters, if someone claims to have faith but does not have works? Surely that faith cannot save, can it? If a brother or sister is naked and lacks daily food and one of you says to them, "Go in peace; keep warm and eat your fill," and yet you do not supply their bodily needs, what is the good of that? So faith by itself, if it has no works, is dead" (2:14–17).

Yes, the major shark in the waters of the higher life, a.k.a. the deeper life, is a tendency to withdraw from the matters of the world, even to disregard both regular and calamitous human suffering. These words of James stand as a mandate to take action in the real lives of real people facing real difficulties and injustices in life.

Another shark in the waters of our efforts to partner with Jesus' Passion for Us to Love God arises out of that central gathering of the people of God for Lord's Day worship—and other days as well. Just what is the right form for worship? At the risk of offending every reader of this book, I'll says it bluntly: there are many. Oh, each and every denomination has brought to focus the role of word and sacrament: the word of Scripture read and expounded, and receiving of the sacraments (a.k.a. ordinances) in the process of doing worship. All include acts of prayer—such as confession of sin, declaration of forgiveness, intercession for others' needs, expressions of praise to God—rightly so. But which acts are essential, and which are optional? Dare I be so bold as to stand with the apostle Paul, when he was addressing differing convictions regarding foods (keeping kosher? abstaining from meats?) and Sabbath-keeping (Saturday? Sunday? every day?):

> Welcome those who are weak in faith but not for the purpose of quarreling over opinions. Some believe in eating anything, while the weak eat only vegetables. Those who eat must not despise those who abstain, and those who abstain must not pass judgment on those who eat, for God has welcomed them. Who are you to pass judgment on slaves of another? It is before their own lord that they stand or fall. And they will be upheld, for the Lord is able to make them stand.
>
> Some judge one day to be better than another, while others judge all days to be alike. Let all be fully convinced in their own minds. Those who observe the day, observe it for the Lord. Also those who eat, eat for the Lord, since they give thanks to God,

while those who abstain, abstain for the Lord and give thanks to
God. (Rom 14:1–6)

The councils of churches worldwide, as well as the nondenominational,
multidenominational, and pandenominational movements seem to have
found sufficient common ground in our day to allow and respect each
other's convictions and practices alongside the role of the sacraments or
ordinances.

However, one very twentieth-century battle has persisted into the
twenty-first: the incessant argument and mutual insulting of one another
over the use of contemporary vs. classical music in worship. Just what is
the right music to play and sing in worship? Again, at the risk of offending
every reader of this book, I'll says it bluntly: all of the above and lots more.

As one trained in classical piano and in choral conducting, and as a
child of the rock and roll generation, and as pastor of a half dozen churches—most of whom employed a full-time, postgraduate educated, classically trained organist-choir director—I have led worship surrounded
by brilliantly presented, God-exalting organ and choir music. In four of
those six churches I have led worship in a second (or even third) service
surrounded by brilliantly presented, God-exalting contemporary praise
music. Sure, we have heard a few snarky comments by someone who
didn't like the other genre of sacred music. But those comments came
seldom, because those uttering them generally let go of their prejudice
under the simple statement, "vive la différence . . . all to the glory of God."

You see, there *is* a right way to worship. It is the way that you were
worshiping when you first sensed the overwhelming, strangely warming,
life-affirming, grace-extending, mystical, visceral presence of God—the
same way you have been worshiping in subsequent times when you have
sensed the overwhelming, strangely warming, life-affirming, grace-extending, mystical, visceral presence of God. You may have been attending
a performance of Handel's *Messiah*. You may have been singing along
with a Michael W. Smith concert. You may have been sitting through Ber-
nstein's *Mass*, or a Taizé folk service, or a performance of sacred ballet.
Deep down inside, when walking into your church sanctuary or meeting
hall, there resides an ever-present holy yearning within you that today's
service will transport you into that same place, that same experience once
again. May it be so this next time you join with your church family!

But if you get shocked by the pastor or musicians taking you to a different place, singing a different tune, flipping the offering from before the

sermon to after the sermon, please be open to allowing a different kind of connection with God to arise. Maybe on this day that the Lord has made, God has something for you that will break with the past encounters. And, if you've been judging and even scorning that other kind of worship music, please cease and desist. The core difference between classical music and contemporary music is each's ethnic origin. From white northern and central Europeans we get classical music. From Africa we get rock rhythms. From hundreds of other places we get hundreds of other genres of music. In all respects and in all worship services, hear the word again, "vive la différence . . . all to the glory of God."

The sharks are circling. May we swim together—all together—and even gather in the net of Jesus' diverse collection of the many diverse swimming things—in worship and in prayer, even whisper-humming that simple folk song, "We are one in the Spirit, we are one in Lord."

Jesus' Passion to Love One Another or a Penchant to Huddle?

Most sharks tend to be solitary fish: when swimming around their summer and winter residences, they hunt and swim by themselves. Not the kind of gathering that Jesus formed when throwing out nets to bring in all kinds of fish. Not the kind he intended when building his church as a carpenter who combines multiple materials to form homes and factories. Not the kind he intended when pulling sheep together in a flock, both in the fields and fenced-in pens. We were made to be in fellowship with one another, with the essential building blocks of the kingdom of God being the local churches.

On the other hand, a few species of sharks, like the lemon sharks, blue sharks, and hammerheads, do school together. What's more, many sharks migrate together.

Many are the followers of Jesus who love to school together. Even when they get aggravated at the sharkish, contrarian attitudes they pick up from those others in the net, they love the ingathering, the building, the eating, the migrating together. "Together" is the operative term for those aiming to partner with Jesus' Passion for Us to Love One Another.

Those communifiers find the inquisitions of the Truth interrogators to be terribly wrought over nothing—or, at most, very little. They find the monastic, solitary instincts of the prayerful lovers of God to be too prayer-closeted (a club of disconnected introverts). They have too much work to do: Sunday school classes to teach, shut-ins to visit, committees to be organized, fellowship dinners to be cooked and enjoyed, budgets to be balanced, security concerns to be solved, bulletins to be typed, websites to be repopulated.

Communifiers can inflict a different kind of damage, however. They can be so intent on taking care of their own that they forget about those outside. They tend to circle their wagons around the home team. They may even throw a cold shoulder in the direction of visitors, lest they disrupt the carefully managed systems of familiarity. They limit conversation topics. Controversial topics are avoided in pulpit and classroom—unless the church is so totally red or totally blue that the pastor can "preach to the choir," blurting what they all want to hear about what they already know.

Communifiers tend to focus their ministry around themselves. One can feel very generous by tithing to one's church, by serving many hours in classes and committees, by singing in choir and serving on governing boards. Communifiers are quick to visit and pray for their fellow members in the hospital or home grieving the loss of a loved one, but at the end of the day, the only ones receiving all that generosity are one's friends, one's own fellowship. Such generosity camouflages what could be categorized as collective selfishness.

Yes, the communifiers build churches. They pursue the unity for which Jesus prayed, they provide enormous service in the local church, and they nurture the growing discipleship of the church family where that family lives: in and around the local congregation. They help resolve the disputes created by the truth tellers and revolutionaries. They pull God-lovers out of their prayer closets to get involved in church life. Nevertheless, their tendency to insulate the church from troubles, and especially from the outside world, too often keeps the church playing safe and staying inward-looking.

The Passion for Us to Love Our Neighbors, or a Penchant to Patronize?

Jesus' Passion for Us to Love Our Neighbors has rallied millions of believers through the centuries to see Christ in strangers, as he expressed it: "I was hungry and you gave me food, I was thirsty and you gave me something to drink, I was a stranger and you welcomed me, I was naked and you gave me clothing, I was sick and you took care of me, I was in prison and you visited me.... Truly I tell you, just as you did it to one of the least of these brothers and sisters of mine, you did it to me" (Matt 25:35, 36, 40).

However, amid such generous and sacrificial forms of service, many of us content ourselves with doing good without acknowledging the source of our kindness.

We've all heard Jesus' words to the disciples just prior to his ascension, "But you will receive power when the Holy Spirit has come upon you, and you will be my witnesses in Jerusalem, in all Judea and Samaria, and to the ends of the earth" (Acts 1:8).

So what kind of witness are we to be? When called into court as a witness, our job is to tell the court what we have seen and heard. What about Jesus' witnesses? The same. But many are those who retort, "I'm a silent witness for Christ." That silence can be rationalized by one's culture—less demonstrative—and one's personality type—introverted. It also gets reinforced by Americans' greatest fear, even more fearful than cancer, stroke, or heart attack—namely, public speaking. Out of such tendencies and fears we say, "I am happy to volunteer in the soup kitchen to feed those experiencing food shortages, but my faith is a private matter." Or "I show the love of Jesus. Others talk about it."

The apostle Peter urges us, "But in your hearts revere Christ as Lord. Always be prepared to give an answer to everyone who asks you to give the reason for the hope that you have. But do this with gentleness and respect, keeping a clear conscience, so that those who speak maliciously against your good behavior in Christ may be ashamed of their slander" (1 Pet 3:15b–16a NIV).

A greater shark problem with those emulating Jesus' Passion for Us to Love our Neighbors is one inherited from missionaries of old, especially those committed to extending charity to the needy. Back in the nineteenth and early twentieth centuries those pursuing such efforts did so with the best of intentions of compassion and care. They were prompted by the very words of the love chapter—or the "charity chapter," as it was then known. The King James Version of the Bible, translated as such in 1611, and the Roman Catholic Douay-Rheims, published in 1899, used the word "charity" to translate the Greek word "agape." The self-sacrificing, perfect agape urged by the apostle Paul in 1 Corinthians 13 extols such charity.

The charity-influenced mission initiatives from the US and Europe, through those centuries and well into the twentieth, bade believers to leave their places and lifestyles of privilege and wealth to demonstrate in action the intentions of the 1890s gospel hymn:

> It may not be on the mountain height or over the stormy sea,
> It may not be at the battle's front my Lord will have need of me.
> But if, by a still, small voice he call to paths that I do not know,
> I'll answer, dear Lord, with my hand in thine:
> I'll go where you want me to go.
> I'll go where you want me to go, dear Lord,
> Over mountain or plain or sea;
> I'll say what you want me to say, dear Lord;
> I'll be what you want me to be.[8]

But such self-sacrificing intentions often did more harm than good. The missionaries went into foreign fields to rescue the lost from sin and perdition, only to turn the indigenous peoples into slaves or servants, or more charitably, to enlighten, educate, civilize, and domesticate them. Trampling on their customs and traditions, the mission efforts too often Americanized or Europeanized those encountered. They were patronized and, in the process, dehumanized.

The book titled *Toxic Charity*[9] summarizes the problem: charitable efforts can backfire wholesale, turning toxic, by providing rescue efforts in a place of adversity, then once having completed that mission, leaving for points unknown. And too often the missionaries who stayed colonized the people there, corrupting their own good intentions by securing profits for themselves. Those allegedly having needed to be rescued were left worse off in spite of the appearance of generous intentions by the rescuers.

Fortunately, the word "charity" has largely been eschewed in most ranges of Christian mission.[10] The new language of "missional church" has taken on far better connotations. Instead of loading trucks with food and clothing on the assumption that we know what others need, missional Christians are venturing out not to save others but to befriend them, learn together with them, and facilitate a process with those to whom they go to assess, diagnose, and determine for themselves how to better address their tangible issues and move forward in life-giving ways.

8. Mary Brown and Carrie Esther Parker Rounsdfell, "I'll Go Where You Want Me to Go."

9. Lupton, *Toxic Charity*.

10. Roman Catholic Charities is a notable exception. They keep the name, but their methods of caring are among the most effective in empowering and partnering with those with whom they serve.

A Passion to Change the World or a Penchant to Blame?

Jesus' Passion for Us to Change the World engages us in exciting and exhausting work for church and world—emphasis upon "world." Such prophetic work provokes itself and others to put faith into action. It names, declares, exposes, and confronts injustices, institutionalized prejudice, entrenched majoritarian advantage, and insider bias. It confronts xenophobia, indicts exploitation, and refuses to allow traditions of insider power to remain in place.

The initial impetus for such activism is the gospel of liberation, as experienced by ancient Israel in its emancipation from slavery in Egypt. The exodus model of life-diminishing exploitation within Pharaoh's slave-supported economic system stands as the symbol, exhibit number one, for the ways that entrenched power brokers have taken advantage of the poor in order to fill their own coffers with riches. The exodus model also depicts a God who feels sorrow—indeed, has empathy for the suffering of God's people and a plan to help the situation change for the better.

> Then the Lord said, "I have observed the misery of my people who are in Egypt; I have heard their cry on account of their taskmasters. Indeed, I know their sufferings, and I have come down to deliver them from the Egyptians and to bring them up out of that land to a good and spacious land, to a land flowing with milk and honey, to the country of the Canaanites, the Hittites, the Amorites, the Perizzites, the Hivites, and the Jebusites. The cry of the Israelites has now come to me; I have also seen how the Egyptians oppress them. Now go, I am sending you to Pharaoh to bring my people, the Israelites, out of Egypt." But Moses said to God, "Who am I that I should go to Pharaoh and bring the Israelites out of Egypt?" He said, "I will be with you, and this shall be the sign for you that it is I who sent you: when you have brought the people out of Egypt, you shall serve God on this mountain." (Exod 3:7–10)

In the time of Jesus, the collective memory of being former slaves liberated by God stood as the central narrative of Israel's identity. The annual celebration of the Passover so carefully and comprehensively choreographed by the directives in the Torah and other readings meant that no children of Abraham, Isaac, and Jacob could lose sight of God's mercy shown their ancestors. Even when teaching the Great Commandment, they are told to love their neighbors—literally the aliens among them—in light of that Exodus story: "When an alien resides with you in your land, you shall not oppress the alien. The alien who resides with you shall be to you as the native-born among you; you shall love the alien as yourself, for you were aliens in the land of Egypt: I am the Lord your God" (Lev 19:33–34).

Accordingly, Jesus' Last Supper being shared within the Passover meal, and Jesus' repeated echoes not only of the two laws of love but also lifting them up as the most important of the laws of Israel, sets the exodus from slavery as not only their identity as liberated, but as the center of their ethic to do the same for aliens.

But this does bring us to the challenge for today's prophets, indeed, the hidden indwelling shark in those emulating Christ's Passion for Us to Change the World. That problem boils down to distance.

One of the failings of the church is living in denial, operating with a distance of oblivion—i.e., numbness that keeps us sufficiently away from the problems others are suffering—and even singing "peace, peace" when there is no peace a mile or two away. That state of smiles and laughter inebriate the church out of compassion and empathy. On the other hand, a second, corresponding failing of those trying to find and broadcast their prophetic voice is their doing so from a state of distance as well. They come across as no more than a noisy gong or a clanging cymbal. It is easy to name others' sins committed a thousand miles away from you. Both kinds of distance—the numbness of the distant, and the distance of the voice—must be addressed.

As Walter Brueggemann states in his 2014 book, *Reality, Grief, Hope: Three Urgent Prophetic Tasks*,[11] the voice of the prophet must speak out, naming the suffering of others, but that prophet must also give personal witness to the reality just as Hosea the prophet gave personal witness to the spiritual infidelities of the nation toward God, by way of himself being married to a woman who was being unfaithful to him. He could only name the reality empathically by experiencing it directly. "The realism of the church is grounded in nothing less than the 'Embodiment' of the life-giving God in Jesus Christ and in the derivative practice of the Eucharist, whereby we refuse the denial of the bodily world that lives by bread."[12]

The second urgent task of the prophet, says Brueggemann, is to share in the grief with the sufferers. An outgrowth of the numbness and

11. Brueggemann, *Reality, Grief, Hope.*
12. Brueggemann, *Reality, Grief, Hope*, 163.

distance of the happy-clappy, easy faith of the privileged is the pattern of supposedly facing our losses by taking on the state of denial. In times of war we deny the grief, indeed, the human existence of those on the other side of the battle. The prophet speaks into that grief and demands that we stop pretending it away. The communal rituals of grieving in and through the church bring that first task—grieving—to the point of mandate to action, to revolution. "Thus it is the church that *practices and performs grief* while the world conventionally denies the power of death among us. It is the church—after the manner of covenant Israel—that has practiced the honesty of mourning that is essential for continuing to live freely in a world of profound loss."[13]

The third urgent prophetic task is that of casting a vision of hope. Rather than simply drowning in the quicksand of despair, instead of the prophet piling grief upon guilt, and terror upon shame, the revolutionary task calls for casting a vision for what God can and will do to bring light to darkness and life to death. "Thus it is the church that *performs hope* in a world of despair. The church regularly performs the rhetoric and gestures of forgiveness with the prospect again in newness."[14]

So What about These Sharks among and within Us?

What about those sharks? They need to be seen, named, called out in full volume among us all.

As ones who are emulating Jesus' Passion for Us to Know the Truth, the truth-tellers need to be proclaiming the truths once revealed and re-framed and continually beg for reconsideration to those emulating Jesus' other passions.

Those emulating Jesus' Passion for Us to Change the World need to be discerning, experiencing, naming, and shouting out on behalf of those suffering the pains of injustice, marginalization, and diminishment for the other lovers of Jesus' other passions.

Those emulating Jesus' Passion for Us to Love God via redemption, adoption, forgiveness, salvation, prayer, praise, worship, and sheer intimacy with God need to be prodding the others to center down on these core acts of the incarnate and crucified Christ.

13. Brueggemann, *Reality, Grief, Hope,* 163. Emphasis in the original.
14. Brueggemann, *Reality, Grief, Hope,* 163. Emphasis in the original.

Those emulating Jesus' Passion for Us to Love Our Neighbors, that is, the strangers, the aliens, the weak, the sick, the dying—to bring healing to bodies, minds, and spirits—need to exhort one another to go out into the highways and byways, out to the communities of loneliness, of poverty, of pain, to extend the empathy of Jesus to help and heal.

And those emulating Jesus' Passion for Us to Love One Another need to be casting their nets on every side of the boat to bring in all swimming things—minnows and whales, St. Peter fish, shellfish, barracudas and flounder, dolphins and sharks—to welcome them in; they need to be building all of the component parts of the household of God, the lumber and stone, the windows and door handles, the furniture and plumbing to be assembled into a home, in fact, a temple made of living stones for the dwelling of God's Spirit; and pull all of the sheep together into one sheepfold, not allowing any to wander away.

Put that all together, and we need followers of Jesus to promote for each others' hearing the Jesus we adore, and for us to listen to their voices to help us no longer have a Jesus we ignore—and so that we do not become so radicalized or so tedious that others will be repelled by us—so that together the body no longer has any resemblance to the singly *red church* or the singly *blue church* that certain politicians would want us to be. Yes, we need to be the full-spectrum church of kaleidoscopic brilliance in the red-and-blue world.

And how do we really make that happen? By becoming the empowering church Jesus designed us to be.

— Part III —

A Fuller Gospel for Empowered
Lives for Unstoppable Churches

---

12 ---

Proclaiming the Fuller Gospel

The Gospel in a Nutshell

WE LIVE WHAT WE believe. And what we believe is built on what we have been taught and trained in (whether we adopt it or repudiate it). Hence, the essence of who we are is found in the teaching itself.

Jesus set the pace for that. He began his ministry with the direction-setting sermon in his Nazareth synagogue, as reported earlier. And his preaching, teaching, conversing, storytelling, prophesying voice dominates the pages of the Gospels.

The apostles reflected back on the insight, wisdom, and power of those preached words. For example, Paul's Letter to the Romans, an advanced introduction to those believers he hoped to soon meet, asks the key question and posits the answer: "But how are they to call on one in whom they have not believed? And how are they to believe in one of whom they have never heard? And how are they to hear without someone to proclaim him? And how are they to proclaim him unless they are sent? As it is written, 'How beautiful are the feet of those who bring good news!' But not all have obeyed the good news, for Isaiah says, 'Lord, who has believed our message?' So faith comes from what is heard, and what is heard comes through the word of Christ" (Rom 10:14–17).

And what was it that Jesus and the apostles preached? The good news, as Isaiah promised and Jesus introduced in his synagogue inaugural address. Not just any generic, pedestrian good news, but *the* good news, the kind that Jesus was talking about in that Sabbath service. The very first words out of his mouth introduced the topic: "The Spirit of the Lord is upon me, because he has anointed me to bring good news to the poor" (Luke 4:18a). *The* good news. It is the evangel (the Greek word was *euangelion*, literally "evangel," which means exactly, "good message" = "eu" means "good" and "angel" means "messenger" or "message").

So what is *the* good news? *The* gospel? Remembering that "gospel" is simply the old English version of "good news," let's ask that question in this way: What Scripture verse comes to mind when you hear the expression, "The gospel in a nutshell"? Martin Luther first came up with the expression. Billy Graham referenced it often.

How did they answer that? Well, think about a football fan holding up a sign behind the end zone: "3:16."

Yes, in a nutshell, those great leaders, along with countless other preachers who have echoed them, have declared that the gospel in a nutshell is what's recorded in John 3:16—"For God so loved the world that he gave his only Son, so that everyone who believes in him may not perish but may have eternal life."

A good response. But I want to suggest that that's not the best biblical text with which to summarize the gospel. I would offer another.

This one is more concise. It has a slightly smaller nutshell; that is, in the Greek manuscript, while John 3:16 takes up twenty-five words, this other uses just twenty. And whereas John 3:16 speaks of God and God's Son, this other includes all three members of the Trinity. Whereas John 3:16 introduces God's motive in sending Jesus, this other verse summarizes the work of all three members of the Godhead.

I propose this gospel in a nutshell: "The grace of the Lord Jesus Christ, the love of God, and the communion of the Holy Spirit be with all of you" (2 Cor 13:13).[1]

If the church is going to exhibit the full breadth of Jesus' passions in its work and witness in the twenty-first century, it must begin—as do all organizations—at the beginning, at the center of the churches' shared identity and calling. For us as Christians of all denominations and movements, that starting point is the existence of the triune God, one God in three persons.

---

1. Some translations number the concluding verse of 2 Cor as v. 14.

What all the major councils and conventions of denominations in the world hold in common as the top and central declaration of their faith is their belief in the triune God. From the ancient Council of Nicea (325) to the Councils of Constantinople (381, 553, 680–81), from the Council of Trent (1545–63) to the Westminster Assembly of Divines (1643–53), from the World Council of Churches (1948–present) to the Second Vatican Council (1962–65), from the National Association of Evangelicals (1942–present) to the National Council of Churches (1950–present). From Eastern Orthodox to Roman Catholic, from Anglican to Assemblies of God, from Church of Christ to United Church of Christ. And virtually all nondenominational, multidenominational and pandenominational churches. All require subscription to the doctrine of the Holy Trinity.

Non-trinitarian churches, such as the Church of Jesus Christ of Latter-day Saints, the Jehovah's Witnesses, and the Unitarian churches, do not believe in the Trinity, and thus they do not qualify for membership in any of the councils.

In fact, after two hundred years of religion scholars showcasing a "hermeneutic of suspicion," constantly challenging every biblical assertion, authorship, and every theological claim imaginable, that massive body of scholars was stunned into a crazy unity in 1980 when German scholar Jürgen Moltmann published his monumental work *The Trinity and the Kingdom*.[2] Building on his earlier work *The Crucified God*,[3] he conceived of the engagement between the three distinct members of the Godhead as being fully united in all matters, including the suffering of Jesus on the cross.

Given the collective anguish felt while living through the bloodiest century in world history,[4] scholars worldwide were looking for some framework to provide a path forward to peace between ideological antagonists. Into this longing came Moltmann, prompting a conversation around the notion that has generated countless other conversations around the trinitarian God who is absolutely three and one at the same time, hence, is inherently social and living in mutual love.[5] After two centuries of scholars living on the edges of the centrifugal forces, regularly

2. Moltmann, *Trinity and the Kingdom*.

3. Moltmann, *Crucified God*.

4. See Ferguson, *War of the World*.

5. Other influential scholars who joined the conversation included Miroslav Volf, Elizabeth Johnson, John Zizioulas, and Catherine LaCugna.

testing the limits of orthodoxy, many of them suddenly felt drawn together by the gravitational pull of the God who is living in togetherness. The wave of resulting social trinitarian studies has been pulling theologians of all labels (evangelicals, progressives, fundamentalists, etc.) to a common core of orthodoxy.

In a new, fresh way, "We are one in the Spirit, we are one in the [trinitarian] Lord."

Put that all together and, in spite of all the battles fought, all the anathemas declared, all the schisms suffered, all the congregational splits and ecclesiastical decamping from home denominations, we Christians on all sides of those divides still stand together on this cornerstone affirmation. Any hope we may have to move past the political divisions, the bitterness of past wounds, and the feelings of estrangement can begin with God's core identity and mission—and one that is not a simple "least common denominator" but is for certain a massively powerful declaration about the God of the universe.

Can I hear an "Amen!"

So, what's it all about? The trinitarian God named *Father, Son, and Holy Spirit,* and categorized as *Creator, Christ, and Spirit,* and described as *Creator, Redeemer, and Sustainer* is the key, the truly essential and effectual tenet of the faith. Some have illustrated the three-in-one as *the One to Whom, the One by Whom, and the One in Whom we offer our praise.* However expressed or illustrated, the Three-in-One God is the answer.

Ironically, the word "Trinity" does not appear in holy Scripture. The earliest known reference to the term comes from the writing of Theophilus of God in 170 CE. The formulation of the term was codified in an incredibly faith-defining gathering in 325, the Nicean Council. They also finalized the choice of books to be included in the New Testament and wrote the Nicene Creed (the most universally affirmed summary of the faith to this day). The doctrine of the Trinity, the triune God, stands strong in faith communities worldwide. Indeed, the full-spectrum church is one that will proclaim the full breadth and individual particularities of the triune God.

So what do all of these conceptual ideas have to do with the day-to-day faith of Christians in the pew? Well, the answer to that is found in this gospel-in-a-nutshell verse. This final sentence in Paul's Second Letter to the Corinthians that's often quoted as the final words in worship services—the Benediction (Latin: "to speak well of," good word)—spells out what the Trinity brings into our very lives.

The Gospel of the Grace of the Lord Jesus Christ

The "grace of the Lord Jesus Christ." Just as the word "Trinity" appears nowhere in the Bible, the word "grace" is nowhere quoted on Jesus' lips. However, the idea of grace permeates Jesus' public ministry. The stories told by him—the good Samaritan, the lost coin, lost sheep, and lost sons—demonstrate it. The stories enacted by him, advocating for the woman caught in adultery, visiting the despised tax collector, conversing with the Samaritan woman, healing the lepers, and so many others depict the gospel not as a paycheck earned, not as a product purchased, not even a prize won for perfect faith expressed in perfect prayer, but as sheer gift. Add in Jesus' pronouncements from the Beatitudes promising unexpected blessings to those lacking them, to declaring of himself, "Those who are well have no need of a physician, but those who are sick; I have come to call not the righteous but sinners" (Mark 2:17), to his words uttered on the cross providing a dying thief admission to paradise and praying for pardon of his murderers: "Father, forgive them, for they do not know what they are doing" (Luke 23:24).

It's in the light of all of the above that Jesus' interpreters spoke repeatedly of his grace. As Peter, defending Paul and Barnabas against legalistic believers, put it, "On the contrary, we believe it is through the grace of our Lord Jesus that we are saved just as they are" (Acts 15:11).

Or as expressed in Ephesians, "For it is by grace you have been saved, through faith, and that not of yourselves, it is the gift of God, not of works, lest anyone should boast" (Eph 2:8,9). Indeed, the final words of the whole Bible say it: "The grace of the Lord Jesus be with all the saints" (Rev 22:21).

So what is grace? The Greek word is *charis*. It is commonly defined as "unmerited favor," but the major theological dictionaries provide many pages of definitions. At the risk of making it too simple, the Sunday school acrostic I learned as a teenager has the best definition I've ever seen: G-R-A-C-E = God's Riches at Christ's Expense. All the riches of God's grace have been given freely: forgiveness, pardon, reconciliation, redemption, adoption, liberation, in-grafting, salvation, blessings, effectual prayer, Spirit-indwelling, sanctification, empowerment, spiritual gifting, commissioning, ultimate glorification—the list goes on and on. And these and many more riches are bestowed upon the children of God. They come neither for cheap nor for free, because a price for all these benefits, beyond all dollars, was paid by Jesus. In his blood.

And, if that sounds to you like a throwback to sawdust trail preaching, please don't dismiss it."

In his willingness to bear the weight of guilt of every sin committed by every person who ever was or will be, Jesus took upon himself all the sins humans have committed, and ever will commit, to forgive them. He took upon himself all the wounds that others' sins have committed against us—the abuse, the brutality, the enslavement, the banishment—and "by his stripes we are healed." "Surely he has borne our infirmities and carried our diseases, yet we accounted him stricken, struck down by God, and afflicted. But he was wounded for our transgressions, crushed for our iniquities; upon him was the punishment that made us whole, and by his bruises we are healed" (Isa 54:4).

Few have expressed this as profoundly and graphically as did Franciscan priest Brennan Manning in his memoirs:

> My life is a witness to *vulgar grace*—a grace that amazes as it offends. A grace that pays the eager beaver who works all day the same wages as the grinning drunk who shows up at ten till five. A grace that hikes up the robe and runs breakneck toward the prodigal reeking of sin and wraps him up and decides to throw a party [with] no if's, ands, or buts. A grace that raises bloodshot eyes to a dying thief's request—"Please, remember me"—and assures him, "You bet!" A grace that is the pleasure of the Father, fleshed out in the carpenter Messiah, Jesus the Christ, who left His Father's side not for heaven's sake but for our sakes, yours and mine . . . This *vulgar grace* is indiscriminate compassion. It works without asking anything of us. It's not cheap. It's free, and as such will always be a banana peel for the orthodox foot and a fairy tale for the grown-up sensibility. Grace is sufficient even though we huff and puff with all our might to try to find something or someone it cannot cover. Grace is enough . . . Jesus is enough.[6]

The Gospel of the Love of God

Unlike "Trinity" not being in the Bible, and "grace" not being mentioned by Jesus, the word "love" is all over the place and most certainly attached to God. In my early years of ministry, being a fanatical trinitarian, I wanted to remind my parishioners of the full gospel implicit in the Trinity.

6. Manning with Blase, *All Is Grace*, 192–94 (emphasis added).

As we ended our services, whether on Sunday or on other occasions, my regular practice was to pronounce the explicitly trinitarian benediction: "The grace of the Lord Jesus Christ and the love of God *our Father*, and the communion of the Holy Spirit be with you all." I added the italics to the two added words, "our Father," to underscore the names of the members of the Trinity.

I should have been scolded by feminists for adding to the yearslong pattern of using words easily inferred to imply gender exclusion. I should have been scolded for inserting my own additions to Scripture. For some reason I was never scolded.

But my inclusion of "our Father" was driven by the belief that Jesus speaking to and about God by using the Aramaic word "Abba," an informal name of address akin to Daddy or Mommy, served both as an expression of intimate closeness and as a word of counterpoint to the more common perspective elevating the otherness, transcendence, impersonal, and frightfulness of God's heavenly identity.

True to Jesus' regular pattern of reframing Truth, he was not the first to suggest that Israel can speak of God as a parent. While the Hebrew Scriptures generally speak of God in more sovereign, majestic, and fearsome ways, on eight occasions God is spoken of as a Father. On the other hand, in the four Gospels, Jesus is quoted as speaking of God as father more than 250 times. Clearly, he was making a point, namely, reframing people's relationship with God in accessible, familiar, interactive, and engaging ways.

The writings of John, especially his letters, declare simply, "God is love." That Greek word of perfect, self-sacrificial love—"agape"—is the term used repeatedly. "Beloved, let us love one another, because love is from God; everyone who loves is born of God and knows God. Whoever does not love does not know God, for God is love. God's love was revealed among us in this way: God sent his only Son into the world so that we might live through him. In this is love, not that we loved God but that he loved us and sent his Son to be the atoning sacrifice for our sins. Beloved, since God loved us so much, we also ought to love one another. No one has ever seen God; if we love one another, God abides in us, and his love is perfected in us" (1 John 4:7–12).

On the other hand, the longtime identification of God as male has been a terrible point of struggle for so many of us—and frankly reflected in the misogyny too common among the males of the race. This I know and stand upon: Jesus' habit of speaking of God as "Abba," Father, was not about genderness. It was about tenderness.

Jesus engaged in prayer to and presented teachings about the God of the universe on a level of closeness beyond that of lovers in love, beyond that of a mother nursing her newborn child. And he was inviting his disciples to emulate the familiar way he talked with and about God. And, lest there be any doubt, in the Genesis account of the creation of humans in the image and likeness of God, the first command given them was to "Be fruitful and multiply and fill the earth and subdue it" (Gen 1:28b). The fulfillment of that command required the male in God's image and female in God's image to procreate children, and hence, both were made equally in God's image. God did not see the male, on the one hand, as like God, and the female, on the other hand, as foreign to God. Both were equally of God and, therefore, God incorporates within God's self all attributes of female and male.

As Jesus taught, the almighty, sovereign, transcendent God of the universe has been revealed also as the shepherd who seeks out lost sheep, the hen who gathers her chicks under her wing, and as the father who runs to the crest of the hill to welcome the prodigal wild child home.

As said by Art Baird, "To know God is not only to know about God. . . . to really know God in the deepest sense, on God's own terms, is to know God personally, immediately, subjectively; to talk to God in prayer, to commune with God in worship and the secret meditation of the heart, to do God's will in living a life of service to others. Because God is person and to know God personally is to know God as he is . . . You can never know God by talking about God. Ultimately, somehow, you have to get down on your knees and talk to God, because God is person."[7]

Without being prodded by fundamentalists or feminists, I stopped adding "the Father" to the benedictions and have pronounced that blessing in the exact language Paul gave us in 2 Corinthians.

The Gospel of the Fellowship of the Holy Spirit

All of this brings us to the third member of the Trinity, as a past pastor of mine called, "What's Its Name" as in "Father, Son, and What's Its Name."

Consider this: What if aliens from outer space fly a UFO over a major US city, and hover over a football stadium, watching the action? What

---

7. Baird, *Rediscovering the Power of the Gospel*, 46, 47.

if, upon returning to their own planet, when asked "What's that sport football all about?" they were to respond, "It is an oblong bowl-shaped coliseum, filled with thousands of humans cheering and shouting, many drinking a yellow drink with whipped cream on top, and eating long, skinny pink things in long, skinny pieces of bread." If we on planet earth heard that report, what would we say? Perhaps, "They've completely missed the point. The point is the ballgame happening on the field!" The activities they saw in the stands are just byproducts.

When it comes to the third member of the Godhead, most people, including many Christian believers, miss the point, too. Some pick up on the Spirit's inspiration, which have led to odd, sometimes eccentric beliefs. Some pick up on the Spirit's elevation, leading to surprising bursts of emotion. Others pick up on the Spirit's revelation, which has sometimes led to odd predictions of major events in church or world. Any and all of those things can go on in the context of the Holy Spirit, but they are byproducts, not the heart of the matter.

The Holy Spirit's essential role in the first-century church, intended to continue through this age, was much simpler than that: namely, fellowship with God and with humanity.

You see, from the time in the garden, humans have suffered from a geographical problem. Having been created in the presence of God, their original sin led to the first humans' banishment from God's presence.[8] All of us since then have been born lacking the connection the first humans enjoyed at the beginning. The unfolding story of God's visitations, interventions, callings, miracles, liberations, prophetic teachings, Psalm readings, etc., in the Hebrew Scriptures show forth the love of God for God's people, and God's desire to dwell with them.

The Christian addendum to that story is that God came to us in the birth of Jesus—Emmanuel, God-with-us—and cultivated an immediate and close relationship with us. Then Jesus was betrayed, denied, and crucified, suffering immediate banishment from that divine intimacy—comparable to the first couple's banishment from the garden—and then he died. But on the third day he rose victorious, paving the way for believers

8. The account of the creation has been interpreted numerous ways, ranging from an exacting literality, to a metaphorical parable, to poetic parallelisms, to myth, to general dismissal. We can't dismiss it. But its meaning and lessons are equally relevant whether it occurred exactly as reported, or the narrative is a story along the lines of the good Samaritan or the prodigal or poetry comparable to a psalm. Please hear this account for the points of meaning, not for any historiographical analysis or scientific arguments.

in him to go to heaven someday, but also for heaven's greatest blessing to come to them: the immediate, close, loving presence of God. He had been promising that that would happen. Now the resurrected Jesus directed the disciples to remain there until it actually happened. And sure enough he ascended to heaven; and about ten days later, Jesus poured out the Holy Spirit, the living Presence of God, to make a home in the lives and community of the believers so that the banishment and estrangement would end forever and all the other promises of Jesus' grace and Abba's love would be theirs.

So what in essence did the Holy Spirit do? The Spirit solved the geographical problem of banishment and exile—so that the dwelling place of God was no longer in a garden nor on a mountain top nor in temples made with hands, but in human lives.

Remember that declaration from 1 John that God is love? The following verse clinches the point: "By this we know that we abide in him and he in us, because he has given us of his Spirit" (1 John 4:13). The Greek word used in the Gospel-in-a-nutshell benediction is "koinonia," which means fellowship or communion. That is to say, "the communing fellowship of the Holy Spirit be with you all."

New Testament scholar Gordon Fee, in his monumental, 967-page-long study *God's Empowering Presence*, says it well in summarizing Paul's teaching: "Absolutely central to Paul's theology of the Spirit is that the Spirit is the fulfillment of the promises found in Jeremiah and Ezekiel: that God himself would breathe on us and we would live; that he would write his law in our hearts; and especially that he would give his Spirit 'unto us,' so that we are indwelt by him. What is crucial for Paul is that we are thus indwelt by the eternal God. The gathered church and the individual believer are the new locus of God's own presence with his people; and the Spirit is the way God is now present."[9]

Hear Paul's simple summary of the story: "God's love has been poured into our hearts through the Holy Spirit that has been given to us" (Rom 5:5b).

To summarize the tripartite promises of the triune God as expressed in this benediction, *Given the love of God who has yearned from eternity past to adopt us as children, and given the grace of the Lord Jesus Christ, who tore down the veil of separation between us and the loving God, the*

---

9. Fee, *God's Empowering Presence*, 6–7.

Holy Spirit has come into our lives to dwell and abide in us—to make us the very body of Christ, household of God, and temple of the Holy Spirit.[10]

To clarify, when the benediction sounds, it may well come off as a fleeting hope, like "I hope you pass your exam" or "I hope you win the lottery." But is the grace of Jesus a fleeting hope, just a big "maybe"? Is the love of God an equally fleeting hope? Just a big, "maybe this time"? No. They are sure things. All the time. So, too, the fellowship of the Holy Spirit. It's not a mere hope. It is a state-of-being sentence.[11] It indicates, "This is what is, has been, and will continue to be."

Which leads back to the central point of this chapter. Any and every church, whether it has thirty members or thirty thousand, will flourish only if it preaches the gospel. Any and every church that characterizes itself as red or blue may spurt with growth when fueled by the adrenaline rush that comes with argumentative preaching against that other party's heresies or imbecilities, but it will not flourish for long unless it preaches the gospel. Any and every church that categorizes itself in any other way, that specializes in any one kind of service, may recruit loyal servant-leaders for the mission, but their energy will wane unless they keep hearing the gospel. And any church that is suffering division between factions, or is being co-opted by a small group of power brokers, or is losing members out of a lack of interest, can find its way back to vitality only if it is preaching the gospel. Get my point? At the risk of extreme redundancy, hear this benediction: "The grace of the Lord Jesus Christ, the love of God and the fellowship of the Holy Spirit are with you all."

---

10. Returning to Fee's work, he says of the 2 Corinthians 13:13 benediction, "In the case of Christ and God at least these [grace and love] are the most characteristic words in Paul's vocabulary to express the essence of their being and activity; the spirit is associated with 'fellowship'" (*God's Empowering Presence*, 362n230). He then adds, "In many ways this benediction is the most profound theological moment in the Pauline corpus" (*God's Empowering Presence*, 363).

11. To be exact, the sentence has no verb, which in Greek and many European romance languages implies "am," "is," "be," or "are"—and often emphatically a continuous present.

— 13 —

Holy Ghosted?

Becoming an Empowerment Church

That Was Then

So, for a church to exercise and carry out the qualities with which Christ founded it—i.e., energy, care, learning, outreach, and influence— it needs to incorporate and give witness to the full spectrum of Jesus' passions in its worship and work. Sunday mornings provide a good start, especially when gifted, trained, and called leaders can set the tone. But to carry out the missions of the congregation requires a multiplicity of ministries led by a diverse team of ministers, carrying them out every day of the week.

Which leads back to the role of the Holy Spirit. Not only did the Holy Spirit bring us into communing fellowship with God, as was just explained. The Spirit endowed us with capabilities with which to extend Jesus' witness to the uttermost. In his public ministry Jesus promised his followers that the continuation of the work he had started would be carried out through them as informed and empowered by the Holy Spirit. He pointed ahead to the coming of the Holy Spirit—dubbed "parakaleo" (literally, "to call alongside"), which is translated comforter, counselor, helper, or advocate, according to the translator's discretion. The parakaleo would:

- ... teach you all things (John 14:25–26)

- . . . remind you of everything I (Jesus) have said to you (John 14:25–26)

- . . . guide you into all truth (John 16:13)

- . . . tell you what is yet to come (John 1:13)

- . . . clothe you with power from on high (Luke 24:53)

- . . . baptize you with the Holy Spirit (Acts 1:5)

- . . . grant you power when the Holy Spirit has come upon you (Acts 1:8).

Sure enough, as the sun rose on the first Christian Pentecost morning, 120 of Jesus' disciples were praying together in the upper room (it was forty-seven days after the resurrection). A sound like that of a mighty wind filled the room, fire descended from on high that divided into multiple candle-sized flames that rested above the heads of the participants, and all began to speak in tongues. They exhibited more drama than the biggest fireworks display ever.

Everything changed. Yes, everything.

Let me summarize it this way: We build our church sanctuaries around a cross, but after Jesus' crucifixion, his disciples returned to fishing. We formulate our church calendars around Easter, but after Jesus' resurrection, his disciples went into hiding. We mostly overlook Pentecost, but after Jesus' outpouring (Acts 2:33) of the Holy Spirit, the disciples went out and turned the world upside down.[1]

Let me put this in yet another way: The coming of the Holy Spirit was not just an appendix to the major story of Jesus' sojourn on earth. It was the ultimate purpose of and the climax to his sojourn here. It launched a new day for the people of God, the massive extending of the kingdom of God, so that "every knee should bend, in heaven and on earth and under the earth, and every tongue should confess that Jesus Christ is Lord, to the glory of God the Father" (Phil 2:10–11).[2]

1. Hear this point from Ralph P. Martin: "Paul invokes the Holy Spirit with one master concern. He is seeking to establish the Holy Spirit as *the authentic sign of the new age, already begun but not yet realized in its fullness*, and he is building his case on the *readers' participation in the Spirit as the hallmark of their share in both the new world of God's righteousness and the Pauline apostolate that represents it*." Martin, *Spirit and the Congregation*, 234 (emphasis his).

2. The study of the Holy Spirit in this and the previous chapters is a brief summary of fifty years of specialized study on the third member of the Trinity, including a doctoral dissertation based on the majestic tome of Old Testament scholar Samuel Terrien,

As a matter of fact, Jesus' ministry had one particular thing in common with that of John the Baptist. Just as John was preparing the way for the one who was to come—namely, Jesus—so Jesus was preparing the way for another one who was to come—namely, the Holy Spirit. The promises of God proclaimed in the Hebrew Scriptures and throughout Jesus' teaching, and made possible by his incarnation, crucifixion, resurrection, and ascension, were made actual by Christ's sending of the Holy Spirit into the lives of his faith family on Pentecost.

Those bright, loud manifestations arrested the attention of the crowds there for the historic Jewish Pentecost festival, leading to a powerful sermon by the apostle Peter, which led to three thousand people repenting and being baptized and filled with the Holy Spirit. And so began the Jesus movement that turned the world upside down.

Yes, the original Jesus movement became the farthest-reaching religious movement in world history—in the apostolic era, and all the more over the next few centuries. And it happened with a minimum of organization, no standardized way of structuring their work, no buildings owned, no armies recruited, no officers commissioned. But what they did have was a force of energy, a source of understanding, an enthusiasm for banding together, a hunger for learning, and an array of particular skills and talents empowered and operative in extraordinary ways; and, underneath all of that, a profound attitude of gratitude for what they had received that motivated them to find ways to share it with others.

About ten days prior to that Pentecost, the resurrected Jesus met the disciples on the Mount of Olives, just across the valley from the Temple on the Mount. They asked him, "Lord, is this the time when you will restore the kingdom to Israel?" (It was a likely question, given the hundreds of times he had previously taught them about the coming kingdom).

He reframed the question to elevate the response. "It is not for you to know the times or periods that the Father has set by his own authority. But you will receive power when the Holy Spirit has come upon you, and you will be my witnesses in Jerusalem, in all Judea and Samaria, and to the ends of the earth" (Acts 1:6–8).

The Elusive Presence: Toward a New Biblical Theology. My dissertation carries Terrien's new biblical theology into the New Testament in a promise-fulfillment motif (not supersessionism, not replacement theory) and is titled, *The Presence of the Spirit: Elusive or Abiding? . . . Toward a Theology of Spirituality,* which Terrien and other scholars applauded. An accessible adaptation of that thesis was published as *Living the Presence of the Spirit.*

Yes, that power—the *dunamis* . . . dynamite—was given them, and within hours their numbers increased by 2,500 percent. Soon they were gathering daily at the temple to learn, to worship, to break bread, to pray, to share their goods with each other, and to give witness to those in the city. Before long, they were fanning out to other communities near and far to, indeed, extend the ministry of Jesus throughout the region and beyond.

The key promise of all of this is the presence and power of the Holy Spirit, which too often has become a dividing line in the historic churches. Clearly, the experiences of the Spirit's work among the apostles was extraordinary, as testified throughout the book of the Acts of the Apostles, and in several of the epistles from apostles to churches.

Gradually the temperature of their gatherings cooled somewhat. In the mid-second century, Montanus appeared as a new prophet determined to revive the electrifying, miraculous character of the faith. Based in the region of Phrygia in central Turkey, he developed a following and was sufficiently credible to draw into the Montanists' membership the leading Christian scholar of the era, Quintus Septimius Florens Tertullianus (160–240), better known as Tertullian of Carthage. But some eccentric prophets in the movement blurted claims that their village Pepuza was the new Jerusalem and soon would welcome Jesus' second coming. The movement was discredited widely and shrank to a tiny remnant. A more tame and temperate style of church then prevailed, and the centralization of power and authority became increasingly institutionalized.

In fact, in their time, Luther and Calvin dismissed a new wave of Radical Reformers as "Enthusiasts." Not so much because of emotionalism but because of "God-withinism,"[3] giving too much credence to the inner light of understanding apart from Scripture.

This all began to change with the rise of Wesleyanism. John Wesley, born in 1703, became an Anglican clergyman, but felt constrained by the formalism there that also was typical of other mainstream churches of the Protestant Reformation, which by that time had been in existence for about two hundred years. He was earnest in religious faith and even went to America to seek to convert the natives, but saw no success there. His faith felt hollow, too. On May 24, 1738, he resisted attending, but did in fact go to a meeting at Aldersgate (a ward in the city of London), which began with a reading from Martin Luther's Preface to the Book of Romans. Wesley reported, "About a quarter before nine, while he was

3. Horton, "Protestantism Is Over and the Radicals Won."

describing the change which God works in the heart through faith in Christ, I felt my heart strangely warmed. I felt I did trust in Christ, Christ alone, for salvation: and an assurance was given me, that He had taken away my sins, even mine, and saved me from the law of sin and death."[4]

As over against the seemingly humdrum religiosity of the church of his ordination, Wesley gave earnest effort to making experiential, encounter-based faith and spiritual disciplines a regular part of his life and influence on others. In the process, he gave rise to the notion of the Holy Spirt being a participant in a person's life, giving special attention to the Spirit's work of sanctification: "But we must always give thanks to God for you, brothers and sisters beloved by the Lord, because God chose you as the first fruits for salvation through sanctification by the Spirit and through belief in the truth" (2 Thess. 2:13).

Wesley's focus on a second experience of encounter with God, akin to Moses on the Mount, the calling of Isaiah, the commissioning of the apostle Peter, and the Damascus Road visionary experience of the apostle Paul, all fed into his teaching of an expectation to connect with God through the Holy Spirit. His brother Charles Wesley's hymns, such as "O for a Thousand Tongues to Sing"; "Love Divine, All Love Excelling"; and "Jesus, Lover of My Soul," certainly encouraged such experiential breakthroughs.

John Wesley's experiences and the growth of the Holiness movement set the stage for the rise of Pentecostalism at the beginning of the twentieth century. There, too, believers experienced a second experience with God, by way of the Holy Spirit, which in these cases were often accompanied by speaking in tongues. Eccentricities abounded. And so did harsh rejections. While they were basically fundamentalist in dogma, the other fundamentalists shunned them as fanatics, as did Christians of most other streams. But they would not be denied their passions for worship, their expectations of God to work miracles in lives, and their enthusiastic evangelistic proclamation. What's more, they took their faith all around the US, spreading into Central and South America, Africa and Asia. Soon they followed patterns of mainline Protestants by establishing colleges, and led the way in utilizing radio, TV, and the internet, and even gaining influence in the White House, so that they developed the institutional

---

4. Bob, "John Wesley's Happy Day."

strength, educated scholarship, and effective pastoral skills to thrive and grow to the level of nearly 600 million adherents worldwide.[5]

Unlike other revivals and awakenings through the past two millennia, the Pentecostal movement has not faded. It continues to grow worldwide. And while all brands of Christianity in the US have been shrinking since the year 2000, these churches overall have nearly kept steady, some even soaring in growth. Why? There are a million reasons as to why Pentecostalism has been so vital, but one of the major reasons is its belief that Jesus meant it when promising, "You will receive power when the Holy Spirit has come upon you."

This Is Now

Pentecostalism continues to thrive in many parts of the world, and so do many denominational traditions that have incorporated pieces of the Pentecostal experience and mindset. As your conversation partner who stated in the introduction that I have been a fundapentacharisgelical, I have had stints in each of those traditions, although my pastoral and preaching style has been fleshed out in mainline churches. Still, I treasure those past experiences, past memories, and lasting friendships. And one aspect of that history and those experiences I hold to be absolutely central to my ministry—and to the success in leading full-spectrum churches— have been my convinced conviction that:

1. the Holy Spirit does indwell all believers;

2. the Holy Spirit's presence makes effectual Jesus' passion for us to love God in expressing our worship of God via divine geography: Jesus' atonement bridged the chasm between heaven and earth, so that the Holy Spirit could be and has been poured out by Jesus via the heaven-to-earth bridge he built, so that the first humans' banishment no longer keeps us apart from God; and

3. the Holy Spirit has come to dwell in us with power, thereby bestowing spiritual gifts, extending callings, and commissioning all believers into world-changing service.

---

5. The total of Pentecostal and Charismatic (neo-Pentecostal) adherents is 584,080,000, which is 26.7 percent of Christians worldwide, according to Pew Research Center's Forum on Religion and Public Life, *Global Christianity*, December, 2021.

Of the many great learning opportunities I've enjoyed, two of them were studying First Corinthians and the Book of Acts under the tutelage of Gordon Fee, the first Assemblies of God minister ever to earn a PhD in biblical studies. He was a scholar who never allowed his faith to become "a watered down understanding that gives more glory to Western rationalism and spiritual anemia than to the living God."[6] He pressed the question most commonly raised in his Pentecostal world: "What is the evidence of the fullness of the Holy Spirit in people's lives?"

He demonstrated, against his denomination's general belief, that speaking in tongues can be an evidence of the Holy Spirit's action, but is not the only nor the most important evidence. He asserted that other spiritual gifts will result from the Spirit's indwelling, but they do not stand as proofs either. He stated that holy living, as elevated in Wesleyan theology, should be an outcome, but it's also not the proof-positive either.

Rather, he asserted, in his booming preaching voice, that the proof-positive of the Holy Spirit's fulness throughout the book of Acts, and throughout the history of the church, was then and is today, "great expectations of what God can and will do among us."[7]

Fee also concluded his forty hours of lectures on Acts with the final exhortation to his students, most of whom were planning to become church pastors: "The book of Acts does not provide any one, single formula on how to lay hold of the experience of the Holy Spirit, but it clearly says that you need it. In fact, please save any future congregation from the mediocrity that you will impose on them if you don't have it. Get on your knees and lay hold of it. Build your life around it. So that you will go out in the power of the Holy Spirit, confident that God will be doing a great work through you, as you set out to turn the world upside down all over again."[8]

Having been thrilled to hear such a great scholar challenge his students to hold to those great expectations, and having already concluded that the early churches' impact in the world was driven by the empowerment and giftedness by the Holy Spirit, I determined that one of the defining marks of my church ministry would be to promote such high expectations of God-with-us via the Holy Spirit's indwelling. In light of that, I would specifically endeavor to help my church members to discern and cultivate their spiritual giftings and callings so they could actively

6. Fee, *God's Empowering Presence*, 9

7. Fee, "Lectures on the Book of Acts."

8. This is not an exact quote, but a paraphrase from memory.

fulfill Christ's Great Commission to make disciples of all nations, being confident that he, by the Holy Spirit, would never leave us nor forsake them or us (Matt 28:18–20).

Today's Spiritual Giftings

In an earnest effort to break away from the contentiousness around spiritual gifts and aiming to eschew the common practice among too many faith communities of ignoring biblical references to them, let us venture into this laboratory of missional invention. The laboratory was formed on that first Pentecost as the necessary mechanism for the fulfillment of Jesus' promise, "You shall receive power when the Holy Spirit comes upon you." The firstfruits of that power were named by Peter's Pentecost morning sermon as he introduced his preaching text:

> Fellow Jews and all who live in Jerusalem, let this be known to you, and listen to what I say. Indeed, these are not drunk, as you suppose, for it is only nine o'clock in the morning. No, this is what was spoken through the prophet Joel:
> "In the last days it will be, God declares,
> that I will pour out my Spirit upon all flesh,
> and your sons and your daughters shall prophesy,
> and your young men shall see visions,
> and your old men shall dream dreams.
> Even upon my slaves, both men and women,
> in those days I will pour out my Spirit,
> and they shall prophesy." (Acts 2:14–18)

Ah hah! The spirit poured out on all flesh . . . prophesying as a result . . . from both sons and daughters . . . the young seeing visions . . . the old dreaming dreams . . . all this to be experienced even by slaves/servants of both genders . . . indeed, filled with God's Spirit . . . and enabled to prophesy. This was a new beginning, indeed. And marked by spiritual gifts being exercised not by religious professionals, priests, Levites, Pharisees, Sadducees, nor rabbis, not handing out business cards touting their academic degrees, but by everyday folk, even slaves—who by definition would be people without credentials on which to brag.

From there the experience of Holy Spirit giftedness was common, referenced in numerous ways through the epistles, and expounded at length in Paul's letters to the Romans (12:3–8) and 1 Corinthians (2:4—3:2, 12:1—14:40). In fact, Paul begins his First Letter to the Corinthians:

"Grace to you and peace from God our Father and the Lord Jesus Christ. I give thanks to my God always for you because of the grace of God that has been given you in Christ Jesus, for in every way you have been enriched in him, in speech and knowledge of every kind—just as the testimony of Christ has been strengthened among you—so that you are not lacking in any gift as you wait for the revealing of our Lord Jesus Christ." (1 Cor 1:3–7)

Such listings of spiritual gifts beg a few questions.

First: what is meant by the term "spiritual gifts"? Well, our English Bibles generally use those two words to translate two distinctly different Greek words. The one most obvious, because it's the root word for the charismatic movement, is *charismata*. The root word of that root word, *charis*, meaning grace, we have explained earlier (in chapter 12) in our discussion on the gospel in a nutshell. To add the "-*mata*" suffix to *charis* means that grace is being expressed in a tangible way.

Another word in this regard is *pneumatikos*. It is an expansion of the root *pneuma* ("spirit," as in Holy Spirit), and with the suffix—*tikos*—it means "spiritual," an adjective. But when the sentence structure puts it into a noun form, it means "an apportionment or expression of the Spirit." Hence, *pneumatikos* references the source of the gifts as being the Holy Spirit. So the one word focuses on grace and the other on the Spirit. Both take the root and make it tangible.

The late John Wimber, founder of the Vineyard Churches and specialist in the theology of the Holy Spirit, coined the term *gracelet* for charisma, and *gracelets* for the plural charismata.[9] In either case, both words seem to be used interchangeably by Paul (Peter, too, who uses each one time: 1 Peter 2:10 and 4:5). Both words speak of ways that the grace of Jesus and the presence of the Spirit get expressed tangibly.

The second question these terms beg is "what" qualifies as spiritual gifts. A common way to list the gifts is simply to look for all the lists given—Romans 12, 1 Corinthians 12 and 14, Ephesians 4, and 1 Peter 4:10–11. These lists overlap in some ways but are different in others. Each is raised as the subject of discussion for different reasons. Clearly the 1 Corinthians 12 lists are intended to stretch the minds of the Corinthians beyond reveling only in speaking in tongues and to recognize other ways the Spirit is working.

---

9. Morphew and Nerheim, *John Wimber's Teaching*.

The list in Ephesians 4 mentions four or five vocational titles: apostle, prophet, evangelist, pastor, teacher (some translators suggest that the last two are really hyphenated: pastor-teacher). Then again other vocational titles appear in Acts and other epistles: elder, deacon, disciple, fellow worker, bishop; most are offered with little definition.

The list in Romans is introductory; Paul is not writing them to correct their errors, as most of his other letters do, but to overview the faith to a community he has never visited (as he had the others). What's more, other gifts are mentioned in other places . . . notably the gift of singleness or celibacy: "I wish that all were as I myself am. But each has a particular gift from God, one having one kind and another a different kind" (1 Cor 7:7). But we all seem to overlook the last phrase, "one having one kind and another a different kind," and if the one kind he's touting is singleness, then the other kind must be marriage.

The very first reference in the Bible to receiving a gift of the Spirit, tracing all the way back to Moses at Mt. Sinai and the reception of the Ten Commandments. While there, Moses was given instructions on how to build a tabernacle (tent) in the wilderness, and then God explained the way for that to be accomplished:

> Then the Lord said to Moses, "See, I have chosen Bezalel son of Uri, the son of Hur, of the tribe of Judah, and I have filled him with the Spirit of God, with wisdom, with understanding, with knowledge and with all kinds of skills—to make artistic designs for work in gold, silver and bronze, to cut and set stones, to work in wood, and to engage in all kinds of crafts. Moreover, I have appointed Oholiab son of Ahisamak, of the tribe of Dan, to help him. Also I have given ability to all the skilled workers to make everything I have commanded you: the tent of meeting, the ark of the covenant law with the atonement cover on it, and all the other furnishings of the tent—the table and its articles, the pure gold lampstand and all its accessories, the altar of incense, the altar of burnt offering and all its utensils, the basin with its stand—and also the woven garments, both the sacred garments for Aaron the priest and the garments for his sons when they serve as priests, and the anointing oil and fragrant incense for the Holy Place. They are to make them just as I commanded you" (Exod 31:1–11 NIV).

Some gift lists add the term "craftsmanship" to their aggregated list. But the text says God has given Bezalel and Oholiab "every kind of skill" to do the work, which includes not just sculpting, sewing, carpentry, oil pressing, and incense formulating, but also architecture, engineering, project management, human resource development, accounting, funds development, and organizational development. And this actual work of Bezalel and Oholiab takes center stage at Exodus 36:30, continuing all the way through 38:31.

Those gifts are dubbed skills, not simply being miraculously imparted abilities but the kinds of skills we acquire via academic study, laboratory experimentation, coaching, training, and apprenticeships.

In other words, given that the point of all gifts is to apportion grace as given by the Holy Spirit, and given that the means of extending those gifts include not just miraculous abilities, but also inherited talents and learned skills and making use of stations in life as obvious as singleness and marriage, then most any capability or life situation or geographical location or ability to travel or just common sense can function as a spiritual gift, a *gracelet,* whenever it is shared in order to extend the grace of the Lord Jesus, the love of God, and the fellowship of the Holy Spirit to others.

Get the point? Do you get the point of Jesus' promise of the outpoured Holy Spirit? Do you get the point of the Holy Spirit's presence in you, around you, and among the "you all" that is your family, your faith community, your service organization, your class, your corporation?

And do you get the idea that maybe the people in your faith community, again whether that entails thirty people or thirty thousand, have all been brought there by the sovereign God to extend the gospel, the full gospel, and to fulfill Jesus' passions out into the community and to the farthest reaches of influence that this—your—faith family, your tribe can go?

Living the Giftedness in the Empowering Church

All of this leads to a bold understanding of the church that is generally out of style these days. The lack of this understanding is fueling the shrinkage of participation in the churches. But the recovery of this understanding (it's not new; this pastor has not invented it) can set congregations—full-spectrum congregations—aflame with motivated believers making an impact on their communities way beyond what they have ever done before.

It goes like this: Given that God has gifted God's people—every one of God's people—with capabilities and life-situations by which God's grace, love, and fellowship can be transmitted to others, and given that the multiple passions of the Christ serve to direct those persons to emulate their Savior on behalf of others—then one of the central roles of pastoral leaders is to urge, to facilitate, and to equip every one of those members to discern their gifts, to find potential partners with whom to cultivate them, to scout out possible recipients and sharers of them, and to go and do accordingly. By so doing, the whole momentum of the congregation can rise like a phoenix.

In order for this to come to pass, the pastor has to stop being a leader and choose instead to be a launcher. Okay, maybe I've spent too many years hanging around rocket scientists, but on this word choice, they get it right. The job of a truly New Testament pastor in the twenty-first century is not to lead a single-file group of followers to go where he or she is going. It is to launch all those folks into whatever direction God is sending them—even if they are going out in ways that are contrary to others on the same team. God's mission is not linear, not a straight, one-dimensional line, but one going in 360 degrees of directions all at once (obviously so when it comes to the spread of the gospel around the earth—actually 360 degrees east and west plus 360 degrees north and south, plus 360 degrees in every other angular direction—you get the point). Call it omnidirectional. Yes, call it omnidirectional leadership in the omnidirectional mission of God, fueled by the omnipotent Holy Spirit, motivated by the omni-benevolent God, and made possible by the omni-gracious Savior.

Hence, the pastor mostly needs to do two other things:

- Preach the fully trinitarian Gospel, and
- Commission the Holy Spirit-filled people to go.

To be clear, in preaching the full gospel, I have been pressing you to focus on the too-often-overlooked third member of the Trinity. Please allow me to reframe my point as: "The Doctrine of the Holy Spirit Infilling, Empowering, Gifting, Calling, and Commissioning of All Believers." Martin Luther had it right when reintroducing the priesthood of all. Well, the apostles also were launching their people into ministry because the empowerment was obvious and unquenchable, and the giftedness just needed to hear the "On your mark; get set; GO!" of their leaders to carry out the mission and calling before them.

In the early apostolic era, the result of such Holy Spirit centeredness, the energy and passion of the Jesus-followers was irrepressible. The level of activity was peddle-to-the-metal. The participation and growth was rapid. At times it all was even chaotic. In the current era, in churches that are affirming the infilling, empowerment, giftedness, calling, and commissioning of all believers also may experience such energy and passion, and such busyness (a full calendar!), and such growth and empowerment. They may experience head-on collisions between folks following contrary paths of mission—but in the process end up learning from each other how best to refine and cooperate in their endeavors. But united by the nutshell gospel, and broadly authorized to follow their callings, this full-spectrum church will have so many points of difference that the red and blue party platforms in political conventions will seem relatively insignificant.

As Andrew Carnegie famously said, "The beauty of empowering others is that your own power is *not* diminished in the process."[10]

So, again, I reiterate my questions: Are you getting my point? Or, I should ask more exactly, are you getting Jesus' point? The coming of the Holy Spirit was not just an appendix to the major story of Jesus' time on earth. It was the ultimate purpose of and the climax to his sojourn here. It launched a new age of the people of God, the massive extending of the kingdom of God, so that "every knee should bend, in heaven and on earth and under the earth, and every tongue should confess that Jesus Christ is Lord, to the glory of God the Father" (Phil 2:10–11).

10. Carnegie, "239 Best *The 360 Degree Leader* Quotes."

14

Leadership

The Not-So-Secret CODE

So, I've got some bad news, some good news, and some great news. The bad news: there are some ferocious sharks in the pool of the church. The good news: most of those sharks are not ferocious at all; they may be persnickety or grumpy or just contrarian, but they have no interest in hurting you or anybody else. The great news, as said in chapter 4, is: Not all nine-inch-high dorsal fins cutting through the waters' surface are attached to three hundred razor-sharp teeth ready to shred human flesh, break human bones, and swallow human organs. Some of those fins are attached to Flipper or one of her cousins. In fact, they not only are tame. They are intelligent, playful, and loving. I know. I've played with one once—just a few months ago.

It was in fulfillment of Barbie's lifelong dream that we signed up for a cruise excursion to swim with dolphins (her dream rubbed off on me). We did our research to be sure that we would be guided by professional, humane-to-the-extreme dolphin caregivers, in a spacious, healthy, natural environment where we would swim with them. So we did, and yes, they were everything we both had hoped for—and they helped my metaphor about swimming with the sharks to take a turn for the better.

Back to the full-spectrum church with its mix of shark species, plus dolphins, plus other creatures of the sea swimming in close proximity to each other: how can we facilitate and equip them all to work and worship together to the glory of God? How can we herd those cats, I mean, those fish—not for catch-and-kill as in the commercial fishing industry, but to bring species of all kinds together in a mutually life-giving community of togetherness—in order to fulfill God's calling upon them individually and upon all of us collectively?

Leaders Don't Just Lead. They . . .

Our faith communities are able to flourish as full-spectrum churches in this red and blue world. But as we have said, to do so requires leaders who are proclaiming the gospel, and who are cognizant of, and respectful toward, all those within their congregations and outside in their communities who are ready to follow Jesus in striving to fulfill any one or more of Jesus' passions for us to serve. We also have said that such churches need to have leaders whose worldview is broad enough to welcome and affirm members who have an infinite variety of spiritual gifts.

Some are inherently wired for such an eclectic leadership style. But even for those so wired, the reality of leading this way tests one's courage and challenges one's principles. Some of the swimming things are difficult to endure and respect. For those not so wired, it can seem impossible, and their highest hopes of having and leading a full-spectrum church can fizzle.

Do not lose hope! The skill sets for church leaders to lead full-spectrum churches are learnable. The white-hot energy of a diverse congregation is attainable, no matter who is in the pews or folding chairs or stadium seats.

Leaders lead, right? It's been nearly forty years since I adopted those two words as one of my life mottoes. I latched onto that maxim when battling the leading member of my church—the teacher of the largest adult Sunday school class, the lead carpenter for church renovations, the coordinator for renewal weekends, and everybody's choice to preach on Laity Sunday. He also was the hit of every party. Plus, he was an early retired, successful engineer, owner of a few patents, and wanting to become a second-career pastor. However, he had been shunned by a bishop in a different denomination, resulting in his feeling resentful toward hot-shot clergy types. When I arrived at his church as a mere twenty-eight year old, he had a hard time addressing as "pastor" a guy younger than four of his five children. You readers from that church will remember him by name, but for the rest I'll dub him Skipper (because I felt like a wet-behind-the-ears Gilligan around him).

On one occasion, having been criticized or challenged by him for something I don't remember (but I do remember the distress and anger I was feeling), I sat down at the living room piano and played old hymns loudly, banging on the keys in fortissimo as a way to vent my anger and to cry out to God, pleading for help.

It was a whining Davidic psalm blaring out in real time.

A few hymns into my complaining, I felt like I heard my answer: *Leaders lead.* I interpreted that to mean, "Don't be intimidated by your youth or by elder members' dismissals of you"; and I remembered Paul's words to Timothy, "Let no one despise your youth, but set the believers an example in speech and conduct, in love, in faith, in purity" (1 Tim 4:12). That in turn led to, "Trust God to lead you as you lead others. And take courage." I did. And though I don't remember the specifics nearly as much as the piano playing and resulting maxim, things worked out.[1]

However, that maxim eventually morphed into a better one: "Leaders launch." Now, you might blame that maxim on the astronauts and rocket scientists I served over twenty-two years of pastoral ministry in my first two churches. NASA-talk was our talk. But "launch" is, indeed, the right word for church leaders. Our calling is not to get out in front to lead the congregation, like the parent pulling their children in a wagon behind them. We don't have a monopoly on discerning God's will for this community of believers, either as a whole entity or as particular individuals, each of whom has their own gifts and callings from God. Instead, our calling is to help fan into flames the gifts of God in every one of our members, as well as their family members and neighbors.[2]

---

1. A blessed footnote to the story: A few years after this incident, Skipper returned to his former denomination, trained, and became a commissioned lay pastor, serving in a church a hundred miles away from mine. Two years into his term, he came back to town, took me out to lunch, and told me about the aggravating situations and members he was serving. Then he stunned me by acknowledging that he had been one of those aggravating members in the ways he had treated me, noting that he hadn't understood the effects of such behavior until he became the one behind the pulpit. He even enumerated specific words and actions. He then asked me to forgive him. He wept as he apologized. I wept as I listened (and weep even now, thirty years later, as I type this). With teary gratitude and joy I forgave him. As I thanked him for it, we rose out of our seats and shared a bear hug—as friends, peers, and partners in Christ's service.

2. 2 Timothy 1:6–7: "For this reason I remind you to rekindle the gift of God that is within you through the laying on of my hands; for God did not give us a spirit of cowardice, but rather a spirit of power and of love and of self-discipline."

Let me put this in business terms. I have learned much from business management books and workshops through the years, and have been able to apply to ministry much of what I have learned. One such application is that people perform their best work when they find their sweet spot, the place where their greatest passions align with other persons' hopes and needs. That is the foundation for vocation, calling, and career. This matches entirely with the spiritual gifting taught and modelled in the New Testament churches. Convergence between Bible and business. Yes!

On the other hand, many a pastor also has built a ministry model that began with their discerning that one thing the congregation is most gifted at; the one style of music the congregation needs most; the one approach to preaching that they must hear; and the one demographic group on which they should concentrate their pastoral care, outreach, and evangelism efforts. But to call that "discernment" is a euphemism for the pastor actually deciding unilaterally which methods the church needs to use; which missional endeavors should be funded; which educational topics should be taught; which demographic the church needs to reach and which ones can be ignored . . . even whether the church should appeal only to blue Democrats or red Republicans.

Harvard Business School teaches its entrepreneurial students to build businesses that way;[3] and indeed, many a Fortune 500 corporation began that way. But most all of them diversified their portfolio a thousand times over as they grew. Moreover, their measure of success was and always will be the bottom line: Is it profitable? How is the cash flow? What are the prospects for increasing profit and growing market share?

The church of Jesus Christ has a different bottom line: Are we teaching the truth? Are we inviting people to grow in God's love, helping them to come together in mutual love, sending them out to love their neighbors near and far, changing the world into a better place for all? Jesus' passions define our bottom line.

In order for the church to join with Jesus in carrying out his passions, God has brought into every congregation individuals with multiple spiritual giftings and callings to be able to carry out the tasks at hand . . . and to invent new ones. Each participant brings spiritual gifts that nobody else has. For example, those called to teach the truth will bring

3. "The essence of strategy is choosing what not to do." And, "Strategy 101 is about choices: You can't be all things to all people." See Li, "10 Famous Quotes by Michael Porter."

different specialty gifts to the task, some gifted to teach elementary children and others gifted to teach young adults and still others gifted to
promote such learning opportunities to the widest possible audience.

And, accordingly, the pastor, the educators, the church officers, the
musicians, the official and unofficial leaders need to team up to find opportunities for the members to pursue their passions and exercise their
gifts and callings to serve one or more of those passions.

Or as Frederick Buechner has famously written, "The place God
calls you to is the place where your deep gladness and the world's deep
hunger meet."[4]

While we may be inspired by Buechner's maxim as it speaks to us,
we also need to pass it on to others. We need to strategize ways to aid all
of the members to find their own callings. Toward that end, I invite you to
adopt another maxim I also adopted early in my years of ministry—back
in the Skipper years—namely, "Go for it." I actually didn't choose that
maxim. I just heard myself saying it so often that it occurred to me, "Hm-
mmm. 'Go for it.' That must be one of my life mottoes, because I keep
saying it."

When folks came into my office, or greeted me in the foyer on
their way out of church, or saw me walking through the supermarket
and stopped to say something like, "Jack, I have an idea," after inviting
them to tell me about it I almost invariably responded, "Go for it!" (unless it needed some refining before giving a total thumbs-up, in which
case I would meet with them first to talk further about it). Then we got
to formulating how to implement their idea, who to recruit to partner in
its implementation, and how to fund it and schedule it; and soon it was
taking shape. Oh, yeah, if it entailed scheduling, we'd talk with the calendar manager. And if it was a big deal, we'd take it to the church board for
approval, or at least to an existing committee to get buy-in. But generally,
it would soon begin to take flight. And while sometimes an idea didn't
bear fruit, usually it did.

Thus, the "Go for it!" maxim remains a life motto unchanged to
this day.

---

4. Buechner, *Wishful Thinking*, 118.

About the Launch of Such Spiritual Gifts

As we stated before, some spiritual gifts are labeled as such in the Bible. Some of our denominations or movements state that what makes them spiritual is that they happen miraculously, untrained, unplanned. Certainly, some of those in Scripture are portrayed like that, for example, speaking in other tongues on that first Pentecost morning and referred to again through Acts and 1 Corinthians.

However, some of the biblical gifts, like leadership and teaching, usually get exercised and strengthened with classroom education enriching their impact and wisdom. Some function in conventional or tangible ways, like contributing to the needs of others (Rom 12:8) and extending help and guidance (1 Cor 12:28 NIV). Some function spontaneously, like gifts of healing, or other miracles, whereas others function as ongoing tasks including paid employment, like pastors, musicians, and apostles. Others, like words of knowledge, wisdom, and discernment include all of the above—and then some. And, if somebody narrows the definition to exclude some abilities, ask them to prove that narrowness based on scriptural terms. They won't be able to do so. The Bible's reporting of the gifts, especially in 1 Corinthians, stresses the multiplicity of inside-the-box and outside-the-box ways that the Holy Spirit is working through people, as over against their particular interest. (In Corinthian's case, Paul lists multiple gifts in order to enlarge their focus from just tongues to many other ways for the Spirit to spread the grace through them; he urges them to aspire to edify as many people as possible in the exercise of their gifts.)[5]

That being the case, it takes little imagination to come up with other comparable ways that the Holy Spirit works (as *pneumatikoi*) to extend grace (as *charismata*)—from neurosurgeons to medical techs, from psychotherapists to drug and alcohol counselors, from farmers to gardeners, from attorneys to judges, from police officers to meteorologists, from school teachers to guidance counselors, from nannies to hospice volunteers, from organists to lead guitarists. In fact, if the Holy Spirit is improving persons' health and wholeness, if the grace of Jesus is changing lives, if the love of God is lifting persons' hopes, then those impacts and changes are gifts of the Spirit, gifts of grace.

Have you disregarded these works of the Holy Spirit? Have your pastors neglected these? Then set your sail to go out into those waters that

---

5. See 1 Corinthians 12—14, reading all three chapters in sequence as a three-point sermon or a five-paragraph essay.

may look unpredictably precarious. Put your hands on some resources that can guide you and your friends into conversations on how to discern each one's spiritual giftings and callings, read and utilize some of the many published resources for gifts discernment (suggestions in the footnote below)—and, as you are doing so, assess which one, two, or three of Jesus' passions swell in your heart as something in which you might seek to participate.[6]

Show Me the Power

When responding to Jesus' final promise, "You shall receive power when the Holy Spirit comes upon you" (Acts 1:8), which we have referenced several times already, one aspect that requires more thought is that of power itself. "Power tends to corrupt. Absolute power corrupts absolutely." So said Lord Acton (1834–1902) in a letter to Bishop Mandell Creighton when discussing abuses of power in the past, especially abuses of some of the popes.[7] Acton's words are widely quoted as if self-evidently true. But are they? In fact, if so, then why was Jesus promising that the Spirit would give such power? He did use that Greek word, *dunamis*, the etymological root of dynamite, to state its ferocity. Was that a creative thing to be promised or a destructive bomb waiting to explode?

Having served in mainline, liturgy-based churches most of my adult life, I can't shrug off the central dynamic of the Pentecostal/Charismatic churches down the street: those folks really believe that Jesus' promise of power to his disciples was fulfilled then and continues to be fulfilled now. Power for praying effectively. Power for God to change lives. Power for their own lives to be changed. Power not only for sins to be forgiven but also for habitual sins to disappear either immediately or gradually. *Power.*

Theologians have rightly outlined benefits of Jesus' salvation, such as justification, sanctification, redemption, and forgiveness. Preachers and theologians have added others such as adoption and emancipation. Luther stressed all of these and added emphatically "the priesthood of all believers." The Pentecostals add one other: the infilling, gifting, calling, commissioning, and empowering of all believers, as introduced in the last chapter. That's a chapter that should be added to all systematic

6. Consider such resources as Kise, Stark, and Hirsh, *LifeKeys*; Prior, "Spiritual Gifts in Business"; and Rees, *S.H.A.P.E.*

7. Letter to Bishop Mandell Creighton, April 5, 1887. Published in Figgis and Laurence, eds., *Historical Essays and Studies*.

theologies of all brands of Christian faith. Jesus promised it. The Acts and Epistles attest to it. We all need to catch up to it.

Yes, playing with power can spark explosions. But disempowerment consumes like moths and rust and mildew. It breaks in to steal persons' hopes and dreams—and diminishes them. And, at the same time—it corrupts the judgment, the self-aggrandizement, the exaggerated sense of superiority of those doing the disempowering.

One of the gifts of the feminist-womanist movement has been the naming of this matter in the worldwide, millennia-long disempowerment that has diminished that majority population. Being treated as less than the men has quashed many a young girl's dreams. I remember well the ways my male mentors and peers and I would speak lovingly of the women in our lives as "gifted in so many ways, but just not to the degree that we men" are, or not in tasks "they simply were not capable of doing as men do." Our male-centric worldview found ways to sound polite. But at best we were patronizing and condescending "to persons of low estate." Many women accepted their place as second class. They were fed out-of-context definitions of the "women's role" in church and life. They knew no alternative. But we men continued—and continue still—to be wrong.

It has been said that of all the amazing civil rights and social justice movements of the twentieth century, that of women's rights, indeed, equality, will long stand out as the most radical and most lasting. Thanks be to God. I welcome being "put in my place" as one among equals in the sight of God.

Which takes me back to empowerment. When it comes to the leadership of churches, there are two kinds of empowerment. The first we've been considering is the empowerment—Greek: *dunamis*—that took center stage with the outpouring of the Holy Spirit. Another comes from the Greek word *exousia,* also translated power, but meaning, specifically, the power of "authority" or "authorization." Examples:

- Jesus spoke as one who had *authority* (Matt 9:8);

- In the Great Commission, "All *authority* in heaven and on earth has been given to me. Go therefore and make disciples of all nations, baptizing them in the name of the Father and of the Son and of the Holy Spirit . . ." (Matt 28:18–19);

- "And he appointed twelve to be with him and to be sent out to preach and to have *authority/power* to cast out demons" (Mark 3:14–15);

- "But to all who received him, who believed in his name, he gave *power/authority* to become children of God" (John 1:12);

- And of the resurrected and ascended Christ, "who has gone into heaven and is at the right hand of God, with angels, *authorities* (*exousion*), and powers (*dunameon*) made subject to him" (1 Pet 3:21b, 22).

Particularly striking is the interplay of the two "power" words in Jesus' final farewell before his ascension: "He replied, 'It is not for you to know the times or periods that the Father has set by his own authority (*exousia*). But you will receive power (*dunamis*) when the Holy Spirit has come upon you, and you will be my witnesses in Jerusalem, in all Judea and Samaria, and to the ends of the earth" (Acts 1:7–8).

So what does that mean for us today? Well, guess which American churches first authorized women to preach, to administer sacraments, to serve as pastors? Apart from a tiny few in among the Quakers, Congregationalists, Wesleyans, Unitarians, and Universalists, in the eighteenth and nineteenth centuries, it was when crossing the threshold into the twentieth century that the Pentecostals opened their pulpits to the 51 percent of us. Charles Fox Parham trained women for preaching ministry in what he called the Apostolic Faith Movement. Notably, his sister-in-law, Lilian Thistlewaite, preached widely throughout the Midwest. The African American preacher William Joseph Seymour brought the Apostolic Faith Movement to Los Angeles, launching the interracial Azusa Street Mission in 1906—and with it: the modern Pentecostal movement—with women and men together providing leadership and outreach.[8]

In short, the exercise of the *dunamis* in women's preaching brought by implication the *exousia*, the authority of God, to do so. And the early Pentecostal men believed that they dare not deny God's work among them; they dare not withhold from women the authority to do so as God has empowered them. Sure enough, the movement mushroomed in the

8. See Robeck Jr., "Women in the Pentecostal Movement." The Mission was even ridiculed on the front page of *The Los Angeles Evening News*, July 23, 1906, for violating Paul's command in 1 Corinthians 14:34 regarding the silence of women. As Robeck Jr. records, Seymour defended his support of women's leadership in a public statement: "It is contrary to the Scriptures that woman should not have her part in the salvation work to which God has called her. We have no right to lay a straw in her way, but to be men of holiness, purity and virtue, to hold up the standard and encourage the woman in her work, and God will honor and bless us as never before. It is the same Holy Spirit in the woman as in the man."

1920s and 1930s, when Aimee Semple McPherson moved to Los Angeles to build Angelus Temple and launch the International Church of the Foursquare Gospel, a major denomination to this day, whose pulpits were dominated by women over those early decades.[9]

Yes, both the power and authority of Jesus, his *dunamis* and *exousia*, were poured out on the first believers to change their lives and change the world—forever.

So shall we worry about its corrupting potential? Michel Foucault, the postmodernist French philosopher suggests otherwise. "We must cease once and for all to describe the effects of power in negative terms: it 'excludes', it 'represses', it 'censors', it 'abstracts', it 'masks', it 'conceals'. In fact, power produces; it produces reality; it produces domains of objects and rituals of truth. The individual and the knowledge that may be gained of him belong to this production."[10]

So, when it comes to leading empowering organizations—especially churches—I hearken back to yet another axiom, this one coming from my mom in my teenage years: "People will readily accept responsibility for their behavior only when they are granted the authority to determine what they are going to do."

I broadened that axiom to a rule of thumb: People will take responsibility and assume accountability for their work to the same level as they are given the freedom and authority to plan and carry out the tasks at hand. In fact, whenever I have lacked the workers willing to carry out tasks in the life of my congregations, I've forced myself to question whether I'm being too controlling to allow them to do the vision-casting, the inventing, the innovating of projects and programs so as to find the internal motivation to do it and to do so with excellence. I also ask myself whether or not I'm asking folks to work in the sweet spot of their giftedness. If not, then I'm asking the wrong people to do the wrong task for that giftedness. When I do find folks' sweet spot and ask them to do so with the promise to authorize them to exercise their gifts—they usually say yes, and they almost always deliver a product far exceeding my initial request.

---

9. Cited in Robeck Jr., "Women in the Pentecostal Movement."
10. Foucault, *Discipline and Punish*, 194. See also Foucault, *Power*.

The Excellence Dividend

I've mentioned my appreciation for some books and workshops on business management. Reading such books and attending such workshops have prompted me and provided me quiet shakedown moments, self-assessments coming from an outside voice that isn't going to publicly embarrass me. The one shakedown voice who has spoken the loudest and clearest has been Tom Peters, the author of many best-selling leadership texts, such as *In Search of Excellence, Passion for Excellence, Thriving on Chaos,* and *The Excellence Dividend.*[11] I commend them to you for your further study on the Empowerment Model of ministry. So many principles I've expounded here from Scripture in the ecclesiastical context find complementary development in the business context.

Another source of counsel has come from a few of the many church consultants who focus on facilitating members' spiritual gifts and callings. Chief among them is the work of Sue Mallory, author of *The Equipping Church.*[12] That title, drawn from the commissioning of church leaders, stresses the purpose of their ministries: "He himself granted that some are apostles, prophets, evangelists, pastors, and teachers to equip the saints for the work of ministry, for building up the body of Christ, until all of us come to the unity of the faith and of the knowledge of the Son of God, to maturity, to the measure of the full stature of Christ" (Eph 4:11–13).

The key phrase there is, "to equip the saints." The work of the church "professionals" is to equip the saints—not dead holy people but living Holy-Spirited members—for them to carry out the mission of the church.

On a side note, when talking with Sue Mallory recently, I asked her what she would change about that book if she were to rewrite it today. She responded immediately that she would speak out more strongly on how the Equipping Church will succeed or fail depending on the advocacy of leadership. "Those pastors need to persevere in teaching this as an ongoing model over time. *And,* then they have to walk the talk. They have to be out in front of the people on this. Where it fails is where the pastors have been equipping church leaders, and then the new pastor comes with a pastor-centric model, and it dies . . . There's an ego-insecurity issue here. They don't have the courage and understanding that others in the congregation have the gifts they are lacking."[13]

---

11. See bibliography for references to Tom Peters' books.

12. Sue Mallory, *The Equipping Church: Serving Together to Transform Lives.*

13. Phone conversation, November 28, 2023.

Hear that final point clearly. Mallory emphatically restated that the surest way for a church to backslide from being equipping is to call or hire a pastor-centric pastor, one who is too proud, which really means too insecure, to allow members to help in their work or be treated as equals to that pastor. She added: "In your new book, urge church search committees to certify that any pastor they recommend be practiced at and committed to the equipping—or empowerment—model of leadership."

The Not-So-Secret CODE

"Control freaks beware!" So I said in this book's introduction. Well now, I reiterate it, but with a huge redirect. "Control freaks, put on your seat belts!" . . . because the more you give up control, that is, the more you transition from being a leader into a launcher, the more you will see Jesus' passions for you come to full fruition, and the more your congregation or your organization will thrive, grow, and flourish.

But must you totally give up control? Not entirely. Church and mission leaders do need to focus their congregations on the proclamation of the gospel, that is, the good news of the grace of the Lord Jesus Christ, the love of God, and the fellowship of the Holy Spirit. In addition, the leaders also need to build up the congregation as a local microcosm of the body of Christ extending his grace, and as a local microcosm of the family of God, extending God's love, and as a local microcosm of the temple of the Holy Spirit, extending the Spirit's communing fellowship and empowerment. In so doing, the leaders need to give shape to the culture of the church or organization. That culture gets shaped by the pastor's personality, by the pastor's ability to model the congregation's sense of identity, and by the tender yet professional interpersonal relationships shared with the congregation.

Plus, the leaders do all of the above by articulating for the congregation the values and missional foci of their work together—not inventing such values and foci, but articulating them in ways that are memorable and measurable, and that reflect Jesus' passions for us together.

On this final point I learned a simple four-point outline in a grad school class with Gordon McDonald (who at the time was pastor of Grace Chapel in Lexington, Massachusetts, later serving as chancellor of Denver Seminary). I turned his outline into a simple acrostic that I introduced as a puzzle to solve ("Can you solve the Secret CODE?"), and thereafter was lifted up repeatedly as categories to address and against which to evaluate our work. The CODE:

C = Caring for one another
O = Outreach to our neighbors near and far
D = Devotion to God
E = Empowering each other to do all of the above

Many churches have developed vision statements and mission statements. Most of those statements produce signs, plaques, and artwork that effectively collect dust. But for my money, these four, simple priorities/purposes became the hooks to hang our coats on, the directives to follow, the rulers with which to measure how we are doing. Note: these match Jesus' passions for us, if we make sure to interpret Outreach as being both loving our neighbors *and* changing the world.

I introduced the "Secret CODE" a few months into my first pastorate in 1984, and did the same in my four subsequent congregations. My state of the church addresses were almost always built on the four-point outline, specifically summarizing what we as a congregation had done in each category, what we had tried to do but didn't succeed at (it's good to applaud unsuccessful initiatives as a way to continue to encourage members' future inventiveness), and what I hoped for us to be improving or innovating in the year ahead. Such addresses have been well received every time. And they have continued to fuel the culture of caring deeply for one another, doing outreach to our neighbors and the world, living lives of devotion in worship and prayer to God, and empowering all of us to exercise our spiritual giftings, and leading with the purpose of being a church on the advance in glorifying God and enjoying God now in anticipation of an even greater glory to follow.

So How Then Shall We Lead the Full-Spectrum Church in a Red-and-Blue World?

. . . by elevating our conversations to a God-inspired level of partnering with and fulfilling of Jesus' passions for us . . .to know the truth, to love God, to love one another, to love our neighbors and to change the world;

. . . by broadening our discussions from the two simplistic party platforms being shaped by leaders who are constantly trimming profound thoughts to sound bites that fit on bumper stickers—outwardly to encompass not just Jesus' five passions, but also the plethora of spiritual giftings, callings, and commissionings that the Holy Spirit and grace have given to those we know and love;

. . . by authorizing others in the church to lay hold of the empowerment of the Holy Spirit to utilize their spiritual gifts to follow their callings, even the ones that sideswipe or even run head-on into some of our gifts and callings;

. . . and by always remembering that at the heart of the matter, we have the good news to proclaim to all those within the reach of our voices, starting with the one we see in the mirror each morning and night.

One Last Shark Encounter

About ten years transpired between Kelly's close encounter with the shark whose two-note melody she couldn't hear, and David's encounter with a shark who couldn't tell the difference between a fish and his foot. Add an additional ten years, and we had a third encounter—thankfully, our last so far. The kids had entered the adult world. We all were living in the NASA community on the south side of Houston. David was now a computer scientist and a married man with two young children (a third would soon follow). Kelly was a physical therapist living in her first postgrad school apartment. We all decided to drive down to jump in the little waves of Galveston Beach.

After walking out to the beach and setting up chairs and blankets, the grandkids rang out their voices of readiness to go into the water. Off came their shirts and sandals. Ours, too. But David was unusually slow to start the disrobing task. After a few moments of silence, with his eyes darting between Kelly's, Barbie's, and mine, he finally pulled his T-shirt up and over his head. He slowly turned around 180 degrees to reveal on the back of his left shoulder an eight-inch diameter tattoo of a ferocious shark.

"Oh, David," we exclaimed with head-shaking squeals of glee—matched with the grandkids' own congratulations of their heroic dad.

Heroic was the adjective to use for the guy who had figured out how to swim with the sharks and survive. Now, after yet another twenty years, the tooth scars on his foot are barely visible, but the trophy he wears on that shoulder proclaims that, in his case, he turned his encounter with the sharks into a victory.

So may it be for you and for your sharks, too.

— 15 —

Epilogue

"Not All Church Management Consultants Need to Be Ignored . . . But Many Do."

A MAGNIFICENT AND GRAND sweep introduction of Jesus' Passion for us to Know the Truth—particularly to reframe truths already learned—comes through to Bible readers in his Sermon on the Mount. In it he begins with a flourish, turning things upside down via the motif he employs in the Beatitudes—"Blessed are . . . for they . . ." Next he launches into five bullet-point topics by using another turning-things-upside-down rhetorical device: "You have heard it said . . . but I say unto you . . ." He delivers them all in Matthew 5, making up the first third of the sermon. Nowhere else in all the records of his speaking does he reuse that second rhetorical speaking motif.

I want to utilize that speaking motif to help clarify and crystallize a few key points that I have shared with you, especially in the last five chapters, where our focus has been on how to lead full-spectrum churches in the twenty-first century. But whereas Jesus' words, "you have heard is said . . ." were mostly referring to misreadings of the Hebrew Scriptures, my sources for what you have heard said will be primarily from management consultants—especially those serving churches—and from generally accepted "common sense." I am going to quote popular maxims, especially ones used so frequently that they have soared past the "cliché" label into the "CW=Conventional Wisdom" category, or even "undeniable truths" category. I am going to question them, that is, refute them.

For review's sake, I'll summarize Jesus' pairings in just a few words each.

You have heard it said:	But I say:
Don't commit murder (v. 21)	*Don't be angry (v. 22)*
Don't commit adultery (vs. 27)	*Don't be lustful (v. 28)*
Don't swear falsely (v. 33)	*Don't swear at all (v. 35)*
An eye for an eye (v. 398)	*Turn the other cheek (v. 39)*
Love your neighbor (v. 43)	*Love your enemy (v. 44)*

That was then and there with Jesus.
This is here and now with you and me:

You have heard it said: Everything has changed. The church must change.	But I say to you: Little has changed.

With due respect to my friend Brian McLaren, who proclaims everything must change,[1] I say, little has actually changed—and little needs to change. Sure, technology has changed rapidly and drawn many other things in its wake: environmental problems have mushroomed beyond the litter and water pollution problems of the 1960s, democracies are teetering on the edge of fascism's pull (again), international relationships are in flux (still). But human nature has not changed. All humans are still created in the image of God. All continue to sin and fall short of the glory of God. We all still need a savior. And, thanks be to God, *Jesus Christ is the same yesterday, today, and forever* (Heb 13:8). Yes, Jesus is the same Savior today that he was two thousand years ago. No change there.

Change is overrated. When pastoral leaders storm into new parishes carrying the mission to disrupt, to overturn, to reinvent that community of faith, they are, by implication, insulting the very people they are called to love and serve. This new pastor is also insulting every pastor who had served this congregation in the past, as if they did not know what they were doing or did not have the courage to stand up for what was right.

---

1. McLaren, *Everything Must Change.*

Such change-agency strategy rings out as the height of arrogance. And yes, church members react against such assaults.

Do you want to see changes there? Begin by applauding all the good things the members have done there, the good things your predecessors did there. When you affirm the work they have already done it gives impetus to do more of the same, even further and better.

Have you ever heard of positive reinforcement? The single best way to influence children's behavior is to applaud, congratulate, and reward their good behavior. They will live up to, or down to, what you say about them. In like manner, a congregation will live up to or down to the reputation pinned on them. Tell them they are bad, and they will do worse. Tell them they are good, and they will do better.[2]

To put it bluntly, any pastor who weaponizes change by dividing the congregation into the two competing camps—i.e., allied early adopters on the one hand vs. tradition-protecting late adopters on the other, splits the congregation and sets in motion the sabotage of the pastor's initiatives. (Reread chapter 2 on the destructive power of binary categorizations.)

You have heard the acrostic: KISS: Keep it simple, stupid.	But I say unto you: There's a reason this is addressed to "stupid."

As stated in chapter 14, it is a good idea for new, small businesses to find a niche, fill it, and thereby make a profit. But that is not the reason for the church's existence. If your congregation's passions and efforts match Jesus' passions for us—if you are loving one another in the congregation so no one strays, if you are outreaching to neighbors near and far so well that they are flocking in the doors and structures of injustice are giving way to equality and opportunity for all, if your devotion to God is generating fortissimo praise in worship, and you are empowering the congregation's members to carry out every volunteer organization's tasks in the city—then maybe you need to trim back just a bit! Otherwise, keep it going.

But if you are doing all of the above then you also know life is complicated. I even wrote a book with a similar title.[3] Over against what I just said above, the one thing that is changing is that life is getting more

2. Griffin, *Mind Changers.*

3. Haberer, *It's Complicated.*

complicated. Those who try to simplify the wind-tunnel pace of issues flying in our faces today, and/or aiming to streamline their faith by trimming it all back to bumper sticker slogans, are trivializing life itself.

The "simplicity" problem becomes especially evident when writing mission statements and vision statements. Every consultant I've known that's guided such an effort has set a maximum word count—like seventeen words or eleven words or even seven words. Rubbish. God has already written a mission statement and a vision statement. It's about a thousand pages long. It's called the Bible. It is filled with nuance, ambiguities, and inconsistencies—not because it isn't all inspired (I do affirm the full Holy Spirit inspiration of the Bible)—but rather, because life is filled with nuance, ambiguities, and inconsistencies. God inspired the writing of the text for it to speak to all aspects of our lives. It's complicated. Wonderfully so.

You have heard it said: Focus, focus, focus.

But I say unto you: Peripherate, peripherate, peripherate, peripherate.

My elementary-school years were haunted by the fact that I was a lousy athlete surrounded by great athletes of my age in the neighborhood. Whenever we'd choose sides to play sandlot baseball, basketball, and football, I would be the last or second-to-last one chosen.

But in the fall of eighth grade, I decided to join the Spartans—the local junior football team. After all the practices, true to form, I gained the status of the third-string fullback (out of three). In the first game of the season, Coach Duff had the first-stringers play the first quarter. In the second quarter, he sent in the second string. And in the third quarter, he sent in the third string. Oh my, I actually got on the field!

Early into that quarter he sent into the quarterback, my friend Scott Getlin, the play being for me to run off tackle to the left. Scott handed me the ball, got in my way, and I tripped over his foot. Lost three yards. But for some reason Coach Duff sent in the same play. Scott again handed me the ball and again got in my way; but this time, I gave him a quick push to moved him aside. A small gap between defenders opened up ahead of me and I darted ahead. Then, out of the right corner of my eye, I saw a pathway open in that direction. I planted my left foot, turned about 65 degrees to my right, and ran, bending back to the left downfield—and all the way . . . fifty-five yards . . . for a touchdown.

My life changed. I suddenly felt like an athlete. By mid-season, I had jumped from third string to first string. I carried the ball often, successfully, and even scored several more touchdowns. The next year, I went out for freshman football, was elected team co-captain by my teammates, and we went on to an undefeated season.

What made me an athlete? Not my athletic prowess. What did it was my peripheral vision. I saw an opportunity that was not in the plan of the play called by the coach.

Likewise, peripheral vision is also one of the greatest keys to church leadership. And peripheral vision stands at the heart of Jesus' parable of the good shepherd.

The "Focus, focus, focus" directive presumes that there's only one thing we need to do and only one target group for whom to do it. Yes, this does work for starting new small businesses (however, if they grow they will need to diversify). But churches are not small businesses. They are the family of God, the body of Christ, the temple of the Holy Spirit. From the start—indeed, in churches of thirteen or twenty-three, and of thirty-three or 333 or 3,333—our calling is not to choose one slice of the population on whom to focus our efforts. Good shepherds don't just care for the sheep close at hand; they will watch out for, and when one is missing, will search hither, thither, and yon to find, rescue and, bring back any stray.

Now, conceiving what "slices" of demographics do exist within our congregation, as well as within the larger population within range of our possible influence, can provide an effective way to measure which of those we are effectively serving, and which ones we are missing. Then, having done so, we need to keep focusing on those already being reached, while at the same time raising up others to focus on those being missed—and then empowering them to find those lost sheep, to love them, care for them, and share the love of God with them.

The key to good shepherding is to peripherate, peripherate, peripherate, peripherate; the fourth one added for emphasis.

You have heard it said: But I say unto you:
You can't be all things   Who says you can't?
to all people.

Do you know who it was that invented that saying about *all things to all people*?

Was it Stephen Covey? No. Oprah Winfrey? No. How about Peter Drukker? No. Maya Angelou? Eleanor Roosevelt? Mark Twain? None of them. How about Ben Franklin? Marie Curie? Martin Luther? Joan of Arc? St. Thomas Aquinas? St. Augustine? None of the above.

How about another saint? How about St. Paul? Uh-huh. Yup. He coined the axiom. But he didn't word it as the bumper stickers do. He wrote:

> For though I am free with respect to all, I have made myself a slave to all, so that I might gain all the more. To the Jews I became as a Jew, in order to gain Jews. To those under the law I became as one under the law (though I myself am not under the law) so that I might gain those under the law. To those outside the law I became as one outside the law (though I am not outside God's law but am within Christ's law) so that I might gain those outside the law. To the weak I became weak, so that I might gain the weak. *I have become all things to all people*, that I might by all means save some. I do it all for the sake of the gospel, so that I might become a partner in it. (1 Cor 9:19–23, emphasis added.)

Paul's passion to be a witness for Jesus was handed a megaphone in the form of his multilingual verbal skills (he apparently was fluent in Hebrew, Aramaic, Greek, and Latin). His readiness to travel and adapt to other cultures and different socio-economic strata gave legs to that mission. And what of that mission? . . . the mission to "save some . . . [via the proclamation] of the gospel . . . to become a partner in it."

Now, Paul didn't learn to speak Swahili or German or Chinese or Cherokee. And, realistically, most American Christians cannot conceive of becoming nearly as multilingual and multicultural as Paul. But when joined together into congregations that are local expressions of the body of Christ, which are aiming to emulate Paul as he emulated Jesus— "Be imitators of me as I am of Christ" (1 Cor 11:1)—if we have even just thirty of us, we can be all things to hundreds of others; if we have three hundred . . . we can be all things to thousands; if we have three thousand . . . we can be all things to millions. That is, if we try to mimic Paul the apostle, and with him, Jesus the good shepherd.

By the way, I do dub as heresy the saying, "You can't be all things to all people," because the Bible warns us about misrepresenting Scripture. The final directive in the Bible says: "I warn everyone who hears the words of the prophecy of this book: if anyone adds to them, God will add to that person the plagues described in this book; if anyone takes away from the words of the book of this prophecy, God will take away that person's share in the tree of life and in the holy city, which are described in this book" (Rev 22:18–19).

Surely the one writing those words was warning against changing anything in the book of Revelation. But biblical Christians long have revered all of the Scriptures as God's word, not mere words to be twisted into different meanings than originally intended. Accordingly, to take Paul's commitment to be all things to all people, and flipping it upside down to repudiate Paul's intended meaning, is wrong. Simply wrong. Accordingly, when others say, "You can't be all things to all people," I say unto them, "Heresy!"

| You have heard it said: Clear the calendar. | But I say unto you: For every gathering canceled, people get canceled. |

Sure, the Sunday school registration may be much smaller than in past decades. If you cancel the third-grade class because there's only one child in attendance, and she misses every other week due to splitting homes between her divorced parents, shall we cancel her? If you cancel the women's Bible study that has shrunk from thirty-five to three or five per week, how dare you decide that those three or five are not worth the effort of attending and taking their turn to read the questions for the others. Go back and read about the good shepherd.

So what if the calendar is crowded. The hardcopy calendars on which every day is limited to four square inches have given way to computer screens, which happen to have an unlimited capacity for enlargement. So what if all the rooms in the building are being used more than once a week or even five times a week. May they all be used day every day—like a public school building in a growing community.

Then again, I can think of a time that a church took this point to an extreme.

In the late 1800s a preteen boy suffered the deaths of his father and, a year later, his two-year-old sister. His mom turned to her faith with such earnest effort that she expected him and his older brother to go to church, the local Episcopal church, every morning. Years later he recounted one particular morning when he was the only person attending the early service:

> I . . . took my place in one of the pews, and waited. When the hour struck for the service to begin, the red-bearded minister came out, in his surplice, went to the altar, and conducted the entire service exactly as if he had had a congregation of a thousand people. I felt some awkwardness when the time for the collection came. I had a nickel for the purpose, but my problem was how to get it on the plate. The minister rose to the occasion. Before time for the offertory, he gravely came down out of the chancel and put the collection plate on the first pew, then as gravely returned to the altar. I went up and deposited my nickel. The minister returned at the proper time, carried the plate to the altar, and offered my gift as solemnly as if it had been gold . . . I saw that morning . . . a man's faith. . . . Young as I was [twelve], that minister's conduct gave me a deep sense of the reality of God; and it has never left me since that day.

That boy grew up, took an interest in the newly developing moviemaking business. He became a movie maker. And he produced a movie that he had dreamed of while sitting in one of those pews. It featured Charlton Heston, Yul Brynner, and Ann Baxter. Its name? *The Ten Commandments*. Yes, the pastor whose conduct of a complete worship service for one solitary twelve-year-old "C.B.," as he was then known, but later known as Cecil B. DeMille, produced "a deep sense of the reality of God" in millions of moviegoers the extent of which we will never know on this side of heaven, but we may well meet some of those beneficiaries when we get there.[4]

It was decades ago that I first heard this story, probably on a Paul Harvey, *The Rest of the Story* radio program, and it has stood before me as the gold standard of what it means to be a pastor. It defines the heart of flesh (to replace the heart of stone) I have aspired to cultivate in my

---

4. Edwards, *DeMilles*, 31.

service to Jesus and his church. It stands as my final answer to those who insist on clearing the church calendar.

You have heard it said:	But I say unto you:
Get the right people on	**Who came up with that**
the bus.[5]	**line? Rosa Parks?**

Please excuse my cynicism, but as a privileged white guy I have to call out any and all of my fellow privileged white guys who say things that are flat-out racist.

But even if, as I imagine, there are no intentional racist overtones in this, the advice flies in the face of God's sovereign call of sinners to come to Jesus to find comfort, forgiveness, healing, wholeness, and empowerment. All of us who have gotten onto that bus have no more right ourselves to be there than anybody else. We are welcomed by the gracious arms of Jesus into the family of God, which gives total rights to all to be there together.

Are there some employees on the church staff who refuse to get with the program? I've had some too interested in their own ambitions and initiatives to be a part of empowering others' spiritual gifts. Or whose manners are simply offensive to and/or mocking of the sincerity of others in the congregation? Or don't have the gifts needed to do the tasks they are employed to do? Ideally, we help them find other roles to play so they can thrive in the fellowship. In some cases, they need to be "counseled out" to help them find another role for which they are better suited. On very, very rare occasions, they violate essential expectations and need to be dismissed;[6] but even at that, they should be led away with as much dignity and hope for recovery as we can possibly extend.

But, please, never use "Get the right people on the bus" as a value for any Christian aim.

5. Collins, *Good to Great*, 41ff.
6. See 1 Cor 5:1–5.

You've heard it said:
Let the search
committee do the
search.

But I say to you:
Make sure the search
committee is peopled
with empowerment
members.

As stated in chapter 14, when flourishing empowerment churches call and employ a pastor-centric pastor—one who is too controlling and/or too proud and/or too insecure to be an empowering-of-others pastor—the empowerment model of leadership will die. The congregation may flourish during the honeymoon stage of that new pastor's tenure, but the giftedness of the members will get squelched and the intrinsic power of the Holy Spirit will be siphoned only through the pastor and that pastor's close inner circle of fans. See to it that your search committee is populated with those who embrace the empowerment model, and will use it as a guide in choosing a pastor who can support, amplify, and flourish within that vision. And then let the search committee do its work.

You have heard it said:
Leaders lead.

But I say unto you:
Leaders launch.

It is so significant that it begs to be repeated. The role of a pastor, a commissioned lay pastor, a CEO, or a leader in any kind of Christian service, is not one to set a direction, leading into it, and dragging the congregation like a little red wagon behind. Rather, a pastor's job is to invite and encourage—yea, urge—the members to discern their gifts and callings, their hopes and concerns, their visions and missions, so they will grasp God's intentions for their lives, whether in the near or even the distant future. The leader may offer counsel to help refine the calling and the strategies to fulfill it, but almost always that call needs to be affirmed, supported, and encouraged. The net effect in a congregation of any size is that people will be going about in different directions, each seeking to faithfully fulfill the call and commission entrusted by God to them, and an enormous array of missional work will ensue.

Hence, leaders launch and partner and resource their members and friends into their pursuits of God's callings before them, together bringing glory to God; and on most days, enjoy God in the here and now, in anticipation of ever greater joy in the forever ahead.

You have heard it said: But I say unto you:
Never swim with sharks!   Go back in the water!

There's way too much adventure awaiting in the ocean to let a mere billion or so sharks deter you from jumping in with them. And, as for me, some of my best friends are sharks.

Bibliography

"1908 Social Creed of the Methodist Episcopal Church." https://www.umcjustice.org/articles/the-1908-social-creed-of-the-methodist-episcopal-church-822.

"2022 PRRI Census of American Religion: Religious Affiliation Updates and Trends." Washington, DC: Public Religion Research Institute, February 24, 2023. https://www.prri.org/spotlight/prii-2022-american-values-atlas-religious-affiliation-updates-and-trends/.

Achtemeier, Mark, and Andrew Purves, eds. *A Passion for the Gospel: Confessing Jesus Christ for the 21st Century.* Louisville: Geneva, 2000.

Baird, J. Arthur. *Audience Criticism and the Historical Jesus.* Philadelphia: Westminster, 1969.

———. *Rediscovering the Power of the Gospel: Jesus' Theology of the Kingdom.* Wooster, OH: Iona, 1982.

Balzer, Klaus. *The Covenant Formulary: In Old Testament, Jewish, and Early Christian Writings.* Translated by David E. Green. Philadelphia: Fortress, 1971.

Beckwith, Dave, with Christina Lopez. "Community Organizing: People Power from the Grassroots." Center for Community Change. http://comm-org.wisc.edu/papers97/beckwith.htm.

Bob, Thomas. "John Wesley's Happy Day." *Banner of Truth*, May 24, 2023. https://banneroftruth.org/us/resources/articles/2023/john-wesleys-happy-day/.

Brueggemann, Walter. *The Prophetic Imagination.* 2nd ed. Minneapolis: Fortress, 1978.

———. *Reality, Grief, Hope: Three Urgent Prophetic Tasks.* Grand Rapids: Eerdmans, 2014.

Buechner, Frederick. *Wishful Thinking: A Seeker's ABC.* New York: HarperOne, 1993.

Calvin, John. *Institutes of the Christian Religion.* Edited by John T. McNeill. Philadelphia: Westminster, 1960.

Campbell, Cynthia, ed. *Renewing the Vision: Reformed Faith for the 21st Century.* Louisville: Geneva, 2000.

Campolo, Tony. *Red Letter Christians: A Citizen's Guide to Faith & Politics.* Ventura, CA: Gospel Light, 2008.

Carnegie, Andrew. "239 Best *The 360 Degree Leader* Quotes." Collected by John Maxwell. https://www.consultclarity.org/post/360-degree-leader-quotes.

Carter, Brody. "New Barna Survey Finds That 38% of US Pastors Have Considered Leaving Ministry." *CBN,* November 16, 2021. https://www2.cbn.com/news/us/new-barna-survey-finds-38-us-pastors-have-considered-leaving-ministry.

The Christian Century. "Mission." https://en.wikipedia.org/wiki/The_Christian_ Century.

Collins, Jim. *Good to Great.* New York: HarperCollins, 2001.

The Constitution of the Presbyterian Church (U.S.A.), Part II, Book of Order. Louisville: Office of the General Assembly, 2023.

Darrow, Clarence. *The Essential Words and Writings of Clarence Darrow.* New York: Random House, 2007.

David, Jim, and Michael Graham, with Ryan P. Burge. *The Great Dechurching: Who's Leaving, Why are They Going, and What It Will Take to Bring Them Back.* Grand Rapids: Zondervan, 2023.

Du Mez, Kristin Kobes. *Jesus and John Wayne: How White Evangelicals Corrupted a Faith and Fractured a Nation.* New York: Liveright, 2020.

Edmonds, Molly. "Shark Facts vs. Shark Myths." Washington, DC: World Wildlife Fund, 2024. https://www.worldwildlife.org/stories/shark-facts-vs-shark-myths.

Edwards, Ann. *The DeMilles: An American Family.* New York: Harry N. Abrams, Inc., 1988.

Fee, Gordon D. *God's Empowering Presence: The Holy Spirit in the Letters of Paul.* Peabody, MA: Hendrickson, 1994.

———. "Lectures on the Book of Acts." South Hamilton, MA: Gordon Conwell Theological Seminary, January 20, 1982.

Ferguson, Niall. *War of the World: Twentieth Century Conflict and the Descent of the West.* New York: Penguin, 2006.

Figgis, J. N., and R. V. Laurence, eds. *Historical Essays and Studies.* London: Macmillan, 1907.

Foucault, Michel. *Discipline and Punish: The Birth of a Prison.* London: Penguin, 1991.

———. *Power.* Edited by James D. Faubion. New York: New, 1994.

Griffin, Em. *The Mind Changers: The Art of Christian Persuasion.* Carol Stream, IL: Tyndale, 1976.

Guyon, Jeanne Marie Bouvier de la Motte. *Le Moyen Court Et Autres Écrits Spirituels (The Short and Easy Method of Prayer).* 1685. Grenoble: J. Millon, 1995.

Haberer, Jack. *GodViews: The Convictions that Drive Us and Divide Us.* Louisville: Geneva, 2001.

———. *It's Complicated: A Guide to Faithful Decision Making.* Louisville: Westminster John Knox, 2016.

———. *Living the Presence of the Spirit.* Louisville: Geneva, 2001.

———. *The Presence of the Spirit: Elusive or Abiding? . . . Toward a Theology of Spirituality.* DMin diss., Columbia Theological Seminary, 1989.

"History of the Cursillo Movement." Diocese of Biloxi, 2007. biloxicursillo.org.

Horton, Michael S. "Protestantism Is Over and the Radicals Won." *Modern Reformation* 26:5 (September 1, 2017). https://store.solamedia.org/products/26-5-reformation-500?variant=44591098364196.

"The Jefferson Bible." *Encyclopedia Britannica.* https://www.britannica.com/topic/ Jefferson-Bible.

Josephus. *Antiquities of the Jews.* Translated by William Whiston. Grand Rapids: Kregel, 1960.

Keck, Leander E. *The Church Confident: Christianity Can Repent, But It Must Not Whimper.* Nashville: Abingdon, 1963.

Kelley, Dean M. *Why Conservative Churches Are Growing: A Study in Sociology of Religion.* New York, Harper & Row, 1972.

Kise, Jane A. G., David Stark, and Sandra Krebs Hirsh. *LifeKeys: Discover Who You Are.* Minneapolis: Bethany, 2005.

Küng, Hans. *The Church.* New York: Image, 1976.

"The Larger Catechism." *The Book of Confessions.* Louisville: Office of the General Assembly, Presbyterian Church (USA), 2016.

Lazzeretti, Craig. "The 30 Greatest Surfers of All Time." https://www.stadiumtalk.com/s/30-greatest-surfers-all-time-d5b3a7ac8d154562.

Leith, John. *Crisis in the Church.* Louisville: Westminster John Knox, 1997.

Li, Edward. "10 Famous Quotes by Michael Porter." Harvard Business School, May 25, 2023. https://www.linkedin.com/pulse/10-famous-quotes-michael-porter-harvard-business-school-edward-li.

Longfield, Bradley J. "Presbyterian Conflict: The Modern Ecclesiastical Context." In *The Nature of the Unity We Seek in Our Diversity,* edited by Theodore A. Gill Jr., 7–20. Louisville: Office of General Assembly, 1999.

———. *The Presbyterian Controversy: Fundamentalists, Modernists and Moderates.* Oxford: Oxford University Press, 1991.

Lovelace, Richard. *Dynamics of Spiritual Life: An Evangelical Theology of Renewal.* Downers Grove, IL: InterVarsity, 1980.

Lupton, Robert D. *Toxic Charity: How Churches and Charities Hurt Those They Help (And How to Reverse It).* San Francisco: HarperOne, 2011.

Luther, Martin. *Luther's Works.* Vol. 34, *Career of the Reformer IV.* Edited by Lewis W. Spitz. Luther's Works (Concordia). St. Louis: Concordia, 1955.

Luti, J. Mary. "The Whole World is Singing: A Journey to Iona and Taize." *The Christian Century,* March 22–29, 2000, 336–41.

Machen, J. Gresham. *Christianity and Liberalism.* New York: Macmillan, 1923.

Maden, Jack. "The Golden Mean: Aristotle's Guide to Living Excellently." Philosophy Break, Ltd., January 2023. https://philosophybreak.com/articles/the-golden-mean-aristotle-guide-to-living-excellently/.

Mallory, Sue. *The Equipping Church: Serving Together to Transform Lives.* Grand Rapids: Zondervan, 2001.

Manning, Brennan, with John Blase. *All Is Grace: A Ragamuffin Memoir.* Elgin, IL: David C. Cook, 2011.

Martin, Ralph P. *The Spirit and the Congregation, Studies in I Corinthians 12–15.* Grand Rapids: Eerdmans, 1984.

McCormick, C. Mark. "Exegesis." In *New Interpreter's Dictionary of the Bible* vol. 2, 366. Nashville: Abingdon, 2009.

McDonald, Glenn. *Glenn's Reflections,* May 11, 2023. glennsreflections.com.

McLaren, Brian. *Everything Must Change: Jesus, Global Crises, and a Revolution of Hope.* Nashville: Thomas Nelson, 2007.

Moltmann, Jürgen. *The Crucified God: The Cross of Christ as the Foundation and Criticism of Christian Theology.* HarperCollins, 1974.

———. *The Trinity and the Kingdom: The Doctrine of God.* Translated by Margaret Kohl. San Francisco: Harper San Francisco, 1981.

Moroney, S. K. "The Noetic Effects of Sin: An Exposition of Calvin's View and a Constructive Theological Proposal." PhD diss., Duke University, 1995.

Morphew, Derek, and Øyvind Nerheim. *John Wimber's Teaching on the Gift and Gifts of the Holy Spirit.* Self-published, 2020.

Niebuhr, H. Richard. *Christ and Culture.* New York: Harper and Row, 1951.

Niebuhr, Reinhold. *Nature and Destiny of Man.* Vol. 2. New York: Charles Scribner's Sons, 1943.

Peters, Tom. *Thriving on Chaos: Handbook for a Management Revolution.* New York: Harper Perennial, 1988.

Peters, Tom, and Nancy Austin. *The Excellence Dividend: Meeting the Tech Tide with Work That Wows and Jobs That Last.* New York: Vintage, 2018.

————. *A Passion for Excellence: The Leadership Difference.* New York: Random House, 1985.

Peters, Thomas J., and Robert H. Waterman Jr. *In Search of Excellence: Lessons from America's Best Run Companies.* New York: Warner, 1982.

Pew Research Center's Forum on Religion and Public Life. *Global Christianity.* December 2021. https://www.pewresearch.org/religion/2011/12/19/global-christianity-exec/.

Prior, Daniel. "Spiritual Gifts in Business." Melchizedek Ministries, 2000. melchizedekchristianchurch.org.

Purves, Andrew, and Mark Achtemeier. *Union in Christ: A Declaration for the Church.* Louisville: Witherspoon, 1999.

Rees, Erik. *S.H.A.P.E.: Finding and Fulfilling Your Unique Purpose for Life.* Grand Rapids: Zondervan, 2006.

Robeck, Cecil M., Jr. "Women in the Pentecostal Movement." Pasadena, CA: Fuller Studio, n.d. https://fullerstudio.fuller.edu/women-in-the-pentecostal-movement/.

Sceurman, Mark, and Mark Moran. "History and Legends of the Mysterious 'Jackson Whites.'" *Weird NJ Magazine,* September 26, 2012. https://weirdnj.com/stories/fabled-people-and-places/jackson-whites/.

Schweitzer, Albert. *The Quest for the Historical Jesus.* New York: Macmillan, 1910.

Sheldon, Charles M. *In His Steps: What Would Jesus Do?* Chicago: Chicago Advance, 1896.

Small, Joseph D. "Who's In, Who's Out?" *Theology Today* 58:1 (April 2001) 58–71.

Stefon, Matt. "Jefferson Bible." Britannica.com. htttps://www.britannica.com/topic/Jefferson-Bible.

Stone, Jon R. *On the Boundaries of American Evangelicalism.* New York: St. Martin's, 1997.

Tannen, Deborah. *The Argument Culture: Moving from Debate to Dialogue.* New York: Random House, 1998.

Terrien, Samuel. *The Elusive Presence: Toward a New Biblical Theology.* New York: HarperCollins, 1982.

Thomas à Kempis. *The Imitation of Christ.* The Catholic Primer, 2004. www.catholicprimer.org.

Tomczak, Benjamin. "Luther Found the 'For You' for You." *Bread for Beggars,* October 30, 2013. https://breadforbeggars.com/2013/10/luther-found-the-for-you-for-you/.

Volf, Miroslav. *Exclusion and Embrace.* Nashville: Abingdon, 1996.

Webster's Ninth New Collegiate Dictionary. Springfield, MA: Merriam-Webster, 1985.

www.ingramcontent.com/pod-product-compliance
Lightning Source LLC
Chambersburg PA
CBHW031056280326
41928CB00049B/770